✾ ✾ ✾ ✾

The Empathic Reader

✾ ✾ ✾ ✾

❀ ❀ ❀ ❀

The Empathic Reader

A Study of the Narcissistic Character and the Drama of the Self

❀ ❀ ❀ ❀

J. Brooks Bouson

The University of Massachusetts Press

Amherst

Copyright © 1989 by The University of Massachusetts Press
All rights reserved
Printed in the United States of America
LC 89–4695
ISBN 0–87023–678–4
Set in Sabon at Keystone Typesetting
Printed and bound by Thomson Shore

Library of Congress Cataloging-in-Publication Data

Bouson, J. Brooks.
    The empathic reader : a study of the narcissistic character and the drama of
the self / J. Brooks Bouson.
        p. cm.
    Bibliography: p.
    Includes index.
    ISBN 0–87023–678–4 (alk. paper)
    1. Fiction—Psychological aspects. 2. Kohut, Heinz—Criticism and
interpretation. 3. Narcissism in literature. 4. Self in literature.
5. Self psychology. 6. Empathy in literature. 7. Authors and readers. 8. Books
and reading. I. Title.
PN3352.P7B68   1989
809.3'9353—dc19   89–4695
                                                                        CIP

British Library Cataloguing in Publication data are available.

To the memory of my father

✿ ✿ ✿ ✿

Contents

✿ ✿ ✿ ✿

Contents

Acknowledgments

I am grateful to those people who, in encouraging me to pursue this project, have provided me with the kind of mirroring approval that has sustained me during many a long and sometimes lonely hour of reading, research, and writing. In particular, I want to thank Meredith Anthony, Yohma Gray, Agnes Donohue, and Patrick Casey. And I am indebted to those people who read portions of the manuscript and helped me, through their questions and comments, to clarify and refine my ideas. They include psychoanalyst Peter Barglow, Frank Cioffi, Deborah Gutschera, Tony LaBranche, Lynne Layton, Bernard McElroy, Matt Naglich, and Barbara Schapiro. And I owe a special debt of gratitude to Bernard Paris and Margret Schaefer for their comments on the entire manuscript and to psychoanalyst Roy Grinker, Jr., for his patient and painstaking reading and rereading of the introductory chapter on Kohut, for his insightful comments on my literary application of Kohut, and for his enduring belief in my work.

I am also indebted to Bruce Wilcox, the director of the University of Massachusetts Press, who provided advice on all sorts of matters related to the manuscript and to Pam Wilkinson, the managing editor, for her editorial expertise and remarkable eye for detail. And I am grateful to the interlibrary loan librarian at Mundelein College, Sr. Frances Loretta Berger, BVM, who helped me track down a score of articles unavailable through other sources. Also I want to thank my students, especially those in my courses on the narcissistic character, Virginia Woolf, and Margaret Atwood, who, in asking challenging questions and sharing my excitement about the approach to literary character that I present in this book, provided the kind of empathic milieu that a teacher finds nourishing.

And, finally, I want to thank my husband, Bob, without whose empathic support this book would not have been possible.

An earlier version of the chapter on Kafka was published in *Narcissism and the Text: Studies in Literature and the Psychology of Self*, ed. Lynne Layton and Barbara Schapiro (New York: New York University Press, 1986), pp. 192–212, and an earlier version of the chapter on Bellow appeared in the *Saul Bellow Journal* 5 (Spring/Summer 1986): 3–14. I am grateful for permission to reuse this material, which I have significantly revised for this study.

* * * *

The Empathic Reader

* * * *

✤ ✤ ✤ ✤

Introductory Remarks

✤ ✤ ✤ ✤

This book is an application of American psychoanalytic theorist Heinz Kohut's "self psychology" and empathic listening techniques to a study of the narcissistic character and the reader/text transaction. It grows out of my fascination with literature and with the very human story that Kohut tells as he describes the dynamics of what is considered by many to be the dominant pathology of our time: the narcissistic disorder. Illuminating in a powerful new way the disconnected lives of increasing numbers of people, Kohut centers his attention on fundamental aspects of human behavior which other accounts of psychological man and woman ignore or minimize: the deep-rooted needs for empathic responsiveness and for a sense of connection with others.

We can hear hints and guesses of this story in comments made by patients suffering from the narcissistic disorder. "[W]hen I am alone, I eat up myself," one such patient tells his analyst. "When you talk," he admits, "I rise in ecstasy, I don't take it in; the ecstasy is that you are talking about *me* and when you are right, such elation!" "I'm just all out of contact with everything," says another to his analyst. "Please say something to me." "I wonder what I look like in your eyes," comments another. "It's a great truth that when I lack a certain type of stimulation I get terrified." "If I perceive you as becoming uninterested, I lose my complete sense of wholeness . . . ," yet another realizes. "When I am talking with a need to talk, there's got to be a listener" (Goldberg,

Psychology 149, 131, 409, 277, 58–59, 62). In these statements, we sense the vast neediness and fragile self-stability of narcissistically defective individuals and their urgent desire for an empathic listener. Because of Kohut, analysts today are better able to understand the communications of these people, described by Kohut as "tragic."

Developing through the psychoanalytic process what he came to call the "psychology of the self," Kohut evolved a new metapsychology, one that provides a radical departure from Freudian psychoanalysis. Shifting away from Freudian drive psychology with its psychobiological description of people as creatures driven by sexual and aggressive impulses, Kohut focuses on the central role of empathy in the formation and maintenance of the self. Kohut's narcissistically disturbed individuals—Tragic Man and Woman—are familiar to readers of twentieth-century literature. They suffer from shaky self-esteem, are prone to intense feelings of loneliness, rage, empty despair, and meaninglessness. They may be arrogant and ruthlessly manipulate others or obsessed with being perfect or clingingly dependent. They may assuage their intense loneliness or feelings of inadequacy with megalomaniac fantasies or harbor secret feelings that they are frauds, impostors. "Disintegration anxiety," which Kohut defines as fear of the loss of the self, is their core anxiety. Self-confirming attention from others—the empathic resonance that Kohut feels is central to self-survival—is one of their most compelling needs. For Kohut, psychoanalysis, the "science of empathy," provides a complex mapping of interior regions of the self through its sustained empathic-introspective immersion into human subjectivity. The basis of this inquiry is an empathic immersion into the complicated self-dramas of a selected group of narcissistic characters and an interrogation of reader interactions with them.

This study is not intended as an exhaustive survey or historical review but rather as a focused investigation of representative narcissistic characters. I've deliberately chosen characters and texts that readers will have puzzled over before and that have generated the kind of critical conversation and debate that lends itself to psychocritical analysis. After an introductory section on Kohut, which is designed to familiarize readers with Kohut's theory of the self, define key Kohutian concepts, and explore the link between empathy and the reading process, I present close readings of individual texts.

Part II begins with investigations of three classic dramatizations of Tragic Man: Dostoevsky's *Notes From Underground*, Kafka's *Metamorphosis*, and Bellow's *Seize the Day*. Providing an exemplary introduction to the narcissistic character, these works give varied form and narrative expression to the drama of the unconfirmed self: in the Underground Man's angry attempt to compel the attention and win the assent of others, including his "gentlemen" listeners, and his enraged response to rejection; in the insect-Gregor's mute appeals for his family's notice and his slow demise when he is ignored; and in Wilhelm Adler's desperate cry for help and his collapse when his plea is rejected. The solipsistic, isolated world of the storyteller and artist, depicted in Conrad's "Secret Sharer" and "Heart of Darkness" and in Mann's *Death in Venice*, is the subject matter of the final two chapters of Part II. Intent on enticing and transforming the listener into an alter-ego "secret sharer," Conrad's storyteller-narrators—the secret sharer captain and Marlow—tell self-referential stories designed to conceal what is revealed: their urgent need for self-rescue. Similarly, Gustave Aschenbach's defensive aestheticism—his conversion of narcissistic needs and fears into literary myths and symbols—signals an attempt to fend off the formless, wordless dread that lies at the core of his experience.

Part III—Tragic Woman—begins with an analysis of Lessing's *Summer Before the Dark*, which dramatizes the long-evaded self-crisis of Kate Brown, a character who experiences a slippage of self when others do not notice her. Woolf's *Mrs. Dalloway*, a novel that defensively poetizes the alien world of the disconnected self, provides another representation of the self-in-crisis in the character of Clarissa Dalloway, a fragile personality who must "collect" the parts of her broken self into "one centre," "one woman." And finally, Atwood's *Lady Oracle* depicts the shapeshifting, mirrored world of the storyteller and artist Joan Foster, who uses comic storytelling to express her exhibitionistic and angry impulses and to compel her listener's attention.

Whether we are maneuvered to experience the insect-Gregor's feelings of powerlessness as we grapple with the resistant, preverbal puzzles underlying *The Metamorphosis*, or induced, like Aschenbach before his demise, to exercise intellectual mastery as we decode the mythic and symbolic overlay of Mann's *Death in Venice*, or prompted to participate in the merger needs and anxieties that underlie Woolf's *Mrs. Dalloway* as we experience the narrative's strange fluctuation between immersion and withdrawal, the works we will examine in this study are designed to bind us in a complicated transaction. In the repeated phenomena of critics replicating, in their commentaries, the narcissistic scenarios and defenses located in these narratives or responding to the needs of these characters for rescue and support or for an empathically attuned listener, we find compelling evidence of the strange power these texts have to implicate us in their unfolding dramas. Enacting the negotiated role of sympathetic listener and advocate, critic/readers may, for example, minimize or even deny a character's negativity or endorse his or her aberrant behavior and self-destructive impulses. Or they may act out, in the critical arena, a need generated by and often depicted in the narrative: the need to see the character rescued. Also suggestive are the critical desires to assert authority over the character, the text, and/or its subsequent readers or to rescue the character or text from what are conceived of as critical misappraisals or misreadings.

My purpose in the following chapters is twofold. In focusing attention on the narcissistic dramas enacted in these narratives, my intent is to tell the strange yet familiar story of Tragic Man and Woman. In listening to the critical conversations surrounding these characters, I aim also to reveal some of the fascinating complexities of the reader/ character and reader/text exchange. The empathic reader, as I describe this person, is also a suspicious critic. A participant-observer, the empathic reader becomes immersed in the illusory world of the fictional text and is actively aware of the text's designs upon its readers. Empathic reading, which locates itself in the transitional space between the subjective and objective, makes us acutely aware of the reciprocal relationship—the empathic event—that occurs between the reader and the text.

In writing this book I have made use of Kohut's books and articles, the work of psychoanalysts such as Michael Basch, John Gedo, Arnold Goldberg, and Ernest Wolf who are careful readers of Kohut, and related psychoanalytic research into the subjects of empathy and countertransference. Although the character analyses I present in this book are an application of Kohut to the study of the narcissistic character, my analysis of the dynamics of the reader/text transaction is an adaptation of Kohut's theory of empathy and recent psychoanalytic accounts of countertransference, which I've attempted to articulate to other, current ways of reading texts. In particular, I've found useful a deconstructive strategy that shows how a critical discourse repeats the textual structures it investigates and psychoanalyst Gail Reed's discussions of the countertransferential aspects of the reading process and of critical reenactments of texts.

✲ ✲ ✲ ✲

Part I
Psychoanalytic Self Psychology

✲ ✲ ✲ ✲

❀ ❀ ❀ ❀

One
Kohut's Psychology of the Self,
Empathy, and the
Reading Process

❀ ❀ ❀ ❀

Heinz Kohut (1913–1981) stated in the last essay he wrote, "psychoanalysis has hardly yet scratched the surface of the fascinating mystery of man. . . . [I]t must turn from the study of Freud to the study of man" ("Introspection" 99). Although Kohut eventually challenged some of the fundamental tenets that govern classical Freudian analysis, his roots were solidly Freudian. In fact, there may have been some narcissistic "anxiety of influence," to borrow Harold Bloom's phrase, in Kohut's initial divergence from Freud. For before 1965, as Charles Strozier observes, Kohut was regarded as "Mr. Psychoanalysis, the most eminent spokesman for classical Freudian thought" but "it soon became painfully clear to Kohut that orthodoxy could not easily contain his developing thought. . . . It is now an almost stale criticism of Kohut that he understood narcissism so well because he was himself so grandiose. No great thinker is humble; and it took real courage and fortitude to move away from a tradition . . . that was so completely a part of Kohut's soul" (10, 11).

In 1966, when Kohut published his initial essay on narcissism, he made only a lateral movement away from Freud. He conceptualized his theory as a minor refinement of Freud's view that narcissism is the "libidinal investment of the self," arguing that the "various forms of narcissism" should be considered "not only as forerunners of object love but also as independent psychological constellations" deserving "separate examination and evaluation" ("Forms and Transformations

11

of Narcissism" 427, 460). And although his first major work, *The Analysis of the Self*, published in 1971, marked a major break from traditional analytic theory and practice, Kohut still framed his findings within the standard Freudian discourse. In the following ten years, until his death in 1981, Kohut came to openly challenge the traditional Freudian ideology in his papers, which are collected in *The Search for the Self*, in his papers and conversations, collected in *Self Psychology and the Humanities*, and in his books, *The Restoration of the Self* and *How Does Analysis Cure?* That Kohut became distressed with the rigid ideological biases of the American analytic enterprise is apparent in many of his public statements. He was bothered by analysts' overidealization of Freud and also by what he called the "tool-and-method pride" of those Freudian analysts who, in their strict adherence to Freud's doctrines, reduced their patients to a predictable set of symptoms. Kohut came to perceive classical analysis as a coercive, overly systematized scientific method that had all but lost touch with its human subjects.

But Kohut's disaffection with the Freudian method also went much deeper. For he, like others, began to recognize a significant shift in the patient population, an increase in the number of narcissistically disturbed patients whom classical analysis was unable to adequately understand or treat. And he, like others, began to cross-question some of the basic tenets of Freudian metapsychology: the theory of the primacy of the drives and drive discharge and the centrality of the Oedipus complex. Kohut did not question the fact of man's biological nature. But he did contest Freud's notion of the biological bedrock of the human psyche as he attempted to dislodge psychoanalysis from the matrix of the libido theory and from its view of the psychosexual constitution of the self.

Kohut's characterization of Freudian man throws into vivid relief some of the fundamental differences between the Freudian and Kohutian views. Kohut perceives the Freudian psychological terrain to be an inhospitable, mechanistic world populated by creatures who are half human, half animal. Freudian man is a "precariously domesticated animal" whose "insecurely tamed drives" are held in check by inner and outer threats: the "fear of punishment" and "guilt" ("Reflections" 539). Conflict ridden, he is hopelessly torn between his biological drives—his primitive sexual and aggressive impulses—and the stern, forbidding "civilizing influences" that emanate "from the social environment" and become "embodied in the superego" ("Introspection" 94). Freudian metapsychology, as it has been described, "rests upon the theory of instinctual drive, deals with the material substrate of subjective experience, and is thus couched in the natural science framework of impersonal mechanisms, discharge apparatuses, and drive energies, all of which are presumed to 'exist' as entities or events in the realm of objective reality" (Stolorow 44).

Prying psychoanalysis away from Freudian psychobiology, Kohut puts self-experience into the center of his view of psychological man and woman. The individual's "essence," he asserts, "is defined when seen as a self" ("Introspection" 94). What Kohut sees as fundamental to the self are not biological drives but rather the desire for a sense of relationship with and responsiveness from others. In place of Freud's conflict-ridden *Guilty Man*, Kohut offers a new paradigm, that of narcissistically damaged *Tragic Man*. Unlike Guilty Man who "lives within the pleasure principle" and "attempts to satisfy his pleasure-seeking drives," Tragic Man's "endeavors lie beyond the pleasure principle" (*Restoration* 132–33). Tragic Man perpetually tries but never quite succeeds in fulfilling the goals, ambitions, and ideals of his core self. Longing to achieve the restoration of his self, he spends his life attempting to repair his defective self, to discover, in an empathic, self-supportive, and self-enhancing milieu, the glue that mends, that binds into a cohesive whole, his broken self.

Kohut's Theory of the Self

While Kohut deviates from classical Freudian theory and has a different view of human nature,[1] he derived his theory of the self through the classical psychoanalytic method, and this is of vital significance to those who view the "psychoanalytic method" and not Freud's "biological speculations" as the "foundation of psychoanalysis" (Basch, "Memorial" 6). Through his analytic work with narcissistically disturbed patients, Kohut slowly fit together the pieces of the "tragic" individual's puzzling condition.

Central to the psychoanalytic transaction is the *transference* in which the analysand, instead of consciously remembering the past, unconsciously reproduces it by repeating and acting out infantile and early needs and relationships with the analyst, who becomes an amalgam of significant early figures—especially parental figures. The patients Kohut treated were generally considered unanalyzable by classical standards. For during the course of their treatment, explains self psychologist Ernest Wolf, "their suffering did not ameliorate, their acting out persisted," and their "transference-like" states "did not yield to the appropriate interpretations of the presumed underlying drive-and-defense constellation" ("Transferences and Countertransferences" 580). In his joint ventures with narcissistic patients, Kohut discovered himself in a strange, archaic interior world where self and other meld, a world that predates the subject/object differentiation central to the classical Freudian transference situation. His patients experienced him not as a separate, autonomous object (person) but as a self-extension or a need-satisfying object to be controlled and used. It was his genetic reconstructions of the troubled lives of such patients that led Kohut to privilege empathy in his metapsychology and in his clinical practice.

Kohut's theory of the *bipolar self* distinguishes between two aspects or poles of the self, which first emerge in the earliest stages of life: the *grandiose-exhibitionistic* and the *idealizing*. The *archaic grandiose self* is rooted in the infant's feelings that he or she is the center of the world and all-powerful and that the parents are there to meet every need and demand. *Archaic idealization* finds its source in the infant's experience of being nurtured, held, and soothed by the parents. By merging with the calm strength of the nurturing caregiver—the *idealized parent imago* who is perceived as all-powerful—the infant finds relief from feelings of helplessness, diffuse depression, and rage. The infant experiences the caregiver not as a separate object but as a *selfobject*, that is, as part of the self.

In normal development, the child's archaic grandiosity and exhibitionism, empathically responded to by the *mirroring* (i.e., echoing, approving, confirming) parents, is gradually tamed as it is undercut by reality. This occurs largely between the ages of two and four. Similarly, idealizing needs are slowly undercut by reality as the child, between the ages of four and six, experiences gradual and phase-appropriate disappointments in the idealized parent imago(s). Over time, as the grandiose-exhibitionistic and idealizing aspects of the self mature, the mirroring, soothing, and stabilizing functions of the archaic selfobjects are slowly internalized through a structure-building

14

process Kohut calls *transmuting internalization.* Ultimately, in normal development of the bipolar self, archaic grandiosity and exhibitionism give rise to the endopsychic resources of healthy self-esteem and assertiveness (the pole of ambition) and archaic idealization to a sense of inner strength and a sustaining relationship with internal ideals (the pole of ideals). Kohut conceptualizes the relationship between the two poles of the self as a "tension arc," that is, as an "abiding flow of actual psychological activity" between the ambitions that drive a person and the ideals that lead him (*Restoration* 180). The "firm self," in Kohut's model, has three basic parts: "(1) one pole from which emanate the basic strivings for power and success; (2) another pole that harbours the basic idealized goals; and (3) an intermediate area of basic talents and skills that are activated by the tension-arc that establishes itself between ambitions and ideals" (Kohut and Wolf 414).

"[I]t is not so much what the parents *do* that will influence the character of the child's self," according to Kohut, "but what the parents *are.*" If the parents' own "self-confidence is secure," they will respond empathically to the child's exhibitionistic displays. The parents' proud smiles "will keep alive a bit" of the child's "original omnipotence" which will consequently be "retained as the nucleus of the self-confidence" that will sustain the individual throughout life. Similarly, the self-confidence of the idealized parents and their calmness and security when they soothe the anxious child will be retained as the nucleus of the inner strength the individual derives from internal ideals (Kohut and Wolf 417). Developing in the matrix of the self-selfobject environment, the *nuclear self* is the "basis for our sense of being an independent center of initiative and perception, integrated with our most central ambitions and ideals and with our experience that our body and mind form a unit in space and a continuum in time" (*Restoration* 177). While Kohut has been accused of reifying his concept of the "self"—for he talks of the self as being "strong," "enfeebled," or "depleted," or as "cohesive," "broken" or "fragmented"—the self is not, for him, "a thing or an entity" but rather "a symbolic abstraction from the developmental process" and an experiential construct. It is "the uniqueness that separates the experiences of an individual from those of all others while at the same time conferring a sense of cohesion and continuity on the disparate experiences of that individual . . ." (Basch, "The Concept of 'Self' " 53).

The Narcissistic Disorder

The *narcissistically defective or deficient individual* never develops the endopsychic resources of healthy self-esteem, inner strength, and resilience because of traumatic empathic failures on the part of the parents during the early stages of self-development. Unlike traditional psychoanalysis which tends to focus on "grossly traumatic events" in the development of pathology—such as the witnessing of the 'primal scene' or the death of a parent—self psychology holds that "such traumatic events may be no more than clues that point to the truly pathogenic factors, the unwholesome atmosphere to which the child was exposed during the years when his self was established" (Kohut and Wolf 417).

Because the self essentially evolves out of the parent-child relationship, parents with defective personalities—those, for example, who are emotionally cold or shallow, severely depressed, or governed by unpredictable mood swings—may undermine the child's development of a healthy self since such parents are typically unable to respond empathically to the child's mirroring and idealizing needs. The child, for example, may experience repeated self-injuring rejections at the hands of the parents when seeking their approval, or may experience massive disappointments in the idealized parents, or may suffer severe separation anxiety. If this happens and the child's development of a healthy narcissistic self is derailed, some normal and necessary transmuting internalizations and self-structure building will not occur.

Individuals who suffer from such empathic deprivations may, as a consequence, be dominated throughout their lives by the regressive needs of the *archaic grandiose self* (which perceives itself as omnipotent, the center of attention, and in control of others) and/or the *archaic idealizing self* (which feels empty and powerless unless merged with an all-powerful other). Because narcissistically defective adults cannot provide themselves with sufficient self-approval or with a sense of strength through their own inner resources, they are forever compelled to satisfy these essential needs through external sources: by extracting praise from or exercising unquestioned dominance over others or by merging with idealized figures. Lacking a *stable cohesive self*—that is, a stable sense of the self as a unitary agent, an initiator of action and a continuum in time—they suffer from a fundamental weakness and deficiency in the center of the personality. They may harbor feelings of greatness side by side with low self-esteem. They may respond to the frustration of their exhibitionistic impulses with shame and to the failure of their grandiose ambitions with rage. They may be prone to states of *understimulation*, a feeling of deadness and empty depression; *overstimulation*, the experience of being overwhelmed by unmodified—and thus frightening—archaic grandiose fantasies or by an intense—and thereby self-threatening—need for merger with an idealized selfobject; *fragmentation*, a frightening loss of a sense of self-continuity and cohesiveness; and *overburdenedness*, a traumatic "spreading" of the emotions, in particular the "spreading of anxiety" (Kohut and Wolf 418–20). And they continue to experience other people as *archaic selfobjects*: "as a part of the self or as merged with the self or as standing in the service of the self, i.e., as utilized for the maintenance of the stability and cohesion of the self" ("Narcissism as a Resistance" 554).

Behind the overt behavior and inner feelings of those suffering from the narcissistic disorder—their hypersensitivity to slights and shame-propensity, their radical shifts in self-perception and self-esteem, their disavowed or overt rage, their intense loneliness and subjective emptiness—lies an urgent need to reconstitute the self. Despite their attempts to repair the self by using others as archaic selfobjects—that is, as substitutes for the psychic structures they lack—the central defect remains. Pathetically vulnerable, they are subject to *disintegration anxiety*—a dreadful fear of the loss of the self (*Restoration* 104–05). Tragic Man and Woman, they are compelled to endlessly enact the same primitive, fixated behavior in their frustrated search for wholeness.

The Self-Selfobject Relationship

At the heart of the analytic situation with the narcissistic patient is the self-selfobject relationship which Kohut locates in an "ambiguous" zone between "endopsychic reality and social reality" ("Selected Problems" 392). Bridging the "inner world of the self and the outer world of the environment," the selfobject concept, observes Ernest Wolf, describes "not a social psychology of relations of objects to each other but a true depth psychology of intrapsychic processes concerning the self—its boundaries, its cohesion, and its fragmentation—under various conditions of correctly attuned or of faulty selfobject responsiveness" ("Psychoanalytic Psychology" 44).

In the analytic transaction, the narcissistic needs of the analysand which were not empathically responded to in childhood become reactivated in a variety of *archaic selfobject transferences*: the need to experience the analyst as part of the self and assume omnipotent control over him or her in the *merger transference* (this is classified as the most primitive form of the mirror transference); the need to receive confirming, approving attention from the analyst and affirmation of the self's greatness and perfection in the *mirror transference*; the need to experience the analyst as similar to the self, as someone who shares the individual's attitudes, concerns, feelings, likes, and dislikes, in the *alter-ego or twinship transference*; and the need to fuse with the analyst, who is perceived as perfect and all powerful, and thus to take on the analyst's power, calm strength, and perfection in the *idealizing transference*. It is important to note here that an individual patient may display a complex mixture of these archaic selfobject needs as the transference unfolds. Fantasies that sometimes emerge in the treatment of such individuals—twinship and superhero fantasies or those of the faceless parent or of body-self fragmentation—reveal the mobilization of archaic needs and fears. Similarly in what Kohut calls self-state dreams, verbalizable dream imagery portrays archaic preverbal states, such as manic overstimulation, a profound drop in self-esteem, or disintegration anxiety (*Restoration* 108–11).[2]

One of the distinguishing characteristics of the archaic selfobject transference is the dramatic intensity of the patient's need for the analyst. When narcissistically disturbed individuals establish an empathic selfobject bond with the analyst, they may feel an infusion of new energy and experience newfound feelings of self-acceptance and wholeness. But any perceived break in the archaic selfobject bond is experienced as a threat to the self. Such patients may feel narcissistically injured and consequently become enraged, emotionally withdrawn, or depressed if they perceive the analyst as nonempathic, emotionally unavailable, or not totally attuned to their often unspoken needs. And they may find it difficult to tolerate even minor disruptions in the therapy, such as schedule changes or weekend interruptions.[3] The response of Mr. M. to an anticipated vacation separation from the analyst reveals his acute neediness: "I have a sense of dying or perishing. . . . I expect this energy to be drawn out of me, it is impossible to generate it." For Mr. E., just thinking about a weekend separation from the analyst makes him "feel a sense of deadness." "My whole life," says Mr. I., "needs an acknowledgement to know I exist; I always need a stamp of approval" (Goldberg, *Psychology* 149, 272, 65). While there are gradations in self-pathology—the self, in Kohut's words, may be "more or less seriously damaged"—what marks the self-disorder is "[s]ignificant failure to achieve cohesion, vigour, or harmony, or a significant loss of these qualities after they had been tentatively established" (Kohut and Wolf 414).

Of course, all of us are subject to occasional and transient feelings of anxiety, depression, or low self-esteem. But in those with the self-disorder, these feelings are more severe and incapacitating and can be triggered by even the minor stresses and failures of daily life. Those with narcissistic personality disorders display a wide range of behaviors and personalities. They may be involved in a lifelong, compulsive search for self-confirming responses from others in an attempt to counteract their innate sense of worthlessness; they may feel worthwhile only if they are attached to someone they can idealize as an embodiment of the human perfection they permanently lack; they may feel valid only in relationships with alter-ego others who conform to and thus confirm their values and opinions; they may demand complete dominance over the selfobject other who functions as a replacement of their defective self-structure; or they may shun contact with others because of their intense selfobject needs, their extreme sensitivity to rejection, and their merger apprehensions (see Kohut and Wolf 421–22). While Kohut, like many others, views narcissistic pathology as the predominant psychological disorder of our time,[4] it is also possible, as some have speculated, that narcissistic symptoms "existed before and were simply not 'heard'" by analysts (Layton and Schapiro 1; see also Kohut, *Restoration* 291).

The Psychoanalytic Cure

Unlike Freudian analysis which views the "essence" of the psychoanalytic cure as the increasing ability "to modify the drives" or as the "expansion of the domain of the ego," self psychology, writes

Kohut, "does not find the essence of the curative process in the cognitive sphere per se" (*How?* 64). Instead, it conceives the *psychoanalytic cure* as a process of structure building and deficit-filling that involves the analysand's gradual internalization of the analyst's soothing, stabilizing, and self-esteem-maintaining selfobject functions.

Again and again in the course of an analysis, the empathic selfobject transference is disrupted by the normal separations involved in the analytic transaction (such as weekend separations) and by the analyst's "unavoidable, yet only temporary and thus nontraumatic, empathy failures—that is, his 'optimal failures'" (*How?* 66). Each separation or empathic failure remobilizes the analysand's archaic selfobject needs and may reactivate old narcissistic injuries and feelings of traumatic rejection which threaten the cohesiveness of the self. The repressed or expressed *narcissistic rage* which often emerges in the analysis of such individuals is a response to traumatic narcissistic injury. As these regressive reactions and retreats are interpreted repeatedly over time, the analysand, via transmuting internalization of the analyst's selfobject functions, slowly acquires the psychological structures he or she lacks. The analysand's self, consequently, becomes more resilient and firm and more resistant to narcissistic injury (see *How?* 66–70).

When the selfobject transference is resolved, the individual is free to pursue the goals, ideals, and ambitions of the nuclear self and thus to lead a more productive and satisfying life. The individual's self is now capable of being sustained by *mature selfobjects*, that is, by the "empathic resonance that emanates from the selfobjects of adult life" (*How?* 70). There is, as we have observed, a quality of drivenness, of addictionlike compulsion, in archaic selfobject needs. Mature selfobject needs, in contrast, are less intense, "less individual and more group oriented, less focused on specific persons and more easily displaceable to other individuals" (Wolf and Wilson 210).[5] Mature selfobjects include one's family, the various groups—peer, political, social, and professional—to which one belongs and also "cultural selfobjects," such as writers, artists, and political leaders (*How?* 220, n.11). "The ordinary person, too, must have sustaining selfobjects in order to be active and productive," Kohut writes. "We need mirroring acceptance, the merger with ideals, the sustaining presence of others like us, throughout our lives" ("Reflections" 494–95; see also Wolf, "On the

Developmental Line" 127–30). Mature selfobjects satisfy the basic human needs for empathic resonance and for a vital sense of connection with others.

The Oedipal Phase

Central to the classical Freudian analytic transaction is the uncovering and resolution of the pathogenic Oedipus complex. Rejecting the Freudian view, Kohut holds that the narcissistically healthy child who is responded to empathically during the oedipal stage will assertively embrace this normal maturational process. The affectionate feelings of such a child will not "disintegrate into fragmented sexual impulses" nor will the child's assertiveness transform into "destructive hostility" (*How?* 14). What breeds oedipal pathology is a flawed self-selfobject matrix. While classical analysts believe that the deepest psychic level has been reached when patients become aware of their sexual and aggressive drives, self-psychologically informed analysts "will be open to the fact that the pathogenic Oedipus complex is embedded in an oedipal self-selfobject disturbance, that beneath lust and hostility there is a layer of depression and of diffuse narcissistic rage" (*How?* 5). In Kohut's view, greed, lust, and rage are *disintegration products* of the self, signals of the self's fragmentation, instability, or enfeeblement. The bedrock of destructive rage is not biological but psychological. Rage is the self's reaction to a traumatic narcissistic injury, one that threatens the cohesiveness of the self (see *Restoration* 113–31; also "Thoughts on Narcissism" 634–57).

In his rereading of the Oedipus myth, Kohut locates behind the tale's "manifest content" of patricide and incest traces of another more fundamental story. "Oedipus was a rejected child," a child unwanted by his parents, and so he was left in the wilderness to die. "[D]own deep the sense of his original rejection must have remained." In place of the story of Oedipus, Kohut offers a new paradigm: that of Odysseus and his infant son. Attempting to avoid being sent on the Trojan expedition, Odysseus feigned madness by yoking together an ox and ass to plow his fields and throwing salt into the furrows. But he was exposed through a ruse. When one of the Greek emissaries, suspecting Odysseus of deception, threw Odysseus's infant son in front of his plow, Odysseus made a semicircle around his son to avoid injuring him. Odysseus's semicir-

21

cle—the "semicircle of mental health"—symbolizes the intergenerational caring and support that Kohut considers "normal and human." Substituting Freud's Oedipus myth with that of Odysseus and his son, Kohut views the "intrafamilial bond," not intergenerational conflict, as the "nuclear essence of humanness" ("Introspection" 97–98, 97, 98).

Empathy

Giving a central place to empathy in his theory of the self and his psychoanalytic practice, Kohut considers "scientific empathy" to be the "highest *ideal*" ("Future" 684). He also insists axiomatically that empathy is fundamental to human life and self-survival. For the self "arises in a matrix of empathy" and it "strives to live within a modicum of empathic responses" to sustain itself ("Remarks" 752, n.5). A "psychological nutriment without which human life as we know and cherish it could not be sustained," empathy is "the accepting, confirming, and understanding human echo evoked by the self" ("Psychoanalyst" 705).

Rejecting the view of the analyst as an essentially detached observer-scientist, Kohut recognizes that in the complex intra- and intersubjective dynamics of the analytic interaction, the analyst is much more than an objective observer.[6] He or she is a deeply involved participant-observer. What is central to the analytic transaction, in Kohut's description, is the *sustained empathic-introspective immersion* of the analyst into the interior life of the patient.[7] Deriving his theory from his empathic grasp of his patients' experiential states, Kohut describes psychoanalysis as "par excellence the science of empathy" ("Future" 678). Empathy—which Kohut defines as *"vicarious introspection"*—is the "capacity to think and feel oneself into the inner life of another person" while "simultaneously retaining the stance of an objective observer" (*How?* 82, 175). Empathy is both a passive mode of immersion and an active mode of perception and understanding, an "instrument of cognition" ("Psychoanalyst" 712).

The processes by which the analyst gains empathic contact with the patient are variously described in the growing body of literature on empathy (see Jaffe 227–30). In one formulation, the core experience of empathy is "transient identification," a "temporary sense of oneness" with the patient which is "followed by a sense of separateness in order to appreciate that one has felt not only *with* the patient but *about* him" (Beres and Arlow 34). Empathy, in a self-psychological formulation, involves some "controlled regression" on the part of the analyst in which the analysand "temporarily" becomes a selfobject for the analyst and thus "aspects of the analysand are experienced as part of the analyst's self and become available for introspective examination" (Wolf, "Transferences and Countertransferences" 586). Empathy, in another description, is the "*position* from which the analyst interacts with the patient": that is, in empathically relating to a patient, the analyst must "choose which imago, or transference object, to stand behind and empathize with" (Schlesinger 201). Empathy is also described as a "listening stance oriented from within" the patient's perspective and feelings (Schwaber, "Self Psychology" 220): the analyst must be able to "step inside the patient's perspective" while maintaining his or her own "autonomy" (Schwaber, "On the 'Self' " 474). Employing the analyst's cognitive, perceptual, and affective capacities, empathic listening involves the analyst's "attunement to and recognition of the perceptions and experiential states" of the analysand (Schwaber, "Empathy" 160).[8] This notion of the empathically attuned analyst stands in stark contrast to the caricatured view of the detached, anonymous, mirror-analyst.[9] A central focus of self psychology is the "interwoven matrix of the patient-analyst as a contextual unit" (Schwaber, "On the 'Self' " 476).

Countertransference

Another important source of knowledge in the analytic transaction is the analyst's awareness of his or her *countertransference* responses to the analysand. In the original and more narrow definition, countertransference refers to the psychoanalyst's unresolved conflicts and spontaneous transference responses toward the patient, which, if unrecognized, can impede or even derail the analytic process. If, for example, the analyst's repressed grandiosity is stimulated by the analysand's idealizing attitudes, the analyst, in a desire to ward off this idealization, may shortcircuit the development of the idealizing transference by denying his or her importance or by making premature interpretations. If, in the merger transference, the analyst's "merger apprehensions" are mobilized, the analyst may react by defensively withdrawing from the analysand's engulfing personality (Kohut, *Analysis* 262–64, 280–81). If the analysand's grandiosity "diminishes the analyst into feeling utterly negligible," the analyst may become bored or angry (Goldberg, *Psychology* 445). And if vulnerable to the analysand's twinship transference, the analyst may react by openly asserting his or her separate identity (Wolf, "Transferences and Countertransferences" 582; see also 581–83).

In the traditional view, then, countertransference may often be considered as evidence of the analyst's residual pathology and thus as a potential hindrance to the analytic transaction. But countertransference, in its broader definition, is considered not only normal but also therapeutically useful.[10] In the "totalistic" definition, countertransference is conceived as the analyst's total emotional reaction to the patient. Since, in this view, the analyst's conscious and unconscious reactions may be induced by the patient or the analyst may experience "the central emotion that the patient is experiencing" (Kernberg 59), countertransference can provide key insights into the patient's emotional states and unconscious fantasies and thus enhance the analyst's empathic contact with the patient. Countertransference is also conceived as a normal "role-responsive" counterpart of or complement to the patient's transference (Epstein and Feiner 12). Countertransference, for example, may involve the analyst's identification with the patient's transference figures and thus lead to the replication of the patient's "early relationship" with significant parental figures. The analyst may, to give a specific example, identify with a forbidding parent figure while the patient is experiencing a renewal of submissive feelings connected to his or her relationship with that particular parent (Kernberg 60, 59). In a self-psychological formulation, "controlled" selfobject countertransference is a process in which the analyst transiently experiences the patient as a selfobject—that is, as part of the self—and thus gains empathic insight into the patient's inner world (Wolf, "Transferences and Countertransferences" 586; see also Köhler 46–48). Countertransference responses to narcissistic patients, which are varied, include overidealization, the desire to control or rescue the patient, fear of intrusion, transient merger anxieties, and feelings of vulnerability, anger, or boredom.

The Reading Process

"What is at work in reading," according to psychoanalyst Gail Reed, "is akin to what psychoanalysis calls countertransference in its broadest sense, the emotional responses of the analyst to the patient which, scrutinized, may provide him with valuable information about the patient or, unscrutinized, may interfere with his understanding of and response to the patient" (*"Candide"* 191). Observing that critics who respond "empathically" to texts "but without conscious under- standing" may "re-enact" aspects of the text's "organizing fantasy" in their critical interpretations ("Toward a Methodology" 39), Reed links this to the clinical phenomenon of "parallelism." Parallelism, as Reed explains, refers to the "well-known but relatively infrequently dis- cussed re-enactments in supervision by the supervisee" of specific as- pects of the patient's "affect, behavior, or conflicts" of which the super- visee "is not consciously aware." Reenactment, in Reed's analysis, can be understood "as a product of empathy untempered by conscious understanding," such empathy achieved "through the transient sharing of fantasy" ("Toward a Methodology" 36–37). Critical reenactments of texts can also be understood as transferential repetitions, as man- ifestations of the compulsion to repeat. Just as the "analyst gets caught up in a repetition of key structures of the patient's unconscious," so reading can be viewed as "a displaced repetition of the structure it seeks to analyze" (Culler 271). In a demonstration of reading as transference repetition, Shoshana Felman offers a deconstructive analysis of *The Turn of the Screw* that shows how certain textual motifs—for example, of a danger that must be avoided, of attack and defense, or of madness and hysterical delusion—recur in polemical discussions of James's work (98–99). She concludes that the "scene of the critical debate" surrounding *The Turn of the Screw* is "a *repetition* of the scene drama- tized in the text. The critical interpretation . . . not only elucidates the text but also reproduces it dramatically, unwittingly *participates in it*" (101).[11] The transient sharing of fantasy, trial or temporary identifica- tions,[12] transferential repetitions, induced affective or countertransfer- ence-like reactions—these are important aspects of the reading process and are at the core of critic/readers' transactions with fictional charac- ters and their unwitting duplication, in their critical interpretations, of the psychodramas encoded in texts.

When Norman Holland claims that readers project their own needs and defenses onto texts and use the text to replicate their own identities,[13] he implicitly denies that readers have the ability to empa- thize, that is, that they can temporarily share the experience of another from *within* that person's perspective. While the capacity to empathize varies from reader to reader, my assumption is that empathy is central to the reading experience and that, despite the wide variation in the ways critics theorize about literature and objectify the reading experience, texts can and do generate a range of similar, collective, and often unconscious responses in readers. In this work, one way I attempt to probe such responses is by focusing attention on academic criticism, which is a public, negotiated response to literature. Because the prevailing critical discourses have long tended to distrust affective responses to literature, such responses have been muted. In the words of Cary Nelson, "[a]cademic criticism works very hard to depersonalize its insights, to mask its fears and wishes in a language of secure authority" ("Reading Criticism" 803).[14] In the view of Jane Tompkins the compulsion to systematize literature or the reader and the desire to be abstract, impersonal, or scientific in critical discussions give evidence of the need of critics to shield themselves from the very literature they describe and the feelings that literature evokes. These critical practices also, I suspect, find their source in the selfobject environment of academic criticism which has evolved during the long struggle and rivalry between the sciences and humanities and has tended to mirror and idealize those critics or metacritics who mimic, or more recently, attempt to dismantle scientific theory or those who assert the critic's grandiosity: his or her power over the text. This is why the more unguarded reactions to literature, typically located in polemicized discussions or in critical obsessions with or avoidances of certain issues, often provide key insights into the fears, fantasies, and defenses generated by texts. Despite what Gerald Graff calls the "routinization of critical discourses," illustrated, for example, in the New Critical "fetish of unity" or in the deconstructive "fetish of disunity" (243, 242), the critical conversations surrounding texts can be psychologically revealing.

Elizabeth Wright observes that "if the patient's 'text', his presentation of experience, can cause a disturbance in the analyst which allows for a new interpretation, this turns upside down the notion that the reader is the analyst and the text the patient. . . . Readers do not only work on texts, but texts work on readers . . ." (17). Thus the "reader-cum-critic's position is . . . vastly complicated" because we are both "subject to the effects the work produces" in us as readers and "committed to the analysis of these effects" as critics (177). Similarly, the model of reading as an empathic event recognizes that the critic/

reader, in the acts of reading and interpreting, is simultaneously cast in the roles of reader/analysand and critic/analyst. Moreover, it also recognizes that the critic's text, in turn, can be subjected to a psycho-critical reading. Like the analyst, the empathic critic/reader focuses attention on the disruptive and disturbing responses—the anger, anxiety, disgust, boredom, fear of encroachment, need to master or desire to rescue—engendered by the characters and texts being investigated. And like the analyst, the empathic reader is aware of the negotiated roles he or she is invited to play when responding to fictional texts. The empathic reader, in other words, is a participant-observer.

Reviewing the current "stories of reading" proposed by reader-response theorists, Jonathan Culler observes that the question of control is central to such inquiries: Is the reader dominant over the text or the text over the reader? In the view of critics such as David Bleich, Norman Holland, and Stanley Fish, the reader is the dominant force; in contrast, Michael Riffaterre and Wolfgang Iser, while admitting the active role of the reader, hold that the text is the controlling force. A "curious feature" of these accounts, according to Culler, "is how easily text and reader can switch places: a story of the reader structuring the text easily becomes a story of the text provoking certain responses and actively controlling the reader" (70). For example, Roland Barthes's "celebrations of the reader as producer of the text are matched by accounts of the text's disruption of the reader's most basic conceptions . . ." (70). Similarly, Stanley Fish's account of reading oscillates "back and forth between a reader who actively takes charge and a hapless reader buffeted by fierce sentences" (71). "The shift back and forth in stories of reading between readers' decisive actions and readers' automatic responses," concludes Culler, "is not a mistake that could be corrected but an essential structural feature of the situation" (73). Describing the "essential, divided quality of reading," Culler comments: "For the reader the work is not partially created but, on the one hand, already complete and inexhaustible—one can read and reread without ever grasping completely what has already been made—and, on the other hand, still to be created in the process of reading, without which it is only black marks on paper" (76). "There must always be dualisms: an interpreter and something to interpret, a subject and an object, an actor and something he acts upon or that acts on him" (75).

Culler's story about the divided nature of reading is incisive. While texts act on readers, readers also make active choices in reading and interpreting texts and thus collaborate in the production of textual meaning. The psychocritical readings presented in the following chapters, for example, are a way of actively retelling, reconstructing the texts discussed in light of the interpretive strategies offered by self psychology. But it is also the case that when we, as critics, "retell"— that is, write a text about another text—we are caught up in an act of duplication. Despite the disproportionate claims of some theorists for the reader's creative role as the producer of the text, texts do act on readers and this is the aspect of the reader/text transaction on which my investigation focuses. The model of reading as an empathic event furnishes yet another "story" of reading. Empathy, in Kohut's view, involves both immersion and cognition. Both subjective and objective, empathic reading is a dynamic process involving the critic/reader's participation in but also active observation and interpretation of the text's intended manipulation of its audience.

One of the primary ways the texts we will examine in the following chapters attempt to manipulate the reader is through the characters they depict. And yet, despite the fact that fictional characters are calculated to evoke a response from the reader, "[c]haracter has not fared well in our century," as Baruch Hochman observes (13). For while the New Critics insisted on the "absolute literariness" of fictional characters, the structuralists and poststructuralists have insisted on their "utter subordination" (20) to the plot or language of the text. It is true that the postmodernist novel works to depersonalize and minimize characters, exposing them to be pure artifice, pure verbal construct, but this does not mean that fictional characters outside this tradition should be retrospectively textualized, pronounced as mere words, mere text.

Because characters are constructed through language and generated in texts, they are, as postmodernist critics like to remind us, in a radical way, *in* and *of* the text. Our experience of the characters we will examine in the chapters that follow, for example, derives from the underlying narcissistic fantasies, needs, and defenses that structure the texts which generate them. And yet there remains something else in our response to character that interests me: what Susan Greenstein has described as "a subversive quality . . . which can penetrate the decorum that generally regulates relations between reader and text" (527). While theorists may insistently reduce characters to the theme or narrative structure or language of the text, many critic/readers, as we shall see, just as insistently respond to the personlike qualities of literary characters. Indeed, one of the primary things that draws us to literature is its *human* element, the selfobject resonance which saturates the literary object and underlies our reciprocal relationships to the fictional characters who populate texts.

"If one insists on seeing all novels as congeries of semiotic systems intricately functioning in a pure state of self-referentiality," writes Robert Alter, "one loses the fine edge of responsiveness to the urgent human predicaments that novels seek to articulate" (21). Kohut's self psychology gives us privileged insight to the urgent predicaments of Tragic Man and Woman. Enticing and eluding us, the narcissistic characters we will meet in the following chapters lead us on the search Kohut conducted throughout his career as both a practicing psychoanalyst and a theoretician: the "search for the self" and for the "nuclear essence of humanness."

✻ ✻ ✻ ✻

Part II
Tragic Man

✻ ✻ ✻ ✻

Two

Narcissistic Vulnerability and
Rage in Dostoevsky's
Notes From Underground

✢ ✢ ✢ ✢

A narrative suffused with rage, Fyodor Dostoevsky's *Notes From Underground* depicts a character who provides a strategic point of entry into the troubled selfhood of Tragic Man. Suffering from shaky self-esteem, "neither a hero nor an insect" (130), the Underground Man is a spiteful individual who harbors a deep sense of injury and attempts to injure others. What will be partially disguised in most of our subsequent encounters with Tragic Man—his urgent need for attention and his enraged or depressed response to what he perceives as rejection—is openly dramatized in this text. That a number of commentators have all but avoided the anti-hero's perverse, angry personality, focusing instead on the philosophic discourse of *Notes*, is telling. In this critical tendency toward textual avoidances and abstractions, we find suggestive evidence of the ability of Dostoevsky's narrative to disturb and implicate its readers.

While *Notes From Underground* is "an abnormally unnerving story to read" and while there is something unsettling about the reader's "experience of proximity" to Dostoevsky's unstable anti-hero (Norman 289), many critics who have responded to this work have centered attention not on the anti-hero's disruptive presence or his shameful autobiographical account in Part 2 but, instead, on the ideological implications of his paradoxical discourse in Part 1. Walter Kaufmann, for example, describes Part 1 of *Notes From Underground*

33

as "the best overture for existentialism ever written" (14). Edward Wasiolek holds that the anti-hero perpetually "redefines himself by contradiction and denial" as a "pledge of his freedom" (43). According to Reed Merrill, "[t]he determined objective of the Underground Man is to prove conclusively that he is free to choose and to act" (515). In Merrill's view, the anti-hero is a "developed thinker" (506) who "*knows* that there are no truths except those temporarily created by his own caprice . . ." (512). Such apologists for the anti-hero, remarks Richard Weisberg, have used Part 1 of the novel "selectively" and have all but ignored Part 2 (554) in their defense of the Underground Man's claim that he acts irrationally and capriciously to assert his free will. We find a dramatic example of these critical omissions in the decision by some editors to publish only Part 1 of *Notes*. Through their textual avoidances and their selective re-presentations of the text, such critics, as they repeat the anti-hero's denials of his utter lack of free choice, use philosophic formulas to shield themselves from his agonistic, destabilizing presence. For "[i]nsult," observes Liane Norman, "is a mode more or less constant" throughout *Notes* and is designed to "provoke defensive responses" from the reader (289).[1] And the fact that the anti-hero's "need for an audience's recognition and confirmation," as Terrence Doody comments, "is constant, desperate, and essential" (27) is also meant to elicit a response from the reader. That a number of critics have played the role of confirming audience for the anti-hero's capricious behavior, reading it as an indicator of his adherence to the principle of freedom, attests to the power of *Notes* to involve the reader in the narcissistic script which it dramatizes.

Casting the "notes" of his anti-hero as a confession, Dostoevsky invites our active listening. Despite the Underground Man's seductive free-will rhetoric, he compulsively performs and reperforms a predetermined plot, as the psychocritics have observed.[2] Now forty, the Underground Man recalls in Part 2 a series of shameful incidents which occurred sixteen years before, when he was twenty-four. Ostensibly, he records his past to obtain "relief" from and to "get rid of" his oppressive memories (156). But it becomes apparent, as he repeats with his "gentlemen" audience the same psychodrama he describes in his reminiscences, that he is condemned to reenact his past in the present. The Underground Man is, as he claims from the outset, a sick man. Literally every word of his paradoxalist's account points to his underlying sense of defectiveness, and his seething anger, floating anxieties, and atavistic urges are forcibly brought to the forefront of the reader's awareness. Despite his noisy declarations that he acts irrationally and capriciously to assert his free will, he is, as he suspects, "impelled," "bound" to act as he does (170, 132). Driven by his archaic grandiose needs, he wants to exert power over others and be the center of attention and when these demands are thwarted, as happens in the separate but interlocking incidents first with the officer, then with Zverkov, and finally with Liza, he reacts with defensive arrogance, grandiose fantasies, depression, and rage. Needing a selfobject totally under his control, he creates his fictive gentlemen audience, acting out with them his desire to tyrannize over and compel the attention of others.

The device of the gentlemen narratees provides the actual reader confronting *Notes* with only a minimal protection from the text's punitive plot against its readers. The use of "you" in the anti-hero's addresses to the gentlemen serves to draw in readers, who are encouraged to identify both against and with the inscribed "you" in the text. Because the gentlemen are characterized as limited and as easily subdued by the anti-hero's superior intelligence, we are partially discouraged from identifying with the narratees in Part 1 and, instead, are urged to take the anti-hero's side in his argument against the rationalists and thus applaud his arrogant intellectualism. The imaginary gentlemen are inscribed as "bad readers." The implied "good readers"—those who accept the anti-hero's philosophy—are invited to temporarily share the anti-hero's illusion of power as he demolishes the rationalist metaphysic, a maneuver apparently attractive to many twentieth-century critic/readers. But while we may be captivated by the prepotent intellectual displays found in Part 1 of *Notes*, the anti-hero's spiteful, sadistic fantasies and behavior, evident throughout the narrative, are designed to assault our sensibilities and thus align us with the gentlemen, who stand in the text as representatives of the normal codes of civilized behavior which the anti-hero so outrageously offends. If we feel unsettled by our close proximity to Dostoevsky's character, it is because we become implicated in the pathological drama enacted in the text, caught up in the same sick narcissistic script the anti-hero stages with the imaginary gentlemen.

The Underground Man's telescoped memory of his relation-

ship with his rejecting caretakers—they "crushed" him with "reproaches" and then, in effect, abandoned him (175)—reveals both the
genesis and recurring pattern of his disordered personality. "If I had
had a home from childhood," he tells Liza, "I shouldn't be what I am
now. . . . I grew up without a home; and perhaps that's why I've turned
so . . . unfeeling" (195). In his radical shifts in self-perception from
arrogant superiority to deep self-contempt; in his intense mood swings
from elated grandiosity to acute depression; in his hypersensitivity to
slights, shame-propensity, and obsessive ruminations over shameful
incidents; in his lack of impulse-control and his need to control or
tyrannize others; in his feeling that he lacks a solid identity, that he
cannot *be* anything—the anti-hero manifests some of the classic symptoms of the narcissistic disorder. Because he has never developed the
inner resources of healthy narcissism, he is condemned to spend his life
in a series of fruitless attempts to extract from others what he permanently lacks: an inner sense of worth and strength. He is also condemned to reexperience with others his early narcissistic injuries.
"There in its nasty, stinking, underground home our insulted, crushed
and ridiculed mouse promptly becomes absorbed in cold, malignant
and, above all, everlasting spite," says the anti-hero in a parodic self-
description. "For forty years together it will remember its injury down
to the smallest, most ignominious details. . . . It will be ashamed of its
imaginings, but yet it will recall it all, it will go over and over every
detail . . . and will forgive nothing" (135). Bound and not free, the
Underground Man is compelled to remember his shameful past and to
act out, again and again, his pathetic, absurd drama. Similarly, the
reader, temporarily bound in a relationship with the anti-hero, is compelled, like the imaginary gentlemen, to listen to his obsessive ruminations, detail by sordid detail. "It is nasty for you to hear my despicable
moans," says the anti-hero at one point, indirectly expressing his mal-
ice toward his gentlemen audience as he describes the attitude of an
educated man suffering from a toothache. "[W]ell, let it be nasty; here I
will let you have a nastier flourish in a minute . . ." (138). Dostoevsky's
Notes reads like an extended exercise in spite directed against those
readers who, like some of the gentlemen narratees, might prefer to hear
a story with something of the heroic or "the good and the beautiful" in
it.

At the age of twenty-four the anti-hero's life, as he explains in his retrospective account, is "gloomy, ill-regulated, and as solitary as that of a savage" (157). Torn between his craving for the approval of others and his fear of rejection, he is "morbidly sensitive" (158). A lower-level government official, he both thinks his fellow clerks superior to himself and despises them as he defensively rejects his potential rejectors. To protect his vulnerable self, he emotionally distances himself from others: he assumes a posture of arrogant hostility in front of his coworkers and so inevitably comes to "loggerheads" with them (161). The fact that he both desires and shuns eye contact with them reveals his need for a confirming response from others and also his underlying anxiety about this need. Consciously experiencing wide vacillations in his self-esteem, he imagines himself as a hero and cultivated intellectual and he perceives himself as a "scoundrel," a "coward," an "impostor" (133, 158, 138), and as subhuman: a spiteful mouse, an eel, "a nasty, disgusting fly" (135, 164). Hating his face and finding it "stupid-looking," he assumes a "lofty expression" so he "might not be suspected of being abject" (158). Just as he hides from others behind a wall of defensive superiority, so he hides from himself behind a wall of fantasied superiority, imagining himself to be a Russian "romantic," one who attempts to "preserve" himself "like some precious jewel wrapped in cotton wool" (160). The jewel image is a signifier of what he lacks and most desires: an inner sense of preciousness and cohesiveness.

Because he lacks the sustaining self-esteem supplied by an inner feeling of worth, the Underground Man is caught up in a redundant narcissistic drama. "[O]ut of touch with 'real life,'" a "terrible dreamer" (218, 167), he retreats to a bookish fantasy world where he, for a time, can overcome his feelings of worthlessness by imagining himself a hero in the world's eyes. In his grandiose daydreams, whose plots are largely plagiarized from books, he fantasies himself triumphant over others: "every one, of course, was in dust and ashes, and was forced spontaneously to recognize my superiority. . . . I was a poet and a grand gentleman, I fell in love; I came in for countless millions and immediately devoted them to humanity, and at the same time I confessed before all the people my shameful deeds, which, of course, were not merely shameful, but had in them much that was 'good and beautiful,' something in the Manfred style" (168). Anticipating that his gentlemen narratees will condemn him for taking pleasure in such preposterous daydreams, he lashes out at them: "You will say that it is vulgar and contemptible to drag all this into public after all the tears and transports which I have myself confessed. But why is it contemptible? Can you imagine that I am ashamed of it all, and that it was stupider than anything in your life, gentlemen?" (168–69). Because on this—and many similar—occasions the inscribed "you" in the text is accused of attitudes and responses the actual reader is likely to share, the anti-hero's condemnation of his narratees is experienced as an indirect attack on the reader. Like the gentlemen audience, the reader of *Notes* is persistently positioned as an antagonist and a coparticipant in the anti-hero's self-drama.

After three months of indulging in escapist fantasies, the anti-hero develops an "irresistible desire to plunge into society" (169). There he uses others as selfobjects by dominating over them or attempting to extract from them the approval he needs to temporarily replenish his enfeebled self. While he craves contact with "society," he also fears, in his encounters with others, both a loss of control and traumatic rejection, for he can become overstimulated and disorganized when he receives the acceptance he desires, and he reacts with angry grandiosity when his demands for confirming attention are frustrated. And thus he is forced, once again, to retreat to his bookish fantasy world where he uses reading to "stifle" all that is "continually seething" inside him: his "wretched passions," "sickly irritability," "hysterical impulses, with tears and convulsions," and bouts of overwhelming depression (161). Taking "refuge" in his daydreams of "the good and the beautiful" (167), he makes up heroic adventures based on literary plots so he can "live in some way" (139). But he remains aware that he, in a fundamental way, does not feel quite real. In his sardonic description of his "golden" dream of becoming "a sluggard and a glutton" with a "good round belly," he inadvertently acknowledges what the men of action have and what he lacks. "[R]eal and solid" (141), they have cohesive selves; a "spindly little fellow" (162), he, in contrast, is narcissistically infirm. A "characterless creature," devoid of "positive" qualities, unable to "become anything" (131, 140, 131), he suffers from an impoverished sense of self.

Attempting to gain a foothold on real life, he writes his confessions and as he writes he deliberately imagines an audience before him—a hostile audience that is totally under his control and that rivets its attention on him. Telling stories so he may "live in some way," the forty-year-old narrator describes in vivid detail, but without deep comprehension, the shame-provoking misadventures of his earlier years. While we are clearly meant to recognize what many critics have avoided—the compulsive aspects of the anti-hero's capricious behavior—and while we may gain some minimal distance from the anti-hero as we observe, in Part 2, how others react to him, his confessions are also designed to bind us in a narrative transaction. The "act of narration," as Peter Brooks comments, can be "far from innocent." "It is not simply, and not so much," writes Brooks, "that confessing excuses but that properly managed it taints." By the time the listener wants to ask "Why are you telling me this?" it is "already too late" for "like the Ancient Mariner's Wedding Guest, he has been made to hear" (261).

"You laugh? Delighted," the anti-hero taunts his gentlemen audience at one point. "My jests, gentlemen, are of course in bad taste, jerky, involved, lacking self-confidence" (138). In the black comedy of his bumping duel with the officer, which reads like an extended joke, the anti-hero purposefully flaunts his perversity as he exposes his self-pathology. Finding himself, after a prolonged period of reading, in desperate need of human contact, he enters a tavern where there has just been a brawl, determined to get into a fight and be thrown out a window. Instead, he is "put" in his "place" and "treated like a fly" by an officer who, finding the anti-hero blocking his path, moves him aside. "I could have forgiven blows," the Underground Man comments, "but I could not forgive his having moved me without noticing me" (162). As he nurses his grudge for *several years* and his resentment grows, he determines to pay back the officer. His self wounded, he responds with narcissistic rage which Kohut characterizes as the "need for revenge, for righting a wrong, for undoing a hurt by whatever means, and a deeply anchored, unrelenting compulsion in the pursuit of all these aims, which gives no rest to those who have suffered a narcissistic injury . . ." ("Thoughts on Narcissism" 637–38).

Finally, the anti-hero decides to retaliate by bumping into the officer during a stroll along the fashionable Nevsky Avenue where the wealthy and distinguished walk. To the anti-hero these strolls are particularly humiliating. He feels he is obliged to "wriggle along" eel-like as he moves aside for those of higher rank. Profoundly ashamed of the "wretchedness and abjectness" of his "little scurrying figure," he imagines himself "a mere fly in the eyes of all this world" (164). His revenge, then, expresses his desire to turn passive suffering into active mastery: he wants to assert his self-worth and to transform the unempathic gaze of the public into an approving one. Determined to be well dressed for his encounter, he chooses, with great care, a new hat, a beaver coat collar, and new gloves. In remodeling his external appearance, he acts out his desire to repair his defective self. Predictably, when he finally does bump into the officer, he gets "the worst of it" for the officer is "stronger" (166). Nevertheless, he feels avenged, elated, triumphant. "The point was," he explains, "that I had attained my object, I had kept up my dignity, I had not yielded a step, and had put myself publicly on an equal social footing with him" (166). Despite his so-called victory, within a few days his ingrained feelings of worthlessness resurface. Again he is driven back to his private underground world where he takes solace in his daydreams and imagines a *"ready-made"* heroic life miraculously opening out before him (167).

In the incident of Zverkov's farewell dinner party, the Underground Man reenacts, with a few minor variations, the narcissistic script rehearsed with the officer. Like the officer, Zverkov is a man of action. In the person of Zverkov—who has wealth, power, and status, is handsome, self-confident and a great womanizer—the anti-hero finds all the "heroic" qualities he secretly admires. After ungraciously inviting himself to the dinner party, he fantasies the role he hopes to play. He dreams of crushing his hated rival, Zverkov, and of "getting the upper hand, of dominating" his friends, "carrying them away, making them like" him. "I knew . . . I did not really want to crush, to subdue, to attract them" (177), he says, consciously denying the wishes that compel him and that he enacts with his gentlemen audience.

At the dinner party, these narcissistic needs are frustrated. The Underground Man feels slighted by Zverkov's condescending attitude, humiliated when his friends seemingly cross-examine him about his lowly job and meager salary, upset about his shabby clothing, and rebuffed when he is mocked for his desire to show off his intelligence. Even worse, his "friends" abandon him to listen to Zverkov's stories. "No one paid any attention to me, and I sat crushed and humiliated" (181), the anti-hero recalls. Attempting to command their attention, he noisily paces before them for some three hours. "But it was all in vain. They paid no attention." While his "enemies" behave as though he is "not in the room" (184), the reader of *Notes* is compelled to act out the scripted role of listening audience to the anti-hero's increasingly pathological account.

Narcissistically injured when his "friends" ignore him, he defends himself by assuming himself superior. "Oh," he thinks to himself, "if you only knew what thoughts and feelings I am capable of, how cultured I am!" (184). Becoming enraged, he wants to flagrantly insult them as they have insulted him. Imagining them to be "pawns . . . inanimate pawns" (183), he experiences them as selfobjects that he wants to have completely in his power, a response in keeping with Kohut's description of narcissistic rage. The "enemy" who provokes a rage reaction, Kohut explains, is not perceived as "autonomous" but rather as "a recalcitrant part of an expanded self over which the narcissistically vulnerable person had expected to exercise full control" ("Thoughts on Narcissism" 644).

Despite his deep anger, the Underground Man also recognizes how shameful his behavior is and how this incident will haunt him for years to come. "[W]ith an intense, acute pang," he recalls, "I was stabbed to the heart by the thought that ten years, twenty years, forty years would pass, and that even in forty years I would remember with loathing and humiliation those filthiest, most ludicrous, and most awful moments of my life" (184). Like the narcissistically defective individual described by Kohut, the anti-hero responds to "the memory of a *faux pas* with excessive shame and self-rejection," his mind returning "again and again to the painful moment, in the attempt to eradicate" its reality (*Analysis* 231). The Underground Man reacts to his humiliating situation with extreme self-rejection. "I was so harassed, so exhausted," as he puts it, "that I would have cut my throat to put an end to it" (184).

In an ugly mood when he confronts Liza at the brothel, the Underground Man looks in a mirror and sees there a reflection of his jeopardized self. "My harassed face struck me as revolting in the extreme, pale, angry, abject, with dishevelled hair." Consciously, he disavows his need for a confirming response. "I am glad," he thinks to himself, "that I shall seem repulsive to her . . ." (189). But his obsessive fascination with Liza's gaze reveals his unacknowledged need to be looked at. Initially, her "wondering" eyes attract him. Later, her "coldly detached" and "utterly remote" look weighs on him, and when she

does finally look at him, he finds "something unnatural" in her gaze
(189, 190). Attempting to capture her attention, he describes, in his
stilted, affected manner, the burial of a prostitute. Soon, however, he
warms to the task and longs to "expound" his "cherished ideas" and
"turn" Liza's "soul." "It was the exercise of my power," he recalls,
"that attracted me most" (193, 194). Through storytelling, he both acts
out his angry grandiosity and reveals his narcissistic wants and fears.
Cast in the role of confidant, made an eyewitness to the anti-hero's
cruelty toward Liza, which culminates in his sadistic assault on her, the
reader of Dostoevsky's narrative becomes subjected to the corrosive
anger that permeates the text.

Trying to get at Liza through "pictures, pictures" (197), the
Underground Man describes, in sentimental detail, first a father's self-
sacrificing love for his daughter and then an idealized vision of love,
marriage, and the family. These romantic stories—the same kind of
stories he tells himself in his corner—both defend against childhood
experiences of abandonment and rejection and reveal the anti-hero's
deep-seated need for a sense of connection with others. He speaks with
"real feeling" and then becomes furious at the thought that Liza might
laugh at him (197–98). When she responds that he speaks "like a
book" (198), he feels not only rebuffed but also thwarted in his desire
to dominate.

Telling another story, one designed to injure her, he describes
her probable fate as a prostitute. As he expresses his angry death wish
toward Liza, he also confesses his own deepest fears about his imperiled self. Despite Liza's pride, he begins, her decline is inevitable. Within
a few short years she will become used up and diseased and when she is
dying others will abandon her. She will be buried in a cold, wet grave,
her name "will vanish from the face of the earth" as though she "had
never existed, never been born at all," and she will be forced to knock
on her coffin lid, begging to be let out to "live in the world again" (201).
In this melodramatic and self-referential story, the Underground Man
reveals the experiential core of his defective selfhood: his feelings of
abandonment, loneliness, worthlessness, depletion, and self-unreality.
Because he, in this instance and in his subsequent confrontation with
Liza, must protect himself from his overwhelming needs, he feels at
once emotionally engaged as he tells his story—"I worked myself up to

such a pitch that I began to have a lump in my throat," as he describes it—and yet sees it as a game, an "exercise" of skill (202).

For the Underground Man, the real crisis occurs when Liza visits him just as he flies into a rage with his servant, Apollon. Mortified by Liza's untimely arrival and anticipating her rejection of him, he rejects her; feeling humiliated, he tries to humiliate her. He tells her he had been laughing at her before when he "talked sentimental stuff" to her. "I had been insulted . . . [and] I had to avenge the insult. . . . I had been humiliated, so I wanted to humiliate; I had been treated like a rag, so I wanted to show my power. . . ." (215). When the anti-hero tells Liza that he shall hate her for having listened to his confessions, he indirectly informs the gentlemen of his deep resentment toward them. Confessing to Liza his feelings of utter worthlessness and shame, he reveals the agonizing sense of injury behind his defensive arrogance and hostility: "I am as vain as though I had been skinned and the very air blowing on me hurt" (216). When Liza responds by embracing him and thus giving him the warm, approving response he desires, he, unable to "restrain" himself, sobs in "genuine hysterics" (217). But this "genuine" response is short-lived. Subsequently, he withdraws emotionally, this defensive retreat feeding into his feelings of fraudulence and unreality. Acting out his need to tyrannize, to exact revenge and humiliate, he has intercourse with Liza and afterwards gives her money. After she leaves, the anti-hero feels remorseful, "horribly oppressed" and then depleted, "almost dead with . . . pain" (219, 221). Although he all but falls "ill from misery," he subsequently divorces himself from his feelings. Through bookish speech—"I remained for a long time afterwards pleased with the phrase about the benefit from resentment and hatred" (221)—he gains temporary mastery over his feelings. He retreats from an outer world that is unpredictable and threatening and takes refuge in his underground world where he maintains a tenuous grasp on his self-cohesion by insulating himself from real life and by reducing self-threatening experiences to bookish phrases.

A "paradoxalist" (222), the Underground Man noisily professes that he is "free." But he also admits that he feels impelled to act as he does, that he acts as "though of design" (139). When he is most aware of the "good and beautiful," he does ugly things, and this behavior seems "not accidental . . . but as though it were bound to be so" (132). Ironically, he avows that he wants to retain his "fantastic dreams" and "vulgar folly" to "prove" that he is not a piano key and that he preserves his "personality" and "individuality" through "caprice" (149, 148). "[W]hat *freedom* is left me," he asks, if "some day they calculate and prove to me that I made a long nose at some one because I could not help making a long nose at him . . ." (147). Through his intellectual displays, his logical exercises, his free-will philosophy, he attempts to defend against his underlying sense of powerlessness, his feeling that he cannot help acting as he does, that he is a piano key. Bound by the compulsion to repeat, he is driven to act out his so-called capricious behavior. And underneath it all—the arrogance, the rage, the demands for attention, the desire to control and hurt others—lies a gnawing sense of injury and pain, a deep "ache" (137). "[W]hy am I made with such desires?" he asks. "I would let my tongue be cut off out of gratitude if things could be so arranged that I should lose all desire to put it out" (153). Though he thirsts for something "quite different" (154), he is condemned to be the anti-hero, a nameless, "characterless creature" (131), and to feel not real and solid, but hollow, fraudulent, invalid—a babbling voice. He is trapped in the prison house of his self-pathology.

"I am a babbler, a harmless vexatious babbler . . ." (140), the anti-hero tells his gentlemen audience. His frantic babbling, his "talk and talk and talk" (153), enacts his instability as it defends against self-fragmentation. For as Kohut points out, the "shift of attention to verbalizable conflicts and anxieties" may be "defensively undertaken" to "stem the tide of disintegration" by focusing attention on "endlessly described conflicts and worries" and away from an "awareness" of the "potentially crumbling self" (*Restoration* 107, 108). The anti-hero writes not only to obtain relief from oppressive memories, as he claims, but also to counteract feelings of self-dissolution. And he writes not only to make up a life for himself, as he says, but also in a thwarted attempt to repair his broken self. He is correct in his speculation that there is something psychological in his need to write his confessions and address himself to imaginary readers. In his gentlemen audience he creates what he lacks in real life: a selfobject totally under his control.

Because the anti-hero is unable to satisfy his selfobject needs in the real world, he creates an imaginary audience that is both the image of his rejectors, the men of action, and a self-representation, a mirror reflection of his own arrogant, mocking attitude. His gentlemen readers laugh at him, find him insolent, contemptible, intrusive. "Isn't that shameful, isn't that humiliating?" he imagines his narratees saying to him as they perhaps wag their heads "contemptuously." "And how persistent, how insolent are your sallies, and at the same time what a scare you are in! You talk nonsense and are pleased with it; you say impudent things and are in a continual alarm and apologizing for them. . . . And how intrusive you are, how you insist and grimace!" (154). Imagining that they are taunting him, he taunts them: "Remember I spoke just now of vengeance. (I am sure you did not take it in)" (140). Rebuffed in the real world for his garish intellectual displays, he exhibits his cleverness and "bookish" intellect to a captive audience. He is perverse, attention seeking, demanding: "(A poor jest, but I will not scratch it out. I wrote it thinking it would sound very witty; but now that I have seen myself that I only wanted to show off in a despicable way, I will not scratch it out on purpose!)" (130); "I want now to tell you, gentlemen, whether you care to hear it or not, why I could not even become an insect" (131). Unable to tyrannize the men of action he encounters in the real world, he assumes complete power over his imaginary gentlemen: "Of course I have myself made up all the things you say. That, too, is from underground" (154). Aware of their probable responses, he makes hostile use of his insights: "Now, are you not fancying, gentlemen, that I am expressing remorse for something now, that I am asking your forgiveness for something? I am sure you are fancying that. . . . However, I assure you I do not care if you are. . . ." (130).

Denied in the real world when he sues for attention, the Underground Man acts out his need to procure the notice of others with his fictive gentlemen. He imagines them, variously, as "looking at" him with "compassion" (147) and as unable to understand him: "No, I refuse to consult a doctor from spite. That you probably will not understand. Well, I understand it, though" (129). Disavowing his need for audience approval, he claims that what they think is "a matter of indifference" to him (136). "[I]f you won't deign to give me your attention," he childishly threatens, "I will drop your acquaintance. I can retreat into my underground hole" (153). Ironically, in every word he writes—most particularly in his avowals of his independence from and indifference toward the gentlemen—he reveals just how dependent he is on them. The Underground Man, observes Mikhail Bakhtin, demonstrates his dependence on the other person through his anticipation of the other person's reply and his response to it (192). In "confessing and condemning himself," Bakhtin writes, the Underground Man "wants to provoke praise and acceptance." His self-condemnation is an implicit appeal that the "other person dispute his self-definition, but he leaves himself a loophole for the eventuality that the other person will indeed suddenly agree with him . . ." (195–96). Moreover, as J. R. Hall comments, the Underground Man attempts to assimilate his gentlemen readers and deny their "feared independence" by turning them "into a mere appendage" of his discourse, an "empty form" (136–37). Despite the anti-hero's claim that he writes as if he were addressing readers "simply because" he finds it "easier . . . to write in that form" (155), he is no more free to choose *not* to use this form of address than he is not to write his notes. He is compelled to create an imaginary audience, to dominate over it, and to attempt to both assimilate it and appropriate from it the narcissistic sustenance he craves so he can "live in some way."

In his interactive maneuvers with his gentlemen audience, we find an indirect disclosure of how storytelling and empathy are used in *Notes* as weapons to assault and trap the reader. The anti-hero recognizes that some of the gentlemen, like him, may use reading to effect a bookish retreat from real life or that they may read literature to temporarily build up the self or to seek refuge in the literary world of "the good and the beautiful." Aware of such needs, he actively mocks and subverts them. Through his confessions—"it's hardly literature so much as a corrective punishment" (221)—he exacts narcissistic revenge upon his narratees. When, as Rene Fortin observes, Dostoevsky's anti-hero, at one point, rejoices in the "nastiness he has inflicted" on the gentlemen and then mocks them by confessing the "pleasure" he takes in his own debasement, the reader who witnesses this behavior is transformed into "an accomplice in an act of psychological perversion" (242). Stories of "the good and the beautiful," the anti-hero implies, are nothing more than grandiose and idealizing fantasies. And stories, an illusory web of words, memorialize what is permanently lost and absent: the loving family relationship. The story he tells Liza of the loving father, mother, and child is covertly sadistic. "[W]hat husband's heart is not touched, seeing his wife nursing his child!" the anti-hero says to Liza as he tries to hurt her through his stories. "A plump little rosy baby, sprawling and snuggling. . . . When its father comes up, the child tears itself away from the bosom, flings itself back, looks at its father, laughs, as though it were fearfully funny, and falls to sucking again. Or it will bite its mother's breast when its little teeth are coming, while it looks sideways at her with its little eyes as though to say, 'Look, I am biting!' Is not all that happiness when they are the three together, husband, wife and child?" (197). Embedded in this peripheral story of the loving family is another: that of the enraged, biting child. This unwritten story recalls a marginalized text found in Part 1 of the anti-hero's discourse—that of Cleopatra "sticking gold pins into her slave-girl's breasts" and deriving "gratification from their screams and writh-ings" (144). A self-styled "retort-made man" (135), the anti-hero ag-gressively encroaches upon and attacks his narratees with his biting, stinging narrative. In his story "all the traits for an anti-hero are *expressly* gathered together . . . and what matters most, it all produces an unpleasant impression, for we are all divorced from life, we are all cripples, every one of us, more or less" (221). Similarly, the narcissistic rage that suffuses *Notes* is acted out on the reader who, in becoming engrossed in the anti-hero's fictional world, becomes the victim of a verbal assault.

While the anti-hero's "word-address," as Mikhail Bakhtin writes, "is capable of agitating and touching one, almost like the personal appeal of a living person" (199), many critics have warded off the text's intended enmeshment of readers in the anti-hero's angry world by reducing his threatening presence to a bookish formula. Edward Wasiolek writes that the anti-hero's "metaphysic implies the psychology; the psychology—empirically observed—confirms the metaphysic" (44). While the anti-hero is a sick, spiteful person, he is, nevertheless, a "hero" according to Wasiolek because his overarching principle is "freedom"; moreover, he is a character Dostoevsky "ap-proves of" (39) and thus, as Wasiolek implies, the reader is meant to approve of. Similarly, Reed Merrill, who describes the anti-hero as an "ethical dialectician" and as a character who has "tragic capability" (509, 507), claims that the Underground Man "can be excused" for being "neurotic, even characteristically paranoid" since he "knows his situation" and wants "to break out of it with a newly discovered dialectic of freedom" (516). In endorsing the anti-hero's aberrant, spiteful behavior by reading it as an expression of some higher philosophic principle, critics such as Wasiolek and Merrill unwittingly enact the inscribed role of confirming audience. And such critics also act out the Underground Man's self-aggrandizing hero fantasy when they laud him as an existential hero (e.g., Kaufmann, Wasiolek) or as a man who "[l]ike the classical hero . . . is willing to stand or fall by his own acts" (Merrill 507). Other critics, perhaps in a desire to diffuse the anger permeating the narrative, reperform Dostoevsky's intended rescue mission by arguing that the passages which were deleted by the censors— those which suggested a Christian solution to the anti-hero's problems—are a central interpretive key to the text and that Dostoevsky's "dominant message" in *Notes* is the necessity of "Christian love and self-sacrifice" for the attainment of "authentic freedom" (Jackson 172; see also Rosenshield).

Because a narrative aim of *Notes* is to make readers feel like passive victims of the anti-hero's affective storms, *Notes* may stimulate in some readers the same fear of passive surrender and helplessness experienced by the Underground Man. Manipulated, taunted, and trapped by the anti-hero's convoluted rhetoric and seductive game of assimilation, readers may be induced to replicate the anti-hero's defensive stratagems: i.e., to assert active mastery over passive suffering by attempting to assume critical dominion and authority over the text. Critics who focus almost solely on the anti-hero's paradoxalist "philosophy" and use intellectual formulas as a kind of shield or those who feel that one must "*see through*" Dostoevsky's character in order to get a "proper understanding" of the text (Frank, *Dostoevsky* 315) may be responding, at least in part, to such pressures. Because the gentlemen readers are "so easily mastered" and stand as the anti-hero's "rhetorical whipping boys" (Doody 31), some readers may form an identificatory bond with the anti-hero of Part 1 of *Notes* and thus partially defend against the text's intended subjugation of the reader. One critic, claiming that the anti-hero "becomes what he is because his life is the *reductio ad absurdum* of the metaphysics of the man of action," argues that the "more repulsive and hideous" the anti-hero portrays his life as being, "the more he underlines the incredible obtuseness of his self-confident judge" (Frank, "Nihilism" 12). In a reading of *Notes* informed by deconstruction that, in effect, rescues readers from the text's game of entrapment, another critic claims that the Underground Man wants his audience to "avoid being trapped by his own tropes or text" and to "recognize the power and limits of all texts, including his own . . ." (Consigny, "The Paradox" 351). Yet another critic, in an apparent desire to rescue the text from the "categories which various critical discourses have imposed upon it," describes how the "independence and self-sufficiency" of *Notes* "reassert themselves each time this work is subjected to an attempted critical domination" (Kavanagh 491). *Notes* may also engender feelings of contempt and anger in readers. One critic, for example, who focuses attention on the anti-hero's insulting behavior, does so in an essay that bristles with insults directed against the existentialist critics who have acted as apologists for Dostoevsky's character (see Weisberg). And yet another claims that "many people praise *Notes from the Underground* without any idea that they are unearthing a caricature of themselves written a century ago" (Girard 262).

A destabilizing story with its abrupt veering from philosophic abstractions to affective intensities, *Notes From Underground* creates in readers "an experienced need for order," as Liane Norman comments (289). It also creates a reactive need for closure, for aesthetic finality. These needs have been acted out again and again as critic/readers, replicating the text's split perceptions of the anti-hero as both a developed thinker and a chaotic personality, have attempted to make sense of his paradoxalist philosophy and/or his capricious behavior. That *Notes* is incomplete is indicated in the abrupt closure in which the authorial narrator, apparently having heard enough, arbitrarily determines to "stop" (222) his transcription of the anti-hero's confessions, this closure repeating a central scene in the text—the dinner party—in which the Underground Man's "friends" refuse to play the role of audience and ultimately abandon him. As Bakhtin states, *Notes From Underground* is an "internally endless speech which can be mechanically cut short, but cannot be organically completed" (197). In the words of Thomas Kavanagh, the anti-hero's endless writing becomes "the attempted yet never successful capture of the self by the self" (505). The narrative incompletion of *Notes* mirrors the anti-hero's incomplete self. When we, as critic/readers, endeavor to explain and interpret the anti-hero's notes, or, as other psychological critics and I have done, describe the psychological mechanisms governing his so-called capricious behavior, we perform a rescue mission. We attempt to capture, stabilize, and make whole through our theoretical constructs and structured critical art the broken self of the Underground Man. And in thinking about rather than with the character as interpreters, we also act out a self-rescue as we ward off the text's enmeshment of us in the anti-hero's perverse personality.

The "[m]an of our time," Kohut states, "is the man of the precariously cohesive self, the man who craves the presence, the interest, the availability of the self-cohesion-maintaining selfobject" (*How?* 61). Fascinated with how artists anticipated the later findings of self psychology, Kohut explains this "anticipatory function of art" quite simply: "when dealing with the psychological world, understanding is of necessity the precursor of explaining" ("Reflections" 519). Dostoevsky is often said to have anticipated Freud. In the character of the Underground Man he anticipates Kohut's broken man, the narcissistically vulnerable individual whose self-cohesion is imperiled. A character we may respond to with intellectual fascination and a fascinated horror, the Underground Man, above all, compels our attention. As readers of *Notes From Underground*, we are maneuvered into providing Dostoevsky's anti-hero with the audience recognition he craves as we witness him carry to an extreme his paradoxalist, narcissistic impulses.

❊ ❊ ❊ ❊

Three
Insect Transformation as a
Narcissistic Metaphor in Kafka's
Metamorphosis

❊ ❊ ❊ ❊

If Dostoevsky's ill-tempered Underground Man belligerently demands the notice of others, Franz Kafka's submissive human-insect, Gregor Samsa, who has lost the powers of speech, mutely signals his urgent desire for his family's attention. What we find openly expressed in the anti-hero's personality—the grandiose needs both to control others and be the center of attention—is repressed and thus expressed in a disguised way in the personality and behavior of Kafka's character. Like the Underground Man, Gregor suffers from a crumbling sense of self. But while the anti-hero only thinks of himself as subhuman, as an insect, Gregor Samsa, in contrast, *is* an insect. Thus to be empathically confirmed, for him, is not merely a way of sustaining his threatened self: it is literally a matter of life and death.

Provoked by the text, critic after critic has puzzled over the meaning of Gregor's transformation. Why is Kafka's character transformed into an insect? readers have long asked. Critical reactions to *The Metamorphosis*, which range from abstract philosophical and linguistic speculations to affective responses, reveal that the fantasies and defenses located in the text have been elicited from a number of its interpreters.[1] The defensive shields of fantasy, black humor, and narrative structure—*The Metamorphosis* is carefully organized around Gregor's repetitive enclosures and escapes—protect against but do not camouflage the horrors of Gregor's insect existence. And yet unconsciously responding to the defensive stratagems of the text or attempting to fend off Gregor's fictional presence, a number of interpreters have likewise veered away from Gregor's situation, focusing attention instead on the sociological, political, philosophical, or religious implications of Kafka's narrative or on its linguistic puzzles or structural features. Other critics, reacting affectively to Gregor's plight, have reproduced in their criticism the angry substructures of this text which originated in Kafka's conflict with his family and his feelings of deep self-rejection. Such critics variously accuse Gregor, his family, or his exploitative economic system for his insect transformation. And still other critics have responded to Gregor's need for confirming attention and rescue. Engendering a potent reader-character transaction, *The Metamorphosis* re-presents and reactively defends against the narcissistic needs, anxieties, and vulnerabilities that inform it. What Kafka so poignantly captures in this story, as Kohut himself commented, is the experience of an individual "who finds himself in nonresponsive surroundings," whose family speaks of him coldly, in the "impersonal third pronoun," so that he becomes a "nonhuman monstrosity, even in his own eyes" ("The Psychoanalyst" 718; "Future" 680; *Restoration* 287). To depersonalize Gregor or turn him into a philosophic or linguistic abstraction, as some interpreters have done, is thus to reenact the narcissistic trauma presented in the text. In the critical conversation surrounding *The Metamorphosis*, we find an unwitting reperformance of key aspects of the text's hidden narcissistic script.

From the very first sentence of *The Metamorphosis* and throughout the narrative, Kafka focuses the reader's attention on the insect-Gregor. The narrator, located both within and without Gregor's subjectivity, acts as an objective reporter of his plight and as an extension of his consciousness. While essentially confined to Gregor's perspective and drawn into his inner world, the reader is also positioned at a slight remove from him, this partial detachment serving to ward off potential reader anxieties about being enmeshed in his claustrophobic insect's world. Encouraged to experience a wide variety of emotional responses, ranging from disgust and physical revulsion to pity and a desire to see Kafka's hapless anti-hero rescued, the reader, above all, is compelled to rivet attention on the insect-Gregor. Inscribed in *The Metamorphosis* is Gregor's protracted attempt to procure the notice of others so he can temporarily sustain his defective self.

The root trope of *The Metamorphosis*, Gregor's insect transformation, is a complex, overdetermined psychosymbol. A reification of his self-state, it reflects not only his inner feelings of worthlessness and powerlessness but also his repressed grandiosity, a grandiosity made distorted and grotesque because it has not been responded to empathically. Like the biblical Samson (the name "Samsa," as critics have noted, is an allusion both to Samson and Kafka),[2] he is at once enfeebled and imbued with secret, magical power. Both the suddenness of his metamorphosis and its magical, fantastic quality signal the eruption of the archaic grandiose substructure of the self and a surfacing of archaic feelings of omnipotence. Significantly, Gregor awakens as a "monstrous" insect (3) and he uses his "gigantic brown" body (36) to frighten others away. Although one of his initial worries, as he rocks himself out of bed, is that he will make a "loud crash" and thus perhaps cause his family "if not terror, at least anxiety" (8), unconsciously he wants to provoke just this response from those gathered outside his door. At the very outset of his ordeal, he, while disavowing his need for attention—he claims he wants to be left alone—listens to the discussion about him between the office manager and his parents, intent on not missing "a word of the conversation" (10). Later, when they stop talking, he imagines that they might be leaning against his door and listening to the noises he is making. Moreover, he is "eager" (12) to learn what they will say when they see him. As the office manager complains, Gregor is determined, albeit unconsciously, on exhibiting himself and "flaunting [his] strange whims" (11). Just as Gregor eavesdrops on his family and imagines his family listens in on him, so the reader is situated as an eavesdropper on the Samsa household. *The Metamorphosis* dramatizes, activates, and fulfills the regressive need for eavesdropping.

In the black comedy of his initial confrontation with the office manager and his family, Gregor satisfies his desire for attention and his grandiose wish to exert magical power over others. For when he makes his first appearance as an insect, his father clenches his fist as if to strike, then falters and begins to sob; his mother collapses; the loathed office manager, obeying Gregor's unconscious wish to get rid of him, slowly backs out of the room, then, his right hand outstretched, approaches the staircase "as if nothing less than an unearthly deliverance were awaiting him there" (17), and finally flees. But Gregor's exhibitionistic display is short-lived. His traumatic rejection at the very moment he shows himself points to a central cause of his self-disorder as it repeats and telescopes his experience of early parental rejection and the long series of similar rejections he has suffered throughout his life, these rejections pivotal in the formation of his distorted self-image.

Just as his family turns away from him, so the reader, while encouraged to sympathize with Gregor, is at the same time prompted to shun him as the text insistently focuses attention on his physically repulsive insect's body. And while we are meant, as one critic has observed, to "respond to the plight of the loathly son" in this scene, it is also true that "our compassion and our understanding seem mocked by the opposing image of a man shooing away a bug." In part, this scene reads like some sort of "grotesque joke" (Eggenschwiler, "*The Metamorphosis*" 206). Replicating the text's split perceptions of Gregor— that he is a repulsive bug and a dependent son in need of his family's support—critics are split on Gregor's nature. "When Gregor first appears before his family," writes Mark Spilka, "they are appalled by his condition, and their revulsion gives the full measure of his deformity" (*Dickens and Kafka* 77–78). While some critics claim that Gregor, as a vermin, remains "morally identical with his former self," which is "sweet, timid, and amiable" (Landsberg 130), others feel that his metamorphosis makes manifest his real parasitic nature (Greenberg 76) or that he "conceals" his "parasitical nature . . . beneath his solicitude" (Henel 254; translated by Corngold 135).

Punished for his self-assertiveness, Gregor is "[p]itilessly" (19) driven back into his room by his father and then made a prisoner. But Gregor's prison is also his refuge. Narcissistically damaged in each of his confrontations with the external world, he retreats to the protective isolation of both his room and his insect's shell. His public display rebuffed, he, from the refuge/prison of his room, attempts to defend his vulnerable self and become the center of his family's attention. Gregor's need for confirming attention is verified by the narrator. When Gregor, just after his metamorphosis, attempts to turn the key of his door, the office manager encourages him, "but," as the narrator comments, "everyone should have cheered him on. . . ." Gregor, in the false belief that they are "all following his efforts with suspense" (14), musters the necessary strength to complete his difficult task. Narcissistically defective, he needs external sources of approbation if he is to counteract feelings of helplessness and find the inner determination to act. In serving as an extension of Gregor's consciousness, the narrator makes Gregor the focal point of and dominant over the reader's perceptions and thus acts out, by proxy as it were, Gregor's repressed grandiose needs.

Two preoccupations which initially emerge in Gregor's sequestered, locked-room existence—a craving for food and for the eye glance—are narcissistic metaphors that express his desire for a nurturing, mirroring response. After his transformation, Grete, the only family member he feels close to, becomes his sole source of narcissistic supplies. When Gregor rejects the milk she brings him, he symbolically rejects his sickly, asthmatic mother who faints, that is, becomes nonresponsive, the first time he displays himself—this being a repetition of his early relationship with this emotionally unavailable and depleted woman. When his mother allows Grete to become his caretaker, she disclaims her responsibility for him and, in essence, abandons him. Disavowing his need to be noticed, Gregor determines he "would rather starve" than draw Grete's attention to his hunger. But he also feels "an enormous urge" to "throw himself at his sister's feet, and beg her for something good to eat" (23–24). When Grete first brings him food, he greedily devours the food that appeals to him. But the fact that what he eats is garbage does more than remind us of his repulsive insect state. It also suggests that his needs are not truly being met and thus serves to indict his family. In effect, he says through this behavior, "I know that this is all I'm worth to you. I'm garbage and so I'll eat garbage." Recognizing that his sister finds him repulsive, he hides under the sofa when she is in his room[3] and he fancies that she gives a thankful look when he covers with a sheet the small portion of his insect's body that protrudes from the sofa. In other words, he must efface and sequester himself—disavow his grandiose needs—to win approval and attention. Gregor's sensitivity to eye glances indicates his unmet, primitive need to be mirrored, to be the "gleam in the mother's eye" (see Kohut, *Analysis* 117–18). While Gregor craves attention, he also is ashamed to have others look at him, his shame a response to his exhibitionistic wishes and his distorted self. Emotionally abandoned by his mother, he finds a mother-surrogate figure in his sister. But tragically when Grete becomes his sole caretaker and thus becomes the center of Gregor's and her parents' attention, she begins to make narcissistic use of him as she asserts her own grandiose needs. Not only does she assume complete dominance over him, jealously guarding her caretaker's rights and flying into a rage when Mrs. Samsa cleans his room, an act that Grete interprets as a threat to her authority, she also begins to lose interest in him. As time passes, she comes to treat him more and more as an encumbering nuisance, an object.

Of perennial fascination to readers of *The Metamorphosis* is Gregor's initial reaction to his transformation. What shocks readers is passively, if not blandly, accepted by Gregor. Instead of reacting with open anxiety, Gregor thinks, at length, about his job and family; he becomes anxious about the passing time and preoccupied with his new bodily sensations and his strange aches and pains. In prolonging the narrative account of Gregor's initial discovery of his transformation, the text acts out what it depicts: Gregor's attempt to avoid confronting his diffuse, preverbal fears. Similarly, readers are shielded from full awareness of the anxieties subtending this scene. Despite this, the text discloses, in other ways, Gregor's sense of body-self estrangement and impending fragmentation: through his initial inability to control the chaotic movements of his insect legs and his later "senseless crawling around" his room (34); through his increasingly disorganized appearance, his growing lethargy and depression; and through his dissolving sense of clock time, an indicator of his loss of a sense of himself as a cohesive continuum in time. Suffering from a crumbling sense of self, he experiences what Kohut describes as the "fragmentation of" and "estrangement from" the mind-body self (*Restoration* 105). Gregor's metamorphosis gives experiential immediacy not only to what Kohut calls the "devastating emotional event" referred to as a "severe drop in self-esteem" ("Reflections" 503) but, more significantly, to the terrifying experience of the breakup of the self. As Gregor's fragile self falls apart, Kafka, as if unconsciously bent on aiding his vulnerable antihero, makes him more and more human in his needs and thus has prompted many readers to respond sympathetically to his character's growing helplessness and need for rescue.

When Gregor makes his second escape from his room, his mother faints and his sister, mirroring Mr. Samsa, responds first with open hostility and then by isolating Gregor, cutting him off from herself and his mother. Similarly, on both this occasion and the first time Gregor shows himself, his mother faints when she sees him, i.e., when he expresses his narcissistic needs and anger, and then he is rebuffed and attacked by his father and subsequently isolated by being locked in his room. Behind the manifest content of these repetitive incidents, which provide a mimetic recapitulation of infantile experiences of parental unavailability, rejection, and narcissistic injury, there lies an intricate cluster of archaic fantasies, fears, and defenses. The fainting mother, for example, suggests a telescoped memory of the nonresponsive mother and the anachronistic fantasy of the depleted mother who is harmed or destroyed through the infant's intense narcissistic neediness and rage. The hostile father and sister, moreover, simultaneously represent a telescoped memory of the angry father, warded-off aspects of the self—Gregor's enraged grandiosity—and a condensed image of the punishing oedipal father and the split-off "bad" mother who causes self-threatening, narcissistic injuries. Intrapsychically, all the authority figures in the novel depict both split-off aspects of Gregor's self and the omnipotent mother-father images. In a series of interlocking, peripheral incidents featuring authority figures, the three boarders assume power over the family only to be sent "hopping" off, insectlike; Gregor imagines telling his remote, godlike boss exactly what he thinks of him and thus making him fall off his desk; and he thinks that the office manager might wake up an insect one day (56, 4, 9–10). This repetitive thwarting of authority figures expresses Gregor's defensive devaluation of, projected rage against, and fantasied depletion or harming of the parental imagoes as well as his abortive attempts to display his own sequestered grandiosity. Narcissistically fixated, Gregor exists in a strange, twilight world of resonating fears and fantasies. When he, in his current situation, reexperiences his primal traumas with his family members, his atrophied self slowly wastes away. Because he lacks a stable, cohesive self, he is deeply threatened by his own narcissistic needs and anger and by any behavior that he perceives as rejecting, neglectful, or hostile.

As Gregor's condition progressively worsens, he briefly succumbs to narcissistic rage, which is expressed as oral greediness. Angered at the "miserable" way he is being treated, he fantasies taking from the pantry the food that is rightfully his. He wants, in other words, to appropriate the narcissistic sustenance that he feels he is entitled to. But as his sister increasingly neglects him—twice a day she "hurriedly" shoves into his room "any old food" available (43)—he loses his appetite, begins to shun the scraps of food that she gives him, and thus slowly starves to death. When Grete becomes a mirror image of his neglectful, rejecting parents, he refuses the food she gives him just as he, at the outset of his ordeal, refused the mother's milk given him. Through his self-starvation, Gregor makes one last, desperate plea for attention as he masochistically complies with his sister's—and family's—wish to get rid of him. In mute protest, he sits in some particularly dirty corner when Grete comes in, attempting to "reproach" her for the filthiness of his room (43). But to no avail. Latent in Gregor's silent reproach is repressed rage which is later voiced by the middle boarder when he gives notice and considers taking some sort of legal action against the Samsas because of the "disgusting conditions prevailing" in the household and family (50). Instead of openly expressing his anger, Gregor responds in a seemingly accepting but really resentful way to his family's neglect when he observes how difficult it is for his "overworked and exhausted" family to find time to "worry" about him more than is "absolutely necessary" (42). Moreover, despite his mother's outrageous neglect of him, he defensively protects her against his anger through splitting: he keeps intact his conscious image of her as the unavailable (absent) but "good" mother and projects her "badness"—her rejecting, narcissistically injuring behavior—onto others. Hovering on the margins of the written text of *The Metamorphosis* is another more potent drama that is split off and evaded: that of the nonresponsive mother. A central cause of Gregor's blighted existence is his relationship with his absent, emotionally vacant mother.

In stark contrast to their neglect of Gregor, Grete and Mrs. Samsa do find the time to bother about, if not dote on, Mr. Samsa; moreover, the three boarders, who dominate the family, become the center of the Samsas' attention. Gregor watches while the family prepares lavish meals for the three boarders who then stuff themselves with food while he, abandoned, is starving to death. But though ignored by his family, he remains the focus of the reader's attention. Because he seems so much the passive victim, some critics have acted as his advocate and denounced his family members. Such critics, speaking for the mute, submissive insect and articulating his disowned hostility, verbally accuse his oppressors. One critic, for example, who describes "consideration" as Gregor's "basic impulse," condemns Grete for her "self-centered meanness" and Mr. Samsa for his "sheer animal hos-

tility" (Rolleston 63). Another critic, who claims that the other characters in the story, especially the authority figures, are the "real vermin,"
comments that the "worst insect among the vermin in the story is . . .
the parasitical father" (Spann 67).

When Gregor hears his sister playing the violin, he makes his
final and fatal escape from his room. Although he is a hideous sight
with his festering wound and filthy, deteriorating body, he feels no
shame as he, in his desperate desire for human contact, advances over
the clean living-room floor. At his most physically disgusting in this
scene, he is also, to many readers, most touchingly human and thus
most salvageable. Compelled because of what he thinks he hears in the
music—authentic emotional expression—he wants Grete's eyes to
meet his. He craves a confirming, healing gaze. Feeling as if the "way to
the unknown nourishment" he longs for is "coming to light" (49), he
wants to take Grete into his room and never let her out so long as he
lives. His desire to exclusively possess Grete reveals his archaic needs.
He wants to extract praise from her (he imagines she will be touched
and admire him when he tells her how he had meant to send her to the
conservatory); he wants to dominate over her (he disavows this need,
imagining that she will stay with him of "her own free will" [49]); and
he wants to merge with her power and strength. Not only does his plan
miserably fail, he is both subject to the unempathic stares of the three
boarders and made aware of how ashamed his family is of him when
his father tries to prevent the boarders from viewing him.

At this point, Gregor, disappointed and weak from hunger, is
verbally attacked. "I won't pronounce the name of my brother in front
of this monster," his sister says to her parents as she pronounces
judgment on him. "[A]nd so all I say is: we have to try to get rid of it.
We've done everything humanly possible to take care of it and to put up
with it; I don't think anyone can blame us in the least" (51). By refusing
to recognize him as her brother, Grete invalidates him. Impaired, enfeebled, Gregor crawls back to his room, his "last glance" falling on his
impassive mother who is "fast asleep" (53). Again, when he displays
himself, his depleted mother becomes nonresponsive, he is punished,
then locked in his room and, on this final occasion, left to die. Disavowing his anger and disappointment, Gregor, just before he dies, thinks of
his family with "deep emotion and love" (54). Gregor's masochistic
compliance and profound neediness have induced many readers to take

his side and pass judgment on the family for their neglect of him. And the question which is asked when Gregor is drawn to Grete's violin playing—"Was he an animal, that music could move him so?" (49)—has prompted critic after critic to, in effect, rescue Gregor from his insect state by suggesting his newfound awareness of his aesthetic and/ or spiritual needs.

When Gregor agrees with his sister's "conviction" that he must "disappear" (54), he expresses, on the family drama level, his feeling that his family is better off without him. This feeling is corroborated by the narrator's description of the family's cold, uncaring response to his death. "[N]ow we can thank God!" (55), Mr. Samsa pronounces when the family gathers around Gregor's emaciated body. "Stop brooding over the past," Mr. Samsa further insists (57). Abruptly, the family members leave off mourning and rejuvenate as they begin to celebrate their liberation from the insect-Gregor, their release from a shameful, secret family burden. In agreeing to "disappear," Gregor also acts out his deep self-rejection and masochistic desire to remedy his situation by effacing himself and thus nullifying his agonizing sense of worthlessness and defectiveness. Moreover, through his death he both punishes himself for his hidden aggression against the family and magically undoes his hidden crime against them. For as an invalid, he has passively exerted power over and devalued family members by obliging them to get jobs and thus assume with their employers the subordinate role he once was forced to play. His death, hence, revitalizes his family. In stark contrast to his sister's transformation—she has "blossomed into a good-looking, shapely girl" (58)—Gregor has been reduced to a thing, an "it." His "flat and dry" carcass (55) reifies his empty, depleted self. It is fitting that the cleaning woman, an embodiment of the neglectful, hostile aspects of the family, disposes of his body. Desperately seeking but never receiving the self-confirming attention, that "matrix of empathy" which Kohut feels the individual needs to form and sustain a cohesive sense of self, Gregor, in the end, is destroyed. His fragile self has been eroded, bit by bit, by the emotionally invalidating responses of his family and by his own sequestered anger. "The deepest horror man can experience," Kohut comments, "is that of feeling that he is exposed to circumstances in which he is no longer regarded as human by others, i.e., in a milieu that does not even respond with faulty or distorted empathy to his presence" ("Reflections" 486–87). In *The Metamorphosis* Kafka conveys, in exacting detail, the horror of such a situation.

Creating a compelling reader-character dyadic relationship, *The Metamorphosis*, which grew out of Kafka's quarrel with his family and with impersonal authority,[4] has incited endless quarreling among the critics. Ignored by his family, Gregor has been the center of a lively critical discussion as reader after reader has been seduced into explaining who is to blame for his condition. Some critics feel that Gregor is responsible. "[T]he final criticism," writes Edwin Honig, "seems not to be leveled against society so much as against Gregor, who sinks into his dilemma because he is unable to find his real self" (67). Franz Kuna, who views Gregor's metamorphosis as symbolic of his submission to the role of "economic man," blames Gregor for "allowing himself . . . to be forced into this subordinate and self-annihilating role" (51–52). Other critics blame the family for his plight. The family frequently has been condemned for their pettiness, their mindless cruelty, their parasitism on the preinsect Gregor, and their failure to love Gregor. Edmund Edel, for example, feels that after the metamorphosis Gregor needs his family's support but they fail "this chance of a humane existence for themselves" (trans. and summarized by Corngold 103). For Douglas Angus "the entire story is one long, varied and agonized appeal for love . . ." (70). Gregor's experience, in Carol Cantrell's view, "emerges as part of a coherent and destructive pattern of family life" (579).

A highly polemicized text, *The Metamorphosis* has provoked critics to make authoritative pronouncements on Gregor's plight—on who or what is to blame for his transformation—as well as on prior interpreters of the text. Stanley Corngold's description of how the "richness and subtlety and fidelity to the text" of a certain critic's commentary makes one "resent the intrusions and dislocations" of other interpreters (74) is not atypical of the irritable tone sometimes found in the criticism this text has engendered. Observing that the many interpretations of *The Metamorphosis* "hardly take account of each other" and "contradict one another in the crassest way," Benno Von Wiese, in an apparent desire to rescue the text from its interpreters, calls for "strict textual interpretation" of Kafka's work (trans. and summarized by Corngold 247–48). Meno Spann's anger against critics who denigrate Gregor is also revealing. Arguing that "the people surrounding the metamorphosed Gregor are the real vermin" (67), Spann denounces those critics who have denounced Gregor and who have, thus, missed the "paradox" which the "skilled reader" understands: namely that the actual vermin in the story are the " 'normal' people" depicted in the text while Gregor "increasingly becomes a true human being in spite of his monstrous shape" (73).

And still other critics, acting out the needs to both ward off and rescue the hapless Gregor, have responded with interpretations which, as Benno Von Wiese aptly puts it, "liberate Gregor Samsa as rapidly as possible from his repulsive image and instead lend him a mysterious metaphysical status" (319; translated by Corngold 247). But some of these approaches, in depersonalizing Gregor, also repeat the central narcissistic trauma dramatized in the text. Wilhelm Emrich, for example, finds Gregor's insect state inexplicable. "The beetle is, and remains, something 'alien' that cannot be made to fit into the human ideational world. That alone is its meaning. It is 'The Other,' 'The Incomprehensible,' pure and simple, beyond the reach of any feeling or imagining. . . . It is interpretable only as that which is uninterpretable" (147). In Stanley Corngold's view, Gregor's insect transformation points to the author's "radical aesthetic intention" (9). "Is it too odd an idea," asks Corngold, "to see this family drama as the conflict between ordinary language and a being having the character of an indecipherable word?" (11). Corngold conceives Gregor "as a mutilated metaphor, uprooted from familiar language" (12). He writes, "In organizing itself around a distortion of ordinary language, *The Metamorphosis* projects into its center a sign which absorbs its own significance . . ." (27–28). Is it too odd an idea to suggest that critics like Emrich and Corngold are responding to the reader's transient sharing of Gregor's intrapsychic world, a world that is frighteningly alien, distorted, and empty?

Kafka, in the words of Theodor Adorno, shakes the "contemplative relation between text and reader . . . to its very roots" (246). "A book for Kafka," writes Silvio Vietta, "should act as a blow on the head of the reader" (211). Temporarily implicated in the incognizable insect world depicted in *The Metamorphosis*, the reader palpably experiences Gregor's feelings of dislocation and self-unreality. No wonder some critics take refuge in the safer confines of abstract philosophic or linguistic constructs. That Kafka's narrative may also engender a wish in readers to escape from Gregor's proximity—a wish the closure acts out—is suggested in some observations made by Roy Pascal. Describing the "intense enclosedness of Kafka's stories," Pascal comments: "There is no escape from the spell they weave, scarcely an opportunity for reflexion, contemplation, for a relaxation of tension, until the spell is broken by the death of the narrator's chief medium, the chief character. And at that point the reader looks back in almost uncomprehending horror, cut off from this strange experience as the awakened sleeper is cut off from his nightmare" (57). While it is true that the narrative "completedness" of *The Metamorphosis* "forces" readers, in Pascal's words, to search out "the coherence of this apparent incoherence" (40), the fact that critics seem to feel strangely helpless before this text, which insistently demands and resists interpretation, suggests that the insect-Gregor's feelings of powerlessness may be induced in readers not only as they share Gregor's perceptions but also as they grapple with the resistant preverbal puzzles encoded in the narrative.

Creating in *The Metamorphosis* a character who is real and unreal, replete with meaning and empty of self, Kafka encourages the interpreter to fill in the deficit, the void that exists at the center of the insect-Gregor's self. Critics have long commented on the repetitive nature of Kafka's fiction. The "form" of Kafka's fiction, as one critic puts it, is "circular": the "basic situation" of a given narrative "emerges again and again like a trauma" (Anders 37). Reading *The Metamorphosis* through the lens of self psychology, we can gain significant insight into both the source of and our reaction to that central, narcissistic trauma.

Four
Empathy and Self-Validation in Bellow's *Seize the Day*

Like Dostoevsky's anti-hero and Kafka's insect-hero, Wilhelm Adler, the protagonist of Saul Bellow's character study, *Seize the Day*, craves the attention of others and depends on others to support his threatened self. But unlike them, he openly voices his sense of narcissistic entitlement and his desire for rescue. "I've never asked you for very much," Wilhelm Adler says to his father in an anguished plea for sympathy. "[O]ne word from you, just a word, would go a long way" (109–10). "I expect *help*!" he insists (53). This impassioned request for an empathic response from his father, which is central to the psychology of Wilhelm Adler, is also central to the critical responses Bellow's text has engendered.

In *Seize the Day* surface illuminates subsurface as Wilhelm's verbal pleas for sympathy shed light on the preverbal depths of his personality. Behind his desperate need for confirmation lie deep-rooted feelings of ambivalence, anger, and disconnection. As he undergoes a harrowing self-crisis, he perceives behind his "pretender soul" (71)—his socially adaptive, compliant counterfeit self—the deficiency at the core of his personality. A chronic mistake maker and a victim, Wilhelm has been variously described as a "*schlemiel*" (Cohen 93–94), a "moral masochist" (Weiss 121), and a symbol of "the failure of the American Dream" (Richmond 15). And yet, despite his overt faults, most commentators have responded sympathetically to Bellow's character. Indeed, the word of confirmation Wilhelm fails to get from his father, as we shall see, has been spoken again and again by critic/readers. Legitimizing his struggles, they find a plenitude of meaning in his defective selfhood and read his suffering as a "mark of the chosen rather than of the rejected" (Cohen 100).

Just as the Underground Man experiences wide oscillations in his self-esteem, perceiving himself alternately as a hero or as subhuman, and just as Gregor Samsa harbors secret feelings of omnipotence when he initially manifests himself as an insect, so we find in Bellow's character the uneasy coexistence of grandiose pretensions and an utter sense of impotence and defeat. When Wilhelm searches his memory on his "day of reckoning" (96), he must sort out fact from fiction, truth from grandiose myth, the "true" from the "pretender" self. His distorted grandiosity is conveyed in the novel's opening scene. Gazing at his reflection in a glass cupboard full of cigar boxes, Wilhelm sees his reflected image "among . . . the gold-embossed portraits of famous men, García, Edward the Seventh, Cyrus the Great. . . . Fair-haired hippopotamus!—that was how he looked to himself" (6). Once impressively handsome, Wilhelm, middle aged, has gone to seed: "He looked down over the front of his big, indecently big, spoiled body. He was beginning to lose his shape, his gut was fat . . ." (29). Because Wilhelm's self is not strong and resilient, he feels overburdened, that he will be "crushed" if he stumbles, that his obligations will "destroy" him (39–40), that he gets "taken" and is "stripped bare" (9–10), that "the peculiar burden of his existence lay upon him like an accretion, a load, a hump" (39). Narcissistically deficient, he looks to others to shore up his sagging self and he looks to his father for support.

When Wilhelm, in his mid-forties and his life at an impasse, comes to the ironically named Hotel Gloriana to be near his elderly father, to be in the parental environment, he seeks some remedy for his situation. In his reiterated attempts to elicit a word of sympathy from his father, he acts out an anachronistic drama. "[I]t's time I stopped feeling like a kid toward him, a small son" (11), Wilhelm thinks to himself as he, clingingly dependent, demanding, and deeply angry, compulsively reenacts his childhood relationship with his father, endeavoring to get from him, somehow or other, the empathic responsiveness he feels entitled to. Emotionally, Wilhelm still is a child. In his crisis situation, his needs for mirroring responses and support from an idealized selfobject—his father and Tamkin—have become acute. What is at stake is his self-survival.

"I'm of two minds . . ." (29, 73) Wilhelm says in an unconscious revelation of his split self. Similarly, the narrator appears to be of two minds about Wilhelm. Mirroring Wilhelm's outer, sympathetic personality and his inner "gruff" voice that typically finds fault with others, the narrator both comes to Wilhelm's support and devalues him. After describing Wilhelm's "odd" habit of pinching out the coal of his cigarette and dropping the butt in his pocket, for example, the narrator makes mention of Wilhelm's ironic notion that he is capable of "outdoing his father" if he wants with his "perfect and even distinguished manners" (28). In contrast, when Dr. Adler's interior voice criticizes Wilhelm for being a "dirty devil," the narrator intrudes to defend Wilhelm: "He was not really so slovenly as his father found him to be. In some aspects he even had a certain delicacy" (42). And while the narrator consistently calls attention to Wilhelm's large, spoiled body, unkempt appearance, and untidy habits, he also describes some of the "slow, silent movements" of Wilhelm's face as "very attractive" (5). Occupying the shifting positions of the narrator, the reader both enters Wilhelm's consciousness and steps back, on occasion, and views him from a slight remove or through the critical eyes of his father.

Installed as an empathic listener and observer, the reader, as the narrative unfolds, becomes aware of Wilhelm's entrapment in his own stifling, interior hell. While the shifting narrative focus does serve to protect the reader from "the oppression of intense identification" with Wilhelm (Opdahl 106), it does not, judging from the critical responses to this text, dilute reader sympathy for him. We are invited to feel a range of responses to Bellow's anti-hero. Like Dr. Adler, we may find things about Wilhelm disgusting, embarrassing, and annoying. But we are also urged to respond favorably to Bellow's character. "It is the neglected parts of Wilhelm," writes John Clayton, "that make us care about the man: the man who receives lines of poetry out of the blue . . . who thinks about the loneliness in New York, who has moments of peace . . ." (41). And while we are forced to acknowledge Wilhelm's physical peculiarities, excessive self-pity, and childish irresponsibility, we are also urged to feel sorry for him and to become progressively concerned about his troubled life and hopeful of his rescue. Sarah Cohen's comments on the novel reflect the collective critical response this text has engendered. Bellow, she observes, "appreciates what Wilhelm is up against and therefore sympathetically pardons his buffoonish deviations and improprieties. . . . [I]t is those who frown upon Wilhelm that meet with Bellow's censure" (93). Indeed, as we shall see, critics have repeatedly pardoned Wilhelm for his faults and denounced his accusers—Dr. Adler and Margaret—for their unempathic treatment of him. Reacting to Wilhelm's need for approval and rescue, most critic/readers have endorsed the conscious project of this text, which suggests Wilhelm's ultimate redemption and spiritual elevation through suffering. And what the text backgrounds, most readers have ignored and avoided. On the periphery of the text, another narrative is recoverable, one that inscribes Wilhelm's split-off anger. The weight of the unspoken, which haunts Wilhelm's interactions with others, haunts the reader of *Seize the Day*, vexing with unanswerable questions those critic/readers who have applied traditional expectations for narrative closure, character development, and resolution of conflict to Bellow's novel.

Providing a remarkable transcription of the strategies and defenses underlying the spoken and unspoken thoughts of Wilhelm and Dr. Adler, the conflict-ridden father-son confrontation that begins the novel gives the reader direct awareness of their colliding subjectivities and irresolvable differences. The narrator, acting the role of empathic listener, on occasion intrudes to explain what was really meant by their miscommunications. "[O]n guard against insinuations" in whatever his father says, Wilhelm studies his father's remarks, looking for hidden insults and nuances. When his father says, "[H]ere we are under the same roof again, after all these years," Wilhelm translates this into a rebuff: "Why are you here in a hotel with me and not at home . . . with your wife and two boys?" When Wilhelm, ostensibly trying to help his father remember how many years have elapsed, asks "[H]ow many years has it been? . . . Wasn't it the year Mother died? What year was that?" (27), he inwardly reacts with anger at what he perceives as his father's excessive self-involvement. His father has forgotten the date, was "set free" by his wife's death, and similarly wants to "get rid of" Wilhelm (29). When Wilhelm describes his mother's death as "the beginning of the end," Dr. Adler is "astonished" and "puzzled." But he defensively refuses to "give Wilhelm an opening to introduce his complaints," having "learned that it was better not to take up" his son's "strange challenges." Pleasant, affable in his response, Dr. Adler is a "master of social behavior." But inwardly he thinks, "What business has he to complain to *me* of his mother's death?" "Face to face," as the narrator describes it, each declares himself "silently after his own way" (28). Each is something of an actor, a pretender, the "great weight of the unspoken" lying between them (6).

In Wilhelm's interactions with his father, we find a typical narcissistic pattern: the thwarting of Wilhelm's demands for an empathic response stirs strong feelings of injury, resentment, and anger. On his "day of reckoning," Wilhelm strips away the protective myth of his happy childhood relationship with his father. "Maybe . . . I was sentimental in the past and exaggerated his kindliness—warm family life. It may never have been there" (26). "[F]illed with ancient grievances" (29), he recalls that his father "never was a pal" to him when he was young, i.e., was emotionally unavailable. "He was at the office or the hospital, or lecturing. He expected me to look out for myself and never gave me much thought" (14). While Wilhelm feels entitled to his father's sympathy and support—"I am his son. . . . He is my father. He is as much father as I am son . . ."—he also is aware that he doesn't "stand a chance of getting [the] sympathy" he craves (43). Nevertheless, he attempts to elicit an empathic response from his father. Wilhelm, trapped in his suppliant's role, is externally conciliatory. But inwardly he criticizes his father, finding him selfish, vain, insensitive. "He had always been a vain man," he thinks to himself. "To see how his father loved himself sometimes made Wilhelm madly indignant" (12). Predictably, Wilhelm's confession that he is "in a bad way" falls on deaf ears. "You might have told him that Seattle was near Puget Sound, or that the Giants and Dodgers were playing a night game, so little was he moved from his expression of healthy, handsome, good-humored old age" (11).

When Wilhelm tries "to unburden himself," he, instead, feels he must "undergo an inquisition to prove himself worthy of a sympathetic word" (52). Seeking sympathy, he ends up feeling rejected and enraged. He senses that he is "being put on notice" when his father comments that he keeps his "sympathy for the real ailments" such as that suffered by Mr. Perls who has a "bone condition which is gradually breaking him up" (42). Dr. Adler is unable to see what the reader recognizes all too clearly: that Wilhelm's fragile self is on the verge of breaking up. Rebuffed by his father, Wilhelm, at first, says nothing but instead compulsively eats, devouring not only his own breakfast but also the remains of his father's. Through this regressive behavior, Wilhelm acts out his desire to appropriate from his father the narcissistic sustenance he feels entitled to. When he, in his openly aggressive demands for sympathy, introduces his well-worn litany of complaints about his wife, Dr. Adler responds that it's Wilhelm's fault, that he doesn't understand his son's problems, and that Wilhelm shouldn't "carry on like an opera" (49).

Inwardly angry, Wilhelm towers and sways, "big and sloven, with his gray eyes red-shot and his honey-colored hair twisted in flaming shapes upward." Outwardly, he assumes the posture of the placater for he wants "an understanding with his father" and so he tries to "capitulate to him" (50). But to no avail. "You have no sympathy" (53), he tells his father. "When I suffer—you aren't even sorry. That's because you have no affection for me, and you don't want any part of me" (54). His urgent plea for sympathy and support—"I expect *help!*" (53)—is rejected. "I want nobody on my back. Get off!" (55), his father says to him.

In this father-son transaction we find important clues to Wilhelm's self-disorder. As we learn in this exchange, Wilhelm is acutely sensitive to what he perceives as his father's affective absence, his affable nonresponsiveness, his self-absorption, his chronic fault-finding, and his covert demand that his son live up to *his* standards of perfection. When Dr. Adler publicly boasts about him, Wilhelm feels that his father is making narcissistic use of him, bragging about Wilhelm's accomplishments for his own self-aggrandizement. "Why, that boasting old hypocrite," Wilhelm thinks to himself. "[H]ow we love looking fine in the eyes of the world . . ." (13). In an attempt to accommodate his father's wishes and driven by his archaic needs, Wilhelm tries to become a success. But his goals—his hypertrophied belief that he could become a Hollywood star, be appointed vice president of Rojax, and make a fortune in the commodities market—are unrealistic. Again and again, Wilhelm's untamed grandiosity overwhelms his reality ego leading to a series of painful and predictable failures. And like the typical shame-prone narcissist, he protects himself through boasts and lies. He lies at "first boastfully and then out of charity to himself" about his Hollywood venture (15); he quits his job at Rojax out of hurt pride—"I told everybody I was going to be an officer of the corporation. . . . But then they welshed. . . . I bragged and made myself look big" (74); he defensively denies that "anything serious" has happened when he is wiped out in the commodities market, the "lie" helping him out (104).

But though such defenses can temporarily shield his attenuated self, they cannot counteract his underlying sense of defectiveness. "Ass! Idiot! . . . Slave! Lousy, wallowing hippopotamus!" (55), he mentally upbraids himself after his traumatic confrontation with his father. He has introjected his father's negative view of him. Years before when Wilhelm went to Hollywood, he, in a symbolic gesture, changed his name in the misguided belief that if he cast off his father's name for him—"Wilky"—he could also cast off his father's negative opinion of him. Ironically, the name he selected in his attempt to assert his identity—"Tommy"—suggests not autonomous selfhood but childlike dependency and arrested development. And "Wilky" has remained his "inescapable self." "You fool, you clunk, you Wilky!" he reproaches himself when drunk (25). In a similar vein, Wilhelm's inner, cynical "gruff" voice—an expression of his split-off anger and his fault-finding, parental introject—unempathically berates others. "Who is this damn frazzle-faced herring with his dyed hair and his fish teeth and this drippy mustache? . . . How can a human face get into this condition?" (31), Wilhelm asks himself when he meets Mr. Perls, an unacknowledged self-representation.

The fact that Wilhelm repeatedly attempts to provoke a reaction from his father through self-pity is also telling. For the self-pity response, explains psychoanalyst Samuel Wilson, expresses an "urgent attempt to counteract feelings of alienation and disintegration accompanying a severe narcissistic wound and to recover selfobject connectedness" (182). "The attack on the self," writes Wilson, "contains the hope that this will subserve the needs of the selfobject, as they are perceived, and therefore restore the tie. The appeal to the mercy of the selfobject subserves the needs for a comforting response." But the combination of "helplessness" and "hostility" underlying this response "provokes the already alienated selfobject into further withdrawal and anger" (183).

While Wilhelm provokes criticism and attack from his father, most commentators take his side in the father-son conflict, even though they may consider his self-pity excessive or confess themselves some-what reluctant to give "sympathy to a man in his physical 'prime' who is asking support of an octogenarian" (Fuchs 80). Even a critic like Jonathan Wilson, who sees many of Dr. Adler's criticisms of Wilhelm as "to some extent justified" and who faults Wilhelm for acting like "an overgrown child," feels that "it is Wilhelm's childishness that primarily recommends itself to us" (97, 100). Given the critical responses to this text, there clearly is something in Wilhelm's urgent need for help that recommends itself to readers and prompts them to come to his support when his father turns away from him. In part because Dr. Adler is so callous in his response to his son's cry for help and also because the text associates him with the material values of a money-obsessed society, reader after reader has acted as Wilhelm's advocate and echoed his— and the text's—accusatory voice and split-off anger. While Wilhelm has been described as a "sensitive individual" who suffers financial failure in a milieu that determines a person's worth "exclusively in monetary terms" (McCadden 93), Dr. Adler, in contrast, has been harshly condemned for being "self-centered, uncompassionate" (Porter 110), "[i]rredeemably selfish" (J. Wilson 103), and for hoarding both his money and his "tight, withered, insulated self" (Rodrigues 85). At one point Wilhelm thinks that "it was the punishment of hell itself not to understand or be understood"; in New York the "fathers were no fathers and the sons no sons" (83–84). Drawn into Wilhelm's interior world, readers are urged, in effect, to enact the "good father" role by sympathetically responding to Wilhelm's need for understanding and rescue.

That Wilhelm's reality is narcissistically constituted is revealed in his involvement some twenty-five years before with Maurice Venice, the Hollywood scout, and his current involvement with Dr. Tamkin. In Venice, Wilhelm unknowingly encounters a reflection of his own split grandiose/enervated self. When Venice talks about how the "down-cast" need a "break-through, a help, luck, or sympathy" (22), Wilhelm is moved. The "obscure failure of an aggressive and powerful clan" (20), Venice, like Wilhelm, is defensively concerned about the impres-sion he is making on others and like Wilhelm he is a braggart and a liar. Physically grotesque, both powerful and weak, Venice is "huge and oxlike" but "so stout" that his arms seem immobilized, "caught from beneath in a grip of flesh and fat" (17). Prophetically, Venice typecasts

Wilhelm as a loser. But he also appeals to Wilhelm's grandiose fantasies. "[I]n one jump," Venice tells him, "the world knows who you are. You become a name like Roosevelt, Swanson. . . . You become a lover to the whole world. The world wants it, needs it. One fellow smiles, a billion people also smile. One fellow cries, the other billion sob with him" (22). Despite the negative results of his screen test and Venice's subsequent discouragement, Wilhelm, driven by his primitive belief in his "luck and inspiration" (15) and by his hankering after admiration, goes to Hollywood. Acting out a preestablished plot, he makes his "first great mistake" (17).

Similarly, when Wilhelm meets up with Tamkin, he is, again, "ripe for the mistake" (58). A "confuser of the imagination" (93), Tamkin is an important figure in Wilhelm's psychic life. In Tamkin, Wilhelm finds a potential need-fulfiller. "I've been concerned with you, and for some time I've been treating you," Tamkin tells Wilhelm (73). Making a hostile use of his empathy, Tamkin pretends he is concerned with Wilhelm so he can gull him. Snubbed by his father, Wilhelm transfers onto Tamkin his need for support from an idealizable selfobject. He sees Tamkin, who has "a hypnotic power in his eyes," as a "benevolent magician" (62, 81). While Dr. Adler says "I want nobody on my back," Wilhelm imagines that Tamkin is supporting him, that he is riding on Tamkin's back, that he has "virtually left the ground" and is "in the air" (96). Narcissistically cathected, Tamkin is a father-surrogate figure. But he is also a complex self-representation.

Is Tamkin a "liar"? Wilhelm asks himself, his question about Tamkin self-referential. "That was a delicate question. Even a liar might be trustworthy in some ways" (57). Like Wilhelm, Tamkin is a braggart who "believes he's making a terrific impression, and . . . practically invites you to take off your hat when he talks about himself . . ." (96). "I read the best of literature, science and philosophy," says the all-but-illiterate Tamkin (72). In Tamkin, Wilhelm finds an exaggeration of his own grandiose pretensions. Tamkin's "hints" about his life—he claims, among other things, to have been part of the underworld, to have been head of a mental clinic and a psychiatrist to an Egyptian royal family—grow "by repetition" into "sensational claims" (80). When Tamkin describes himself as a "healer" who belongs to humanity, Wilhelm's inner cynical voice calls him a "[l]iar . . . a puffed-up little bogus and humbug with smelly feet" (95–96). An incarnation of Wilhelm's distorted grandiose/vulnerable self, Tamkin is a "rare, peculiar bird" with his "pointed shoulders, that bare head, his loose nails, almost claws, and those brown, soft, deadly, heavy eyes" (82). Potent and weak, he seems to achieve the "hypnotic effect" in his eyes through "exertion" (62), and when his "hypnotic spell" fails, his "big underlip" makes him appear "weak-minded" (96).

When Wilhelm gives Tamkin power of attorney over his remaining funds, he acts out a complex psychic script. To make or have money is to attempt to supply oneself with an external source of self-worth and power. Money also is a symbol of his father's power. When forced to accompany the self-involved and demanding Mr. Rappaport to the cigar store, Wilhelm displaces his angry feelings about his father onto Mr. Rappaport. "He's almost blind, and covered with spots, but this old man still makes money in the market," Wilhelm's angry inner voice complains. "Is loaded with dough, probably. And I bet he doesn't give his children any. Some of them must be in their fifties. This is what keeps middle-aged men as children. He's master over the dough" (101–02). At one and the same time Wilhelm believes that Tamkin will magically make a fortune and thus save him, and he expects to lose all his money. To be divested of his money is to make reparation for his covert angry impulses. But to be bankrupt is also to be rendered helpless, the hidden fantasy being that his father will relent and give him the money—i.e., the narcissistic support—he needs to sustain and strengthen his flagging self. As Wilhelm tells his father, "It isn't all a question of money—there are other things a father can give to a son. . . . [O]ne word from you, just a word, would go a long way" (109–10). Wilhelm is deeply angry with his father and afraid of his anger. But he also craves the healing response that only his father can give. Transferring his needs onto others, Wilhelm wants Mr. Rappaport to give him a winning tip on the market, "to speak the single word" that will "save him" (87). Similarly, he wants Tamkin to "give him some useful advice" and thus "transform his life" (72).

"How did you imagine it was going to be—big shot? Everything made smooth for you?" says Wilhelm's wife, Margaret (114). In his strained relationship with his wife, Wilhelm repeats the narcissistic drama he enacts with his father. Like Dr. Adler, Margaret is contemptuous, unempathic, fault-finding. Her emotional absence is reflected in her "hard" voice (112). Irritated with Wilhelm's hyperbolic talk, she tells him to "stop thinking like a youngster" and sardonically says that he deserves the "misery" he feels (112, 113). Also a self-representation, Margaret is an amalgam of Wilhelm's clinging dependency and disavowed anger. "A husband like me is a slave, with an iron collar," Wilhelm tells his father (49). "Whenever she can hit me, she hits, and she seems to live for that alone. And she demands more and more, and still more" (47). Her angry thoughts are lethal. "She just has fixed herself on me to kill me. She can do it at long distance. One of these days I'll be struck down by suffocation or apoplexy because of her" (48). "This is the way of the weak," Wilhelm says to himself in a self-referring description of his wife. "[Q]uiet and fair. And then smash! They smash!" (112).

While the portrait of Margaret is extremely unsympathetic, Bellow's narrator explains and thus softens her hard words: "She had not, perhaps, intended to reply as harshly as she did, but she brooded a great deal and now she could not forbear to punish him and make him feel pains like those she had to undergo" (114). At one and the same time Bellow expresses his own dislike of the Margarets of this world and depicts himself as the empathic and mediating authorial presence behind the text. Critics, in their discussions of Margaret, follow the text's mandates and echo Bellow's anger as they, taking sides in the husband-wife conflict, come to Wilhelm's support and harshly judge Margaret. She has been depicted variously: as "parasitic" (Raper 166), as a "resentful sadist" (Fuchs 85), as a "murderer of the spirit" (Mc-Cadden 106), and as a "termagant wife" who endeavored to "rob" Wilhelm of his "identity during [the] marriage" and "is now determined to rob him of his waning funds" (Cohen 91).

"I was the man beneath; Tamkin was on my back, and I thought I was on his," Wilhelm reflects when he, after his commodities loss, searches for Tamkin. "He made me carry him, too, besides Margaret. Like this they ride on me with hoofs and claws. Tear me to pieces, stamp on me and break my bones" (105). His money gone, Wilhelm, desperate, seeks out his father. When, in this final father-son confrontation, his father disowns him, Wilhelm is struck by Dr. Adler's wide-open, "dark, twisted" mouth (110). A concentrated image, the angry mouth depicts not only the fault-finding father but also Wilhelm's split-off anger. Standing over his father in the massage room, Wilhelm also sees, in his father's "pale, slight" deteriorating body (108), a reflection of his own enervated, crumbling self. From the beginning of his "day of reckoning" Wilhelm has felt himself drowning in his quelled tears, this sinking sensation giving experiential immediacy to his crumbling self and the line from "Lycidas" which he recalls—"Sunk though he be beneath the wat'ry floor" (13)—giving further evidence of this feeling-state. Through his reiterated complaints that he feels congested and as if his head were about to burst, he communicates his feelings of strangulating anger and incipient fragmentation. "New York is like a gas. The colors are running. My head feels so tight, I don't know what I'm doing" (50). Sensing that he is about to confront "a huge trouble long presaged but till now formless" (4), he focuses on his verbalizable troubles to shield himself from what lies behind them: unbearable feelings of preverbal dread, rage, and despair.

"The past is no good to us" (66), says Tamkin, the self-styled "psychological poet" (69). "The future is full of anxiety. Only the present is real—the here-and-now. Seize the day" (66). All too often, Tamkin's advice to Wilhelm has been construed by critics as the novel's serious message. But is it? Wilhelm, in a moment of anguish, prays to be let out of his "thoughts," to be let out of the "clutch" he is in and "into a different life" (26). This prayer, significantly, follows his realization that he lacks "free choice," that "there's really very little that a man can change at will" in his life (25, 24). While Tamkin's seize-the-day advice reflects Wilhelm's *wish* to be different, Wilhelm cannot change merely because he wishes to do so. Just as years before Venice seemed to promise Wilhelm freedom from the "anxious and narrow life of the average" (23), now Tamkin seems to promise him freedom from his anxiety-ridden middle age. Claiming that he wrote his poem, "Mechanism vs Functionalism," with Wilhelm in mind, Tamkin describes the hero of the poem as "sick humanity," which, if "it would open its eyes . . . would be great" (77):

> If thee thyself couldst only see
> Thy greatness that is and yet to be,
> . . .
> Witness. Thy power is not bare.
> Thou art King. Thou art at thy best.   (75)

After reading the poem, Wilhelm is "dazed, as though a charge of photographer's flash powder had gone up in his eyes." Consciously, he is enraged because he recognizes that Tamkin is illiterate. Unconsciously, he is angry because in the "mishmash, claptrap" (75) of Tamkin's poem he finds a parodic expression of his own grandiosity. Forced to "translate" Tamkin's words into "his own language," Wilhelm finds himself unable to "translate fast enough or find terms to fit what he heard" (68). "[W]hy do people just naturally assume that you'll know what they're talking about?" he asks himself after reading Tamkin's poem (76).

Through his writing, Tamkin attempts to win the approval of, gain leverage over, and aggressively encroach upon Wilhelm. A subject of much critical discussion, the enigmatic Tamkin has been read as a coded representation of the literary artist. It is interesting that Gilead Morahg, one critic who pursues at length the Tamkin/artist parallels, transforms Tamkin into the novel's moral center and actively splits off his bad qualities. Describing Tamkin as a "morally motivated person who uses fiction in order to affect, and hopefully transform, the life of another," Morahg claims that Tamkin "is similar to the artist, the estimation of whose work is to be completely disassociated from any moral judgment concerning his personality and conduct" (116). While some critics claim that the "grotesque and eccentric Tamkin" gives voice to Bellow's "most-cherished ideas" (J. Wilson 98), others hold the opposite opinion, feeling that he "combines in caricature all the worst perversions of Modernist belief" (Cronin 21). Latent in this critical split, one can speculate, is Bellow's own ambivalence toward his role as an artist. This text seems to suggest that the empathic artist who gives voice to healing ideas may also be a cold-blooded manipulator and an impostor.

In the novel's final, climactic scene when Wilhelm, searching for Tamkin, suddenly finds himself at the funeral of a stranger, he completes a drama whose script is largely unknown to him and one that actively fosters reader interpretation. "On the surface, the dead man with his formal shirt and his tie and silk lapels and his powdered skin looked so proper; only a little beneath so—black, Wilhelm thought, so fallen in the eyes" (117). In the psychic notation of the novel, the dead man represents the affectively absent father, the empty self that is subjacent to the social, pretender self, and Wilhelm's own self-demise. "What'll I do?" he asks himself. "I'm stripped and kicked out. . . . Oh, Father, what do I ask of you? . . . And Olive? . . . you must protect me against that devil who wants my life. If you want it, then kill me. Take,

take it, take it from me" (117). Behind Wilhelm's verbalizable troubles lies a profound sense of vulnerability and despair. Soon "past words, past reason, coherence," he cries "with all his heart" (117–18). As the "flowers and lights" fuse "ecstatically" in his "blind, wet eyes" and the "heavy sea-like music" pours into him, Wilhelm, his self dissolving, hides himself "in the center of a crowd by the great and happy oblivion of tears." He sinks "deeper than sorrow, through torn sobs and cries toward the consummation of his heart's ultimate need" (118).

This final, ambiguous description has been read positively, as the inception of a healing process through mourning. But it also suggests both a loss of self-cohesion and a regressive retreat into the world of earliest childhood. Significantly, when Tamkin earlier enjoined Wilhelm to do "here-and-now" exercises, Wilhelm recalled how, years before when he was ill, his wife had nursed him and read to him the lines from Keats which haunt him on his day of reckoning: "Come then, Sorrow! / Sweetest Sorrow! / Like an own babe I nurse thee on my breast!" (89). These lines suggest not only Wilhelm's mourning for his lost self but also his regressive urge to return to the blissful world of earliest childhood, the "Mt. Serenity" described in Tamkin's poem: "At the foot of Mt. Serenity / Is thy cradle to eternity" (75). A narcissistic nirvana, Mt. Serenity is the introjected world of the good mother. In Wilhelm's mind this is the place inhabited by Olive, his mistress, whom he associates with the peaceful, sunlit landscape of Roxbury (43). In the final scene, as Wilhelm's enfeebled self collapses, he returns to the formless oblivion and the oceanic oneness of this primal world. But this return offers him only a momentary respite. For Roxbury is but a stone's throw from the hell of New York where people howl like wolves from city windows and where it is impossible to communicate; Mt. Serenity is within reach of the "ruins of life . . . chaos and old night" (93). Wilhelm's introjected world of "the good things, the happy things, the easy tranquil things of life" (78) and his fantasy of merging into a mystical "larger body" where "sons and fathers are themselves" and "confusion is only . . . temporary" (84) are but fragile defenses against—and retreats away from—his more immediate feelings of anger, unrelatedness, and inner chaos.

"Let me out of my trouble. Let me out of my thoughts. . . . Let me out of this clutch and into a different life" (26), Wilhelm prays at one point, though he is fully aware that he lacks "free choice," that he cannot liberate himself from his "inescapable self" (25). While the tone of the closure is positive and suggests the possibility of Wilhelm's redemption through suffering, the weight of the novel conveys the opposite message. Critic Ihab Hassan questions whether the "particular mode" of Wilhelm's revelation "does not seem rather gratuitous, rather foreign to the concerns . . . most steadily expressed throughout the action" (316). The reader is enticed to believe, as does Bellow's hero, that Wilhelm can make a new beginning; can change midstream; can free himself from his introjects, his crippling dependencies, his defensive boasting and his masochistic self-depreciation; that he can be "let out of" his "troubles" and "thoughts" into a "different life." One critic who is seduced by the positive rhetoric of the closure writes: "Because he is able to transcend his personal grief, Wilhelm's tears are also tears of joy. In destroying the pretender soul, Wilhelm prepares the way for the coming of the true soul, who will not lead him to torture himself over an unworthy father, will not persuade him to go to Hollywood or marry unwisely or seek a quick fortune with a charlatan" (Porter 125). Wilhelm's "uncontrollable crying," writes another critic, provides a "release from the insoluble problems that tear at his heart" and marks the "beginning of his creative re-birth" (McCadden 91–92). "Seize the day," free yourself from the past, Tamkin enjoins Wilhelm. How ironic such advice is in a novel whose protagonist is bound up in an ongoing process of consciously remembering and unconsciously reenacting his past.

What is the typical critic/reader's overall response to Wilhelm? Clinton Trowbridge's comments are illuminating. "Even when Wilhelm is being depicted least sympathetically, when he is most in the wrong, most the slob," he writes, "we are continually made aware that we are witnessing the strugglings of a drowning man and we want to see him rescued" (65). " 'I expect *help!*' " Wilhelm says to his father, only to be rebuffed. But many critics have responded to Wilhelm's need for rescue by elevating and spiritualizing his struggle. While a few critics acknowledge and then excuse Wilhelm's anger, claiming that it results from his "sense of persecution" (Porter 114), most keep intact their image of Wilhelm as a passive victim by totally ignoring it. They see Wilhelm as Keith Opdahl does, as a "good man" in a world "antithetical" to goodness (112). While critics, as we have observed, echo Wilhelm's accusatory voice and the text's anger as they harshly condemn Margaret and Dr. Adler, they regard Wilhelm as an innocent buffoon who is "exposed to the world's sharkish materialism" (Cohen 90). "Wilhelm's only weapon," writes Daniel Fuchs, "is love, and this is why he is in such a bad way among the money men . . ." (97). Wilhelm's drowning is interpreted as a "baptism, a rebirth" (Porter 125), his collapse as a "triumph" (Opdahl 115). Beneath the novel's "profound and moving sense of despair" Trowbridge finds "the birth of a soul" (62). Wilhelm is described as resisting modernist pessimism and as "[h]olding fast to his transcendental dream" (Cronin 23). "Wilhelm's sobs," as Fuchs comments, "have gained a following" (95). Indeed, they have. Wilhelm's suffering enhances his worth and gains the reader's attention and sympathy.

That the reader's impulse was shared by Bellow is suggested in Daniel Fuchs's analysis of Bellow's revisions of the novel. Particularly revealing is Fuchs's observation on how the "language of outrage" in the novel became "balanced somewhat by the development in the language and imagery of love and spiritual resurrection, most notably in the novella's conclusion" (94). The first version of the closure, unlike the final version, focused on Wilhelm's regressive collapse: "The lights and flowers fused in his blind wet eyes and the music shuddered at his ears. Wilhelm choked his sobs in his handkerchief, and bit his thumb but he failed to check his weeping" (Fuchs 96). Here attention is drawn, observes Fuchs, to the "neurotic, childish thumb in the mouth," an image totally eliminated from the final version with its suggestion of ecstasy and transcendence (97). "Words such as *consummation* [and] *ecstatically*" and the "slow, deliberate, majestic rhythms" of the final paragraph, in the words of one critic, "compel the reader to participate in Wilhelm's moment of . . . transcendence" (Rodrigues 105–06). Moreover, the measured speech of Keats, Milton, and Shakespeare which haunts Wilhelm serves to elevate his struggle. In effect, Bellow provides the healing word Wilhelm seeks through yet another type of father figure—the literary father. But the contrast between literary speech and Tamkin's garbled, illiterate romanticism works to subvert the author's intended literary reclamation of Wilhelm. We find a similar subversion in Bellow's description of Wilhelm's repudiation of his visionary "blaze of love" for all the "imperfect and lurid-looking people" he sees in the subway: "It was only another one of those subway things. Like having a hard-on at random" (84–85). This has led at least one commentator to cross-question the positive tone of the closure and wonder if Wilhelm's "sour dismissal" of his subway experience isn't "predictive of a parallel dismissal" of his funeral home experience "once his tears have dried" (Sicherman 14).

While the closure can be viewed as a reparative gesture derived from Bellow's need to rescue the troubled self of his anti-hero, it also can be read as a reaction formation against his covert desire to "kill off" his hapless character. Tamkin, who, as we have observed, can be read as a clandestine representation of the author, is described as a storyteller who invents a woman, kills her off, and then calls himself a healer (95). Two contrasting but associated signifiers in the novel—the healing word and the angry mouth—can be read as coded references to the author who expresses his anger through his characters while enacting, in his narrator's guise, the role of mediator and empathic listener. "I can sympathize with Wilhelm," Bellow commented in an interview, "but I can't respect him. He is a sufferer by vocation. I'm a resister by vocation" (Roudané 279). Fuchs asks, "Isn't Wilhelm the victim Bellow wants to delete from his own typology?" (79). While the closure of this text may represent a gesture toward resolution of conflict and aesthetic finality, its very abruptness and incompleteness undermine such an authorial intention. For just when the reader "expects the falling action to unravel and explain," comments J. R. Raper, "the book ends" (158). The closure is "unresolved," observes Richard Giannone, baffling reader expectations for "clarification and completion" (203). While the final potent image of Wilhelm in the funeral parlor provokes the reader's sympathy for his redundant suffering, it also, in effect, puts the reader in the place of the other mourners whose curiosity is provoked by his unexplained lament. The closure forces the reader to interpret and explain. It is also possible that the abrupt closure answers the secret wish of some readers—and the author—to abandon Wilhelm, to be let out of his troubles, and thus escape his stifling fictional presence.

Speaking informally on the novel, Bellow once described one of the novel's themes as the city dweller's attempt to fulfill his personal needs through strangers (Opdahl 108). That Wilhelm craves empathic resonance is revealed in his open, compulsive sharing of his problems with others. "Other people keep their business to themselves. Not me," he realizes (35). For him it is "the punishment of hell itself not to understand or be understood" (83–84). Despite this, Wilhelm finds it impossible to communicate, living as he does in a world in which "[e]very other man" speaks a language "entirely his own" and where the fathers are "no fathers and the sons no sons" (83–84). When he, at the end, finally breaks down, it is at the funeral of a stranger and in a roomful of strangers who observe him from a psychic distance. Ironically, one of the bystanders comments that he must be "somebody real close to carry on so" (118). The tragedy is that Wilhelm, who wants to be "close," is so totally alone. "Howling like a wolf from the city window" (98), he knows the awfulness of living in an unempathic environment and in a world populated by reflections of his own distorted self. In a fantasy borne of deep necessity, he can imagine a world in which "sons and fathers are themselves" and "confusion is only . . . temporary" (84). But he also realizes that if he stops suffering, he will "have nothing" (98). For behind his verbalizable troubles is a formless oblivion, the wordless dread and inner emptiness of Tragic Man. His self defective, Wilhelm inhabits not the glorious here-and-now fantasied by Tamkin but the bleak here-and-now of his own crippled self.

✻ ✻ ✻ ✻

Five
Storytelling as Attempted Self-Rescue in Conrad's "Secret Sharer" and "Heart of Darkness"

✻ ✻ ✻ ✻

In his two famous tales of the double—"The Secret Sharer" and "Heart of Darkness"—Joseph Conrad gives fictive expression to his obsession with the lonely, isolated individual in complex narratives that have incited seemingly endless critical discussion. Insight into the psychodynamics of these texts is found in the fierce critical polemics they have engendered. In their at once self-revealing and self-concealing narratives, Conrad's narrators—the captain and Marlow—convey their urgent need for self-rescue and for mirroring responses from others. These needs have been responded to by the vast majority of critics who have tended to romanticize and idealize Conrad's story-teller-characters and censor awareness of their negative depths. In this chapter, as we turn to a consideration of Tragic Man as storyteller, we will examine the narcissistic urgings that prompt Conrad's storytellers. Both subject and object of these tales is the desire to entice the listener, to find a selfobject secret sharer, one who hears, sees, understands, and becomes assimilated to the storyteller's point of view.

"The Secret Sharer," as one critic aptly puts it, is "criticism-riddled" (Dussinger 599). Critics have often observed that the text prods the reader to ask questions and openly invites a psychosymbolic reading. While a handful of critics, like Lawrence Graver, feel that the text seduces them "into hunting for a complex symbolic consistency" which

82

it "does not possess" (152), most critics have attempted to decode Conrad's tale and make sense of its central mystery: the shadowy figure of Leggatt. Conrad's covert ambivalence toward Leggatt is mirrored in the two classical interpretations of the story: Albert Guerard's analysis of Leggatt as the dark, criminal self and Daniel Curley's description of him as the ideal self. Although "there is adequate evidence to deny Leggatt's villainy," as Graver observes, there is also "proof to smudge his status as an ideal figure" (151). Just as Conrad's narrator denies the manifest brutality of Leggatt's criminal act, many critics have evasively minimized Leggatt's crime. Equally revealing is the fact that almost all readers have unquestioningly accepted the triumphant tone of the closure. The closure, and much of the criticism surrounding this tale, as we will see, repeats its central action: the concealment of Leggatt and the denial of the captain-narrator's split-off negativity.

As "The Secret Sharer" begins, the young captain is assuming the stress-ridden responsibilities of commanding a ship for the first time. His underlying narcissistic vulnerabilities are activated when he finds himself in a hostile environment: the crew members resent his presence and are prepared to find fault with him because he is young and inexperienced. He reacts defensively by imagining himself as a brooding, isolated hero and by establishing an alter-ego relationship with Leggatt, a chance companion who becomes his fantasied double. Initially, the captain hovers between two responses to Leggatt. He perceives him as an individual in need of help who is "not a bit" like himself (105) and as his selfobject "double." At first, the captain identifies with the fugitive because of the similarities in their physical appearance and in their social, educational, and professional backgrounds. More important, both are essentially secluded loners, outsiders who are distrusted and resented by their crews. Like the captain, Leggatt desires an approving gaze. Describing how he felt when the captain first looked at him, Leggatt recalls, "I didn't mind being looked at. I—I liked it. . . . It had been a confounded lonely time. . . . I was glad to talk a little to somebody that didn't belong to the *Sephora*. . . . I don't know—I wanted to be seen, to talk with somebody, before I went on" (110–11). In his desire to understand Leggatt's situation and save him from the cold stares of judge and jury, the captain acts out his own need to be responded to empathically.

While the captain is depicted as introspective, he responds to

Leggatt without apparent psychological insight or self-recognition. It becomes the task of the reader to ferret out the dynamics of the captain's transactions with the mysterious outlaw. From the outset, the captain feels attuned to Leggatt, as if a "mysterious communication was established" between them (99). Experiencing Leggatt as his "alter ego," he develops an archaic twinship relationship with the fugitive, this type of relationship, in Kohut's explanation, emerging from a need to experience others as essentially similar to the self, a need often found in lonely, isolated individuals like the captain (see *How?* 194–99). Reading himself into the fugitive, the captain unknowingly encounters in his counterpart an embodiment of his own split grandiose/vulnerable self. For while Leggatt is a strong swimmer, he is also so weak that he must be helped into bed; he is "well-knit," "resolute," and a "strong soul" (100, 99) and yet his face looks "sunken in daylight" (114). As Leggatt sits "like a patient, unmoved convict," with his "bowed" head "hanging on his breast" (127, 115), he is the image of extreme withdrawal, depression, and rigid self-containment. The captain, in his desire to help the defenseless, weak fugitive, reveals his unacknowledged need to safeguard his own shaky sense of self; in his intense identification with the manly, self-assured aspects of his alter ego, he reveals both his hidden grandiosity and his need to merge with an idealized figure of power and strength. While Leggatt does represent aspects of the narrator's "ideal conception" of self, as critics have observed, he also incarnates the captain's disowned feelings of vulnerability and rage. What the narrator splits off and denies, a large number of critics have avoided in their readings of the text.

Self-possession and a threatening loss of self-control—these contrasting behaviors are found in the savior/murderer Leggatt who savagely kills an unruly seaman as he saves a crew of twenty-four. Without hesitation, the captain accepts and identifies with the murderous behavior of his double. When Leggatt confesses, "I've killed a man," the captain responds, "Fit of temper," in a confident way. "The shadowy, dark head, like mine, seemed to nod imperceptibly. . . . It was . . . as though I had been faced by my own reflection in the depths of a sombre and immense mirror" (101). While one of the narrative aims of this text is to foster reader endorsement of Leggatt, Leggatt's account of the murder, which some critics have seized upon to prove the fugitive's criminality, works to partially subvert this conscious intention.

84

Although Leggatt refuses to go before judge and jury, a number of critics, seduced into playing a negotiated role, have been preoccupied with trying his case.

Without apparent remorse, Leggatt tells his "fierce story" (103). In a monotonous voice, he describes how, during a violent storm, he attacked a disobedient hand—an "ill-conditioned snarling cur," one of those "[m]iserable devils that have no business to live at all" (101)—for his "cursed insolence at the sheet." After felling his victim "like an ox," Leggatt then grabbed him by the throat and "went on shaking him like a rat," holding him by the throat until he was "black in the face" (102). "I wonder they [the crew] didn't fling me overboard after getting the carcass of their precious ship-mate out of my fingers. They had rather a job to separate us . . ." (103), Leggatt sardonically comments. Leggatt's description of the storm—"it was a sea gone mad! I suppose the end of the world will be something like that" (124)—depicts the fragmenting depths of narcissistic rage. Denying the savagery of Leggatt's deed, the captain condones his behavior. "I knew well enough . . . that my double there was no homicidal ruffian. . . . I saw it all going on as though I were myself inside that other sleeping-suit" (102). Leggatt, as one critic has observed, is "more disturbingly violent than the narrator seems able to admit. By evasion and restatement the narrator repeatedly softens or intellectualizes impressions of his double's actions. . . " And he strategically ignores the fact that the murder apparently occurred *after* the saving foresail had been set and thus that the hand's "insolence did not literally obstruct the act that saved the ship" (Eggenschwiler, "Narcissus" 29–30).

"It's a great satisfaction," Leggatt later tells the captain, "to have got somebody to understand. You seem to have been there on purpose" (132). Assuming the same role as the captain—that of understanding listener—a number of critics have similarly sympathized with Leggatt and acted as his advocate. In his well-known defense of Leggatt, Daniel Curley compares Leggatt's felling his victim like an ox to "throwing a glass of water in the face of a screaming child." When the wave breaks over the ship, in Curley's view, it is "Leggatt's reflex" that leads him "to hold fast to anything" and "[u]nfortunately" he happens to be holding "a man's throat." Though a "murder in form," this is not, argues Curley, "a murder in fact" (81). "The victim and the circumstances of the crime," according to another commentator, "may help explain Leggatt's want of self-reproach, but to condemn him for not feeling remorse is presumptive; one cannot impose an obligation to feel. The absence of remorse is part of his character" (Ressler 206). Leggatt's "insistence that the price of exile is enough to pay 'for an Abel of that sort,'" writes another critic, "gains the admiration of the captain and should gain ours" (Graver 154). And yet another lauds Leggatt for "escaping the law and transcending its hollow forms of authority" (Stallman 285). While Albert Guerard is taken to task for "doing what Conrad clearly did not wish to be done" by using the "epithet 'criminal'" to refer to Leggatt (Kirschner 125), even Guerard describes Leggatt's crime as "marginal" and says that the reader "incorrigibly sympathizes" with the fugitive (23). "In a sense," writes Bruce Johnson, "sharing Leggatt's crime is far too easy: witness the surplus of critics who have . . . made a kind of festival out of doing so" (138–39). Despite this, some critics have resisted the narrator's promptings and recognized "the moral obliquities of Leggatt's position" (Daleski 271) and the "macabre violence" of the fugitive's account of the murder (Eggenschwiler, "Narcissus" 30).

This persistent and irresolvable critical disagreement over Leggatt's nature points to the ambiguities and inconsistencies of the text. The captain's hiding of Leggatt and his later feigned deafness are unconscious indicators of his defensive denials of Leggatt's—and, thus, his own—negative depths. Invited to identify with the captain-narrator, the reader is urged to collude in his evasion of Leggatt's violence. The fact that so many critics have responded sympathetically to Leggatt gives evidence of Conrad's amazing ability to bind his readers in a narrative transaction even in a tale containing the "Nietzschean" implication that "certain men constitute a bold élite with the right to override customary ethical principles" (Watts, "Mirror-tale" 35). Critics who gloss over or ignore the text's contradictions, who reproduce Leggatt's and the captain's version of the murder and provide glowing testimonials on behalf of the fugitive, inadvertently become accessories to and coparticipants in the captain's plot to conceal Leggatt.

Because the narrator focuses on Leggatt's self-possession and manliness, some critics also have been led to misread the captain's increasingly aggressive behavior after the appearance of the outlaw as a sign of his newly found inner strength or of his desire to imitate his double's manly qualities. Such readings ignore the open discrepancy between the captain's assertive public behavior and his appalling loss of self-control.

Through his assertiveness, the captain attempts to shield against his underlying feelings of inadequacy and rejection as he acts out his buried need to dominate others. The emergence of his primitive grandiosity causes him public shame and humiliation, for his crew becomes even more leery of him as his behavior becomes progressively demanding and unpredictable. The reader, too, comments one critic, "who has been vicariously identifying with the captain," soon begins to feel "uneasy and embarrassed" (Cox 146) in witnessing this behavior. As the captain becomes increasingly isolated from and condescending toward the crew, his "frigid dignity" (113) chills the others. Fearing, as time passes, that the crew suspects him of "ludicrous eccentricities" and that he appears "an irresolute commander" to those observing him "more or less critically" (126), he becomes more and more domineering. The steward bears the brunt of his unacknowledged need to control others: "It was this maddening course of being shouted at, checked without rhyme or reason, arbitrarily chased out of my cabin, suddenly called into it, sent flying out of his pantry on incomprehensible errands, that accounted for the growing wretchedness of his expression" (128). Hypersensitive, the captain easily feels slighted. When Captain Archbold says that the "very smart, very gentlemanly" Leggatt was not "exactly the sort" for a chief mate of the *Sephora*, the narrator feels as if he "were being given to understand" that he, too, "was not the sort that would have done for the chief mate of a ship like the *Sephora*" (119). The crew's response to Archbold's query about Leggatt—"As if we would harbour a thing like that"—gives voice to the narrator's deep sense of rejection. "[T]he elements, the men were against us—everything was against us in our secret partnership . . ." (123), as he puts it.

Preoccupied with Leggatt, the captain suffers severe disintegration anxiety. He becomes "distracted . . . almost to the point of insanity" by the "dual working" of his mind. "I was constantly watching myself, my secret self, as dependent on my actions as my own personality. . . . It was very much like being mad, only it was worse because one was aware of it" (113–14). As self/other boundaries blur, he begins to lose his grip on reality. Panic-stricken when he thinks that the steward has discovered Leggatt, he projects his rage onto his double: "Had my second self taken the poor wretch by the throat?" (129).

When, in the rescue scene, the captain orders the ship to move perilously close to land, he acts out his covert rage toward his unempathic crew members and terrifies them in the process, causing his "thunderstruck" mate to moan at his elbow and the helmsman to cry out in a "frightened, thin, child-like voice" (140, 141). In an uncanny reenactment of Leggatt's murder of the unruly hand—Leggatt shook his victim like a rat—the captain "violently" shakes his mate's arm. " 'You go forward'—shake—'and stop there'—shake—'and hold your noise'—shake—'and see these head-sheets properly overhauled'—shake, shake—shake. . . . I released my grip at last and he ran forward as if fleeing for dear life" (141). Subjacent to the narrator's ideal, heroic self-conception are the primitive substructures of the self. In his frenzied approach to the Koh-ring, as his ship seems almost "swallowed up" by its "great black mass" (140–41), the captain glimpses an interior world that cannot be mastered verbally. He teeters on the brink of self-dissolution and then protectively retreats to the "real world," the world of the isolated, grandiose hero which he occupied at the outset of the tale.

Because he succeeds in his dangerous and needlessly reckless maneuver with the ship, the young captain becomes, in the eyes of the crew—and of many readers—the daring hero he imagined himself to be. In the "cheery cries" (143) of the crew as the ship comes round and the crew's hostility turns to admiration, he finds, in his social environment, the mirroring responses he needs to buttress his self. As he acts out his rehearsed heroic role, he claims that his "conscience" (141) compels him to take the ship in as close to the land as possible. Imagining himself in Leggatt's situation, he gives Leggatt his hat, and it is the hat—an "expression" of his "sudden pity" for Leggatt's "mere flesh" (142)—that saves the ship. The white hat, as one critic astutely observes, is interpreted for the reader as a "reward" for the narrator's "compassion and fidelity" while the word " 'conscience' is a nobler and simpler term for the motives behind this act" (Eggenschwiler, "Narcissus" 37, 36). The narrator moralizes and romanticizes his narcissistic urgings. He anesthetizes himself through heroic deeds and through moral justification. And he deflects his attention away from his inner sense of isolation, vulnerability, and neediness. His story, then, denies what it exposes. His fantasy of the exiled Leggatt "hidden for ever from all friendly faces" (142) expresses a fear that Kohut describes as "greater than the fear of death": the "fear of being permanently deprived of 'human meaning, human contact, human experience'" (*How?* 213, n. 10). In his contrasting, self-referential descriptions of Leggatt—Leggatt as a needy person banished from all friendly faces and as "a free man, a proud swimmer striking out for a new destiny" (143)—the captain reveals the persistence of his own defensive isolation and need for human closeness.

The triumphant rhetoric of the closure—which suggests that the defective self can be magically and instantaneously cured—urges readers not to interrogate but to collude in the narrator's defensive denials, to believe, as most critics do, that the captain has healed his self-division and moved "to a more mature reintegration resulting from self-knowledge and self-mastery" (Joan Steiner 184). Like the rest of the story, the closure acts out the concealment of the narrator's Leggatt-self. It also dramatizes the narrator's *enduring* need for self-rescue, this need transferred to many readers who have been seduced into sharing the young captain's wish to see Leggatt rescued. The cry of success at the end signals the triumph of the grandiose self while it masks the implicit suicidal nature of Leggatt's act, which the narrative indirectly discloses in the initial, vivid depiction of Leggatt as a drowned corpse. Leggatt is too proud—and too ashamed—to go before judge and jury with his "fierce story" (103). When Leggatt initially describes his alternatives—to come on board ship or to swim till he sinks from "exhaustion"—the captain misconceives this as "no mere formula of desperate speech, but a real alternative in the view of a strong soul" (99). Despite the narrator-captain's claim, Leggatt, behind his hubris, displays the self-destructive impulses sometimes observed in the shame-prone narcissist. Kohut reads such impulses as the attempt "of the suffering ego to do away with the self in order to wipe out the offending, disappointing reality of failure" (*Analysis* 181, n. 10). That such suicidal feelings emerge, as Kohut claims, not from depression but from rage is evident in Leggatt's bitter comment: "I didn't mean to drown myself. I meant to swim till I sank—but that's not the same thing" (108). The narrator, in his description of Leggatt as "free" and "proud," exposes his own wish to be autonomous and invulnerable. But he remains overly dependent upon selfobject others to confirm his self. What the text dramatizes—

the captain's craving for a mirroring response from others—is also indirectly disclosed in the way the reader is directed to respond to his narrative.

Situated as a "secret sharer," a sympathetic listener, the reader becomes absorbed in the captain-narrator's story, which compels attention, mystifies, intrigues, excites. Enmeshed in the narrator's private world, the reader is encouraged to sympathize with his plight and to disapprove of those who dislike him, in particular Captain Archbold. Unlike Archbold, who "wouldn't listen" to Leggatt (107), the reader is coaxed to listen empathically to the fugitive's story. When the captain openly reveals his contempt for Archbold—for example, he faults the older man for his "spiritless tenacity" and describes his manner as that of a "criminal making a reluctant and doleful confession" (116)—the reader is meant to become aligned with the narrator's point of view. When the narrator refuses to listen to Archbold's version of the murder—"It is not worth while to record that version," as he puts it (117)—the reader is urged to discount it. Identifying with the narrator and following the text's directives, commentators have similarly typecast Archbold as the "villain" of the story (Graver 156) and harshly criticized him for his "moral sclerosis" (Kirschner 127) and "zeal for vengeance" (Bidwell 27) and for being "narrow-minded, muddled, [and] soulless" (Dobrinsky 38).[1]

While turning a deaf ear to Captain Archbold—this a repetition of the captain's gesture—the reader is prompted to identify with the narrator, who is characterized as a sensitive young man caught up in a difficult situation. The fact that the narrator's situation mirrors, in a significant way, the reader's, may work to reinforce reader involvement with Conrad's character. For like the narrator, the reader, during the reading act, is secluded from others and yet experiences, in the world of fiction, the illusion of human companionship with characters who, like Leggatt, are both real and unreal.[2] The pull and tug toward empathic identification, which is so central to the story, is also central, as we have observed, to many a reader's response to it. For the most part, critics have responded favorably to Conrad's narrator, finding him "likable," his loyalty to Leggatt appealing to "our romantic and liberal instincts" (Watts, "Mirror-tale" 32). That Conrad intended this effect is suggested by his reaction to a reviewer who called Leggatt a "murderous ruffian." "Who are those fellows who write in the Press?" a bewildered Conrad wrote in a letter to Galsworthy. "Where do they come from? I was simply knocked over . . ." (Jean-Aubrey 2: 143).

Despite Conrad's bewilderment, despite his intention that readers sympathize with Leggatt, his story does send a mixed message to readers and hence the endless and unresolvable critical split over Leggatt's nature. A common and revealing feature of critical discussions of this text is each new critic's almost ritualized condemnation of his critical forerunners. Sometimes the tone of such criticism is quite splenetic. Gloria Dussinger, for example, complains that another critic has turned Conrad's tale "inside out" and through this "violence" has both "destroyed Conrad's art and drained the story of any significance" (600, n. 4). Lawrence Graver claims that an earlier interpretation "sinks under its own extravagance" and describes the "average reading" of the story as "[p]olemical and highly selective" and "easily open to charges of partiality or distortion" (150). In their often angry reactions to earlier interpreters, such critics unwittingly reenact a central psychodrama of this text: the splitting-off of anger and its displacement onto a substitute figure. Aware of how critics often "blame one another" when confronted with a work "improperly understood," Graver instead shifts the blame onto the text, arguing that in the case of "The Secret Sharer" the "work itself is at fault" (151). Frederick Karl simply avoids the text's contradictions and uncertainties by claiming that the "surface in this case *is* the story" (234). And Dussinger seems intent on rescuing the text by finding a way of reading it that "forestalls plaguing contradictions" and allows us to see it as "coherent, unified" (599–600). In their appropriation of the text and attempt to make it yield a coherent, stable message, critics reenact the narrator's assertion of authority and his ultimate denial of his contradictory, destabilizing impulses. Moreover, those critics who moralize or romanticize the tale or those psychological critics who see, in its closure, resolution of conflict, replicate Conrad's defensive censoring of the text's dark negativity. "Is it perhaps true that this story meant so much to Conrad," speculates C. B. Cox, "because it enacted his own need to exorcise his mirror-image, to jettison those fantasies of alienation and suicidal loneliness which were disturbing his own balance of mind?" (149–50).[3] The fictional portrayal of Leggatt also provides suggestive evidence of Conrad's deep anxiety about and need to split off and evacuate his own angry impulses. To reiterate a point made earlier, the cry of exaltation at the end rings hollow, barely masking, as it does, a disturbing impulse toward isolation, banishment, and suicide. The obverse side of the isolated, grandiose, public hero in Conrad's story is the needy, shame-ridden, suicide-prone inner self. In his closely related story, "Heart of Darkness," Conrad lifts the heroic mask even further as he stages his boldest and thereby most self-endangering journey into the shuttered, alien world of the narcissistically damaged self.

Like "The Secret Sharer," "Heart of Darkness" is a criticism-riddled and criticism-split text. Despite Kurtz's manifest depravity, he is the subject of the narrator's split perceptions, his "mingled admiration and disdain" (Thorburn 123). Mirroring Marlow's—and the text's—ambivalence, some critics describe Kurtz as "the man of genius" tragically spoiled by the jungle (Meckier 373) or find him, though "evil" at the end, still "much more admirable" than the other Europeans depicted in the text. While he ends a "hollow" man, he "has not always been 'hollow.' He has lost a fullness not approached by any other character in the story . . ." (Montag 95). "It is a recurring critical view," writes one critic, "that Kurtz is not degraded at all" but nevertheless "[h]e is. . . . Paradoxically, to the extent that Kurtz's 'unlawful soul' has aspired to godhead and assumed it, to that same extent Kurtz as a human being becomes debased" (McLauchlan 13). Kurtz, observes Cedric Watts, "seems to split under thematic pressure, so that to some commentators he presents the face of a contemptibly hollow man, while to others he offers the face of an impressively full man" (*Deceptive Text* 14). Exposing in the character of Kurtz the unacknowledged side of the values seemingly celebrated in "The Secret Sharer," "Heart of Darkness" reveals the grandiose core of isolated heroism.

As critics slowly have come to recognize Marlow's bafflingly complex role in the narrative, the initial misreading of Marlow as mere narrator, as a "transparent medium" through which the reader learns of the "exploitation of the Congo natives and the degradation of Mr Kurtz" (Hewitt 104), gradually has been revised. W. Y. Tindall's early insight that "[r]eality in a Marlow story is in Marlow's head, not somewhere else" and that in this Marlow story Kurtz and the savages represent Marlow's "doubles" (125, 130) has led to Garrett Stewart's more complex awareness that in "the psychic scheme" of the narrative, "all things external seem to radiate from Marlow as percipient center"

(323). The "psychological crux" of this tale, in Stewart's words, "is a vexing crisscross of doubles that lingers in the imagination until it sorts itself into shape" (322). In the novel, observes Jerome Meckier, Conrad "raises doubling to a fine art," making the opening, unnamed speaker into Marlow's "final *döppelganger*" (375). The effect of such rereadings has been an appropriate undermining of the story's surface drama, as critics have edged toward a recognition of the narcissistic nature of Marlow's narrative.

In "Heart of Darkness" Conrad journeys far into the strange, interior landscape of the storyteller, Marlow, an uncanny place of self-reflections that exists on the outer reaches of language. The reader of "Heart of Darkness," in joining Marlow in his circuitous, self-reflexive journey, slowly gropes toward the "dead center" of the novel—the utter point of solipsism. Entering that claustrophobic world is like entering the mirror world of the dream in which everything—scene, setting, characters—emanates from the dreamer. As in "The Secret Sharer," Conrad, in this tale of the double, reveals the selfobject needs of his storyteller-protagonist. Through the storytelling frame—Marlow tells the story to an unnamed listener who, in turn, tells it to us—Marlow's narcissistic needs are made manifest, the unnamed listener-narrator, as we shall see, being slowly transformed into Marlow's selfobject double. A story that is also about the act of storytelling, "Heart of Darkness" dramatizes Marlow's on-going attempt to repair his broken self through the process of telling a story. "[M]ine," says Marlow, "is the speech that cannot be silenced" (110). Speaking an encoded dream-speech, Marlow tells his story in a compulsive, trance-like way, inviting his listener not only to understand and share his perceptions but also to become his selfobject alter ego.

Marlow's narcissistic adventure begins where it ends—in the "sepulchral city" where he first confronts a premonitory figure from the deeper recesses of archaic memory: the old woman knitting black wool. When she looks at him "with unconcerned old eyes," the "swift and indifferent placidity" of her look troubles him (64–65); later she intrudes upon his memory at a moment of peaked horror when he finds Kurtz crawling on hands and knees back into the haunted, dark forest, the place of ancient dreams (161). Though a marginalized character, she stands at the psychocenter of Marlow's tale. She is the archaic maternal imago. Her expressionless, unempathic eyes are a portent of psychic death, for the developing self which is not responded to empathically is, like Kurtz, damaged, fixated in an anachronistic world of grandiose and idealizing illusions. The journey that begins in sight of the unempathic maternal figure who guards "the door of Darkness" (64) is a journey to the uttermost brink of self-dissolution.

Perceived as a brooding, animate female presence, the African landscape is a kind of dreamscape that reflects the shifting feeling-states and fantasies of the dreamer, Marlow. Variously, Marlow perceives it as empty, silent, oppressive, treacherous, and a place of "hidden evil" (104). To him its "stillness of life" is "the stillness of an implacable force brooding over an inscrutable intention" (105–06). Marlow's only defenses against the sinister power of the wilderness are the trivial distractions of work, "the mere incidents of the surface" (106). In such a world, the remembered past takes "the shape of an unrestful and noisy dream" (105). "It seems to me," Marlow says at one point to his listeners, "I am trying to tell you a dream—making a vain attempt, because no relation of a dream can convey the dream-sensation, that commingling of absurdity, surprise, and bewilderment in a tremor of struggling revolt, that notion of being captured by the incredible which is of the very essence of dreams. . . ." (94). During his journey to Kurtz, which Marlow describes as a "weary pilgrimage amongst hints for nightmares" (71), that dream becomes increasingly oppressive. Through his slow and grinding journey and his narrative postponements, Marlow enacts his unacknowledged need to defer confronting the Kurtz within him and thus to avoid full recognition of the archaic anxieties encoded in his tale.

In the remote African dream-terrain, as reality slips and slides from under his feet, Marlow confronts cast-off images of self and haunting fantasy figures from his surfacing past. Kurtz's selfless disciple, the Russian harlequin, for example, is an embodiment of the archaic idealizing self. Behind the harlequin's boyish innocence, Marlow perceives the "loneliness" and "essential desolation" (143) of the threatened self. The harlequin's motley dress, sudden mood shifts and fragmented speech—he tells his story "in interrupted phrases, in hints ending in deep sighs" (147)—are portents of self-instability. In the African natives Marlow observes at the outset of the journey, he confronts a monitory image of the narcissistically impaired and impoverished self. Mistreated and starving, the natives are "[b]lack shapes" found in "all the attitudes of pain, abandonment, and despair"; they are "black shadows of disease and starvation" and images of "weariness" and "contorted collapse" (75–76). Attempting to feed a starving native—"[t]he black bones reclined at full length . . . the sunken eyes looked up at me, enormous and vacant" (76)—Marlow rehearses his later attempt to rescue the imperiled self of Kurtz. Recognizing the restraint of the hungry cannibals in his employ, Marlow muses on the "devilry of lingering starvation, its exasperating torment, its black thoughts" (120). Starkly contrasted to the natives are the European exploiters: the members of the Eldorado Exploring Expedition who are openly reckless, cruel, and greedy; the manager of the Central Station who appears "great" but perhaps has "nothing" inside him (84); the Central Station brickmaker who seems a "papier-mâché Mephistopheles" with "nothing inside" (92). In Kurtz, Marlow finds a single embodiment of these various characters and split-off aspects of self: the heady romanticism and desolate isolation of the harlequin, the illusive grandiosity, plundering greed, and hollowness of the white exploiters, the depletion of the starving natives, the devouring hunger of the cannibals. Inhabiting a strange interior world of proliferating self-reflections, Marlow, in his descriptions of others, provides an unacknowledged description of self.

The nightmare of Marlow's choosing and the figure found at the innermost circle of the "heart of darkness," Kurtz becomes the focal point of Marlow's and the reader's attention. Because of Marlow's fascination with Kurtz, as Cedric Watts observes, the reader is "led into a kind of complicity with the tale's central figure of corruption." Watts describes Kurtz as Januslike for he "presents two contrasting faces to Marlow and to commentators. One face has a vacuous expression: he's a hollow man. The other face has a ferociously intense expression: he's a remarkably full man." Against the "explicit" evidence of Kurtz's hollowness, "the text quite as firmly suggests that in the extremity of his ambitions, of his corruption and of his depraved appetites, Kurtz in ontological fulness offers a challenging *contrast* to the long line of hollow men" depicted in the text and thus "commands awe rather than dismissive contempt" (*Deceptive Text* 21–22). Both full and empty, awe-inspiring and contemptuous, Kurtz engenders in the reader a feeling of fascinated horror. The reader, like Marlow, wants to penetrate the hidden mysteries of Kurtz's sequestered self. But to do so, the text seems to warn, is to be implicated in and thus risk being contaminated by the horror of Kurtz's existence.

Like Marlow who is represented to the European dignitaries as "an exceptional and gifted" man, "[s]omething like an emissary of light, something like a lower sort of apostle" (67), Kurtz is similarly described as a "prodigy," "a special being," "an emissary of pity, and science, and progress" (90). Marlow, appalled by the "philanthropic pretense" and "imbecile rapacity"(88–89, 86) he observes in the ivory trading posts, becomes increasingly preoccupied with Kurtz as his steamboat slowly moves toward the Inner Station on its rescue mission. In Marlow's imagination, Kurtz evolves into an idealized fantasy figure. In reality, as Marlow discovers, Kurtz is an apostle of light gone to the devil, an image of the archaic grandiose self gone mad.

Kurtz initially exposes his distorted thinking in his noble, eloquent report written for the International Society for the Suppression of Savage Customs. In his "moving appeal to every altruistic sentiment," Kurtz argues that the Europeans, since they are perceived as "supernatural beings" by the natives, "can exert a power for good practically unbounded." He later appends this postscript to his report: "Exterminate all the brutes!" (134–35). To the African natives, Kurtz becomes a potentially terrible godlike being. Ruthless and savage, he destroys those who thwart him. The unspeakable rites he participates in—cannibalism is suggested—reveal the extent of his psychic regression, while the fierce and mournful behavior of his native followers dramatize the magnitude of his narcissistic rage and despair. In a dark parody of the grandiose self's need to be the center of confirming attention, he surrounds himself with his native worshippers and the chiefs crawl on hands and knees when approaching him, a detail Marlow finds particularly unsettling because it activates his own disowned wants and fears. Similarly, Marlow's steamboat crawls toward Kurtz (108, 111), and the Russian harlequin, in Marlow's view, crawls "as much as the veriest savage of them all" (150). This image, which repeats and circulates in the text, suggests an enactment of an early fantasy/memory of the helpless child crawling before the omnipotent and dangerous parent. Later a horrified Marlow finds Kurtz crawling back into the threatening embrace of the savage wilderness which seems "to draw him to its pitiless breast" (163). In this archaic scenario we find the source and prototype of the damaged, encrypted self.

Both potent and exhausted, Kurtz acts out, to the end, his narcissistic script. The "wastes" of Kurtz's "weary brain," Marlow discovers, are "haunted by shadowy images . . . of wealth and fame revolving obsequiously round his unextinguishable gift of noble and lofty expression" (167). Marlow finds something "contemptibly childish" in the fantasies of the dying Kurtz: "[h]e desired to have kings meet him at railway-stations on his return from some ghastly Nowhere, where he intended to accomplish great things" (168). Kurtz's moving eloquence barely masks his overarching possessiveness. "You should have heard him say, 'My ivory'. . . . 'my Intended, my ivory, my station, my river, my ———' everything belonged to him" (132). "My Intended, my station, my career, my ideas—these were the subjects for the occasional utterances of elevated sentiments" (167). Kurtz's devouring greed is encapsulated in a potent image: "I saw him open his mouth wide—it gave him a weirdly voracious aspect, as though he had wanted to swallow all the air, all the earth, all the men before him" (152). Kurtz, in his obsessive search for the precious and valuable ivory, has acted out his urgent need to supply himself, through external means, with a sense of self-worth and power. But instead of filling his inner emptiness, he has become an image of the void within. "[H]ollow at the core" (149), his "disinterred body" (131) withered and consumed, he is an "animated image of death carved out of old ivory" (152).

"His was an impenetrable darkness. I looked at him as you peer down at a man who is lying at the bottom of a precipice where the sun never shines," Marlow says of Kurtz (169). Something is "wanting" in Kurtz, Marlow recognizes; he has a basic "deficiency" (148–49). Suffering from a self-deficit, Kurtz is trapped in the "heart of darkness" of his own inescapable self. The heads on stakes that surround his station are a perfect emblem of his wrathful, impulsive grandiosity and impending body-self fragmentation. Just before his death, Kurtz's features outwardly express his distorted, tormented selfhood. "It was as though a veil had been rent. I saw on that ivory face the expression of somber pride, of ruthless power, of craven terror—of an intense and hopeless despair" (169). In Kurtz's illusion of power, his devouring greed, his boundless rage, his inner emptiness and depletion, we find the dark core of the damaged grandiose self.

In Kurtz, an "initiated wraith from the back of Nowhere"

(134), Marlow comes face to face with his own deep fear of self-disintegration. This slowly surfacing fear is adumbrated in the text's frequent references to death: the Swedish captain's report of a suicide by hanging, Marlow's confrontation with dying natives, the ubiquitous reports of dying traders, the death of Marlow's helmsman, and, most particularly, the fate of his predecessor, Fresleven. A gentle, quiet man, Fresleven, "probably" feeling the need to assert his "self-respect," as Marlow describes it, flew into a rage during a quarrel over two black hens and was consequently killed (61), his skeletal remains being found by Marlow. The text's recurrent messages that one should retreat from anger—"Avoid irritation. . . . keep calm" (66); "Danger—Agitation" (91)—point to Marlow's defensive avoidance of his negative depths. Because Marlow's own brush with death is a passage through an "impalpable" (171) gray twilight world, he identifies not with his own near-death experience but with Kurtz's death, and he is willing to exchange Kurtz's black horror for his own gray postmortem existence. But while Kurtz's death strips away the veneer of grandiose pretense to reveal the lurking, awful truth of the indescribable "horror" within, Marlow evades full awareness of that horror by moralizing, by pronouncing Kurtz's final words an affirmation, a moral victory. Peter Brooks observes that Marlow's "moral rhetoric appears in some measure a cover-up" (248). "To present 'the horror!' as articulation of that wisdom lying in wait at the end of the tale, at journey's end and life's end, is to make a mockery of storytelling and ethics, or to gull one's listeners . . ." (250). Despite this, many critics, directed by the text and in an unwitting mimicry of Marlow's defensive evasiveness, have likewise affirmed and moralized Kurtz's demise. But "[t]o romanticize Kurtz because he has experienced the abyss," writes Suresh Raval, ignores "the reality of his degeneration . . . ; the abyss is privileged and idealized, made into an oracle of modern art" (39).

The horror that Marlow attempts to stave off resurfaces when he returns to the "sepulchral city." In the people "hurrying through the streets to filch a little money from each other, to devour their infamous cookery . . . to dream their insignificant and silly dreams" (172), he sees trivialized versions of Kurtz. When he visits Kurtz's Intended, a vision of Kurtz, "a shadow insatiable of splendid appearances, of frightful realities" (176), enters the house with him. This unbidden reliving of the past signals the repetition of a trauma. The Intended is the storyless, supplementary female, an echo to Kurtz's male grandiosity, and she is also a sinister presence. Behind her idealism, Marlow discovers shades of Kurtz's narcissistic pride and possessiveness. The sound of her voice evokes the wilderness and Kurtz's presence, and the room grows darker as she makes her insistent narcissistic claims, "I knew him best!"; "He needed me! Me!" (179, 183). A study in chiaroscuro, she has an "illumined" forehead which contrasts with the deepening darkness that envelopes her stately form (179). In the Intended, Marlow sees the living image of the woman portrayed in Kurtz's painting, the "draped and blindfolded" torchbearer who is depicted against a dark background, the "effect" of the light upon her face being "sinister" (90). In the Intended, Marlow also sees a reflection of the goddesslike African woman, whose face is "tragic and fierce" and whose walk is "ominous and stately" (154). When the native woman throws up her open arms "rigid above her head, as though in an uncontrollable desire to touch the sky," her grandiose, stylized gesture brings forth the brooding shadows of the dark wilderness (155). Marlow's journey, which begins in sight of the unconcerned gaze of the indifferent old woman who knits black wool, ends in his confrontation with the Intended. When Marlow lies to the Intended, telling her what she wants to hear and prompts him to say—that the "last word" Kurtz pronounced was her name (183)—he tells an unacknowledged truth. For the Intended is both the idealized, mirroring lover and Kurtz's dark nemesis, a self-reflection, part of the horror he discovers within himself. Ironically, while Marlow says that the women are "out of it" for they exist in a "beautiful world of their own" (131; also 67–68) and while the Intended is relegated to the periphery of his narrative, his story reveals a deep-rooted ambivalence toward woman in all her guises: her placid indifference, her tragic and fierce sorrow and concern, her menacing presence, her possessive neediness and love. The fact that the female is backgrounded, all but excluded from the text, points to Marlow's unconscious stratagem of avoidance. On the fringes of Marlow's tale exists another fragmentary text: that of the absent and self-threatening female. The account of Marlow's confrontation with the Intended, then, is palimpsestic: it encodes a deeper drama of the narcissistically damaged self. At the psychocenter of the heart of darkness is the absent female, the beloved who is, at once, the revered and feared love object—a reflection of the earliest love object—and a selfobject alter ego.

The critical controversy surrounding Marlow's visit to the Intended provides suggestive evidence of readers' half-awareness of the dark significance of the Intended and of the text's evasiveness. Taking issue with the traditional view of the Intended as the prototypical innocent female who lives in her own idealistic dream world, some recent critics have identified her as the "horror." She has been described, variously, as Kurtz's destroyer because she is the cause of his African adventure (Montag 96), as the embodiment of the cultural ideals that corrupt Kurtz (Geary 505), and as "the essence of the European darkness" that invades the jungle (Stark 555). This final scene, as Conrad cryptically described it in a letter, "locks in" the narrative (*Letters to William Blackwood* 154) but in a way unrecognized by earlier critics. The reader is stage directed in this appended scene. For while Marlow insistently claims that the Intended is pure and innocent, he depicts her as sinister and indirectly names her "the horror." The fact that Marlow lies to the Intended has also made critics uneasy. While some critics have defensively read the final scene as proof of Marlow's honesty—he "proves his honesty" by telling his listeners that he told a lie (Meckier 377)—others have found his lie subversive and contaminating (see, e.g., G. Stewart) or felt that it puts in doubt his reliability as a narrator. "Suppose we are missing the whole point of the story," writes one critic as she describes the "uneasy doubts" many commentators have about the final scene (McLauchlan 3). The appended lie, like the appended postscript in Kurtz's essay, insistently subverts the censored text to which it is attached. A signifier of the text's evasiveness, the appended lie points to the existence of other largely undisclosed dramas: the "horror" of the Intended and the "horror" Marlow discovers within himself.

That Kurtz is Marlow's self-reflection is indirectly revealed in the final scene when Marlow, standing before the mahogany door of the Intended, seems to see Kurtz, with his "wide and immense stare," looking at him "out of the glassy panel" (177). Resembling the empty, depleted Kurtz, Marlow is worn and hollow, his expressionless, self-contained appearance masking his persisting fear of his disowned angry and terrifying impulses. The "culminating point" of Marlow's experience and yet an "inconclusive" experience (58), his harrowing rescue mission into the ominous wilderness is an excursion into the hidden recesses of the archaic self. Having once entered that haunted

dream world of reverberating self-reflections and archaic fantasy figures, Marlow, like Kurtz, is an "initiated wraith," a voice existing in an
alienated present. Through the inconclusive act of storytelling, Marlow
verbalizes and thus attempts to master and neutralize the narcissistic
anxieties expressed in his tale. While "Heart of Darkness" gives voice
to archaic fears, it also diffuses them through what F. R. Leavis dis-
paragingly describes as the "adjectival insistence" of this tale which
works not to "magnify but rather to muffle" Marlow's descriptions of
human horrors (177). Marlow's fears are displaced onto others and
dispersed throughout the text. By confronting and then symbolically
divesting himself of the Kurtz within him, Marlow attempts to rescue
his own threatened self as best he can. But while Marlow desires to
relegate Kurtz to the oblivion of the past, his vivid recapitulation of his
adventure reveals his enduring and obsessive fascination with his self-
reflection. "I can't choose," says Marlow. "He won't be forgotten"
(135). Similarly readers, told that the unspeakable lies at the center of
the story, are compelled, as one critic observes, to "return time and
again to the words" of the text in order to "speak about" what they are
"repeatedly told . . . is unspeakable" (Yoder 77, n. 4).

"A voice! A voice! It rang deep to the very last. It survived his
strength to hide in the magnificent folds of eloquence the barren darkness of his heart" (167), says Marlow as he recalls Kurtz's "unbounded
power of eloquence" (135). "[O]f all his gifts the one that stood out
preeminently, that carried with it a sense of real presence, was his
ability to talk, his words—the gift of expression, the bewildering, the
illuminating, the most exalted and most contemptible, the pulsating
stream of light, or the deceitful flow from the heart of an impenetrable
darkness" (129–30). As a storyteller, Marlow is an opaque, restrained
version of Kurtz. Like Kurtz who finds an audience in the harlequin and
surrounds himself with his native worshippers, Marlow is surrounded
by a circle of listeners. Idol-like, isolated, Marlow variously cajoles,
mystifies, and berates his listeners. At times, Marlow's acerbic wit
barely conceals his deep, underlying anger. At one point, for example,
he lashes out at his narratees for "performing" on their "respective
tight-ropes for—what is it? half-a-crown a tumble———" (106). "You
can't understand," he complains to them. "How could you?—with
solid pavement under your feet, surrounded by kind neighbors ready to
cheer you or to fall on you . . ." (132–33). To his listening audience,

Marlow, like Kurtz, becomes a disembodied voice. As the initial warm bond between the narratees slowly dissolves, the night's darkening shadows concretize the unidentified narrator's emerging mood of inner dread and isolation and the excavation of his buried anxieties. "It had become so pitch dark," the unnamed narrator says at one point, "that we listeners could hardly see one another. For a long time already he [Marlow], sitting apart, had been no more to us than a voice. . . . I listened, I listened on the watch for the sentence, for the word, that would give me the clew to the faint uneasiness inspired by this narrative that seemed to shape itself without human lips in the heavy night-air of the river" (94). While Marlow recognizes that many people go to books because they can provide the "shelter of an old and solid friendship" (113), his story frustrates such reader needs. Through the changing perceptions of the unnamed narrator-listener, we learn of the power of storytelling. Defamiliarizing the familiar through his mediated dream-tale, Marlow urges his narratees to replace their perception of the world with his, to replicate the unnamed narrator's inner transformation. Empathically attuned to Marlow's story, the unnamed narrator-listener—the reader's surrogate and Marlow's selfobject double—becomes aware of his own central isolation as he, in the final moment of the novel, looks into the black night, newly cognizant of the menacing inner world that exists within and beyond the world of representable dreams and nightmares.

Like the young captain in "The Secret Sharer," Marlow tells a story that conceals as it reveals. And like the young captain, he is deeply conflicted between his selfobject needs and his defensive desire for isolation. "I don't want to bother you much with what happened to me personally . . ." (58), Marlow begins his story, disarming his listeners and implicitly disowning the Kurtz within him. Marlow does not openly say, "I have a secret desire to be idolized, to manipulate and have power over others." Instead, he reenacts his grandiose desires while confessing them by proxy, for as a storyteller he is surrounded by a group of listeners who feel "fated" to hear his "inconclusive" tale to the end. Marlow tells his story because he must. In telling his story, he attempts to repudiate the Kurtz within him and thus render him powerless. And like Kurtz he needs an audience. But Marlow is also ambivalent toward himself and his craft. He fears that he is an "impostor" and that storytelling might be little more than a hollow sham, a "deceitful flow from the heart of an impenetrable darkness."

"We live, as we dream—alone. . . ." (94), Marlow comments at one point, describing his own persisting feeling of isolation. Through storytelling, Marlow attempts to alleviate his empty isolation. For to tell a story is to find someone who understands and thus involve the listener. "Do you see the story? Do you see anything?" (94), Marlow asks his narratees at one point, revealing his urgent need to be responded to empathically, this need communicated to the reader who is urged, like the unnamed narrator-listener, to listen for the "sentence," the "word," that will give a "clew" to the "faint uneasiness" inspired by Marlow's narrative. While Marlow's detached, idol-like appearance suggests that he is autonomous and self-contained, his interactions with his audience reveal his need to be understood and acknowledged. To be nothing but a voice is to feel unreal and to exist in the inner gray void of the empty self. The fact that some critics have described *Heart of Darkness* as "epistemologically vacuous" (see Levenson 154–55) or have found in it a deconstructionist "suspicion of personal identity" and "critique of voice as the sign of presence" (Pecora 998, 1001) suggests the ability of Conrad's text to transmit to readers at least a latent awareness of the subjective emptiness that lies at the core of Marlow's experience.

As a storyteller, Marlow acts out his own need for self-rescue. For to implicate and initiate the narrator-listener is to temporarily transform the other into a selfobject alter ego. By sharing Marlow's perceptions, the listener certifies Marlow's self. The listener also becomes the future teller of Marlow's tale, as Peter Brooks observes. An inconclusive tale whose meaning "will never lie in the summing-up but only in transmission" of the horror, Marlow's tale traps the narratees in a "dialogic relationship." Similarly, the inability of readers "to sum up—the frustration promoted by the text—," writes Brooks, is "consubstantial" with their "dialogic implication in the text" (260–61). Many critics have attempted to retell or sum up the text through their critical narratives and thus repair Marlow's broken self and evacuate the horror. While the evasiveness and inconclusiveness of the tale ultimately frustrate such critical gestures, critic/readers, through their persistent empathic interest in Conrad's storyteller, act out the negotiated role of critic-rescuer and thus, as it were, become the ultimate guarantors of Marlow's self. In so doing, they enact a self-rescue as they, positioning themselves as interpreters, situate themselves at a safer psychic remove from the text and thus fend off its intended implication of readers in the corrosive and inhospitable world of the heart of darkness.

Criticism-riddled and criticism-resistant texts, "The Secret Sharer" and "Heart of Darkness" are tales of the double that reveal the narcissistic needs and anxieties of the storyteller-protagonists. Masterful storytellers, Conrad's narrators command our attention. Binding us in a narcissistic transaction, they urge us to hear and understand—to become empathically attuned listeners, secret sharers, and, thus, critic-rescuers.

✿ ✿ ✿ ✿

Six

Defensive Aestheticism and Self-Dissolution: The Demise of the Artist in Mann's *Death in Venice*

✿ ✿ ✿ ✿

The horror that reverberates through Conrad's tale of darkness, a horror partially camouflaged by the narrative indirection and prolix style of Conrad's text, also permeates Thomas Mann's *Death in Venice*, the work we will now consider as we move on to an analysis of Tragic Man as artist. Mann, as he renders the horror of Aschenbach's demise in rich and allusive prose, draws attention to the literary features of the text. Encouraging readers to decode and exercise intellectual mastery and deflecting attention from the painful emotional content of what he describes, Mann prompts us to participate in the text's defensive aestheticism: its translation of narcissistic anxieties into literary discourse.

Despite the disturbing subject matter of *Death in Venice*, critics typically have centered their attention not on the artist's disintegrating personality, but instead on the novel's complex and proliferating network of symbols and myths, its elevated and parodic style, and its examination of the plight of the artist. In Eric Heller's description, Mann is preoccupied with "the problems besetting the relationship between 'life' and 'art,'" and his special style, which Heller calls "ironical traditionalism," is modeled on "the classical products of literary history," which Mann "could not help 'parodying'" (126, 127). Aschenbach, according to Ignace Feuerlicht—and Feuerlicht's assessment is typical—is both the representative artist "whose downfall and death exemplify the impossibility of an artist's ever achieving perfect beauty and dignity" and a "special type of artist who forgets that art demands dissoluteness as well as discipline" and who ultimately "succumbs to frantic dissolution, as if life (or death) were cruelly taking revenge for being neglected" (120). In Daniel Albright's view, Mann's novel "is disquieting because it calls into question no single abuse of art but Art itself" (227). Albright sees Aschenbach as an example of the "aesthetic man" who sees "style and type instead of things in themselves" and who looks at life "as if it were governed by the rules of novels" (228). Following the text's directives, critics of *Death in Venice* have focused, by and large, not on what is disconcerting, even threatening, in the novel—the unraveling of Aschenbach's personality and the surfacing of feelings of shame, anxiety, revulsion, and horror—but instead on the intricate and allusive literary puzzles located in the text.

Myths, symbols, hymnic speech, literary and philosophic discourse—in *Death in Venice* these hang over an abyss of nothingness, of formless, wordless narcissistic anxiety and dread. *Death in Venice*, observes Heller, is "thoroughly organized": through the use of recurrent leitmotifs Mann gives form and structure to a "story of increasing disorder and decomposition" (121, 120). For Mann's artist, Aschenbach, despite his success in the eyes of the world, lives the half-life of broken man. In Aschenbach, as in the other examples of Tragic Man we have encountered, we find the copresence of feelings of greatness and powerlessness. Aschenbach's special brand of hero—those who are "great in despite" (384)—is a self-characterization, a depiction of his own enfeebled, grandiose self. As his artistic powers wane, he experiences increasing disintegration anxiety. His surfacing anxiety is signaled by the redundant strangers, their recurrence an indicator of deep trauma and the return of the repressed. But this same repetition compels the reader, after a momentary sense of dislocation and a discomforting sense of being in sight of the uncanny, to observe and interpret. Made privy to the aging artist's thoughts and perceptions and invited to focus on the literary, allusive qualities of the descriptions centering on his self-dissolution, the critic/reader fends off full awareness of the nameless dread at the core of Aschenbach's experience.

A famous, highly successful artist, Aschenbach has always depended on the approbation of the public to maintain his self-esteem.

We learn that "Aschenbach's whole soul, from the very beginning, was bent on fame . . ." (382); his career has been a "conscious and over-weening ascent to honour, which left in the rear all misgivings or self-derogation which might have hampered him" (385). As Kohut himself observed in his remarks on the novel, Aschenbach has used his art "to create replicas of the perfect self" and thus supply himself with a needed feeling of psychological wholeness and perfection ("Creativeness" 821).[1] And yet, despite the "applause and adulation of the masses" (387), the aging artist undergoes an unavoidable decline. His life "on the wane" (380) and suffering from "growing fatigue," he becomes enervated by his daily efforts to write and no longer gets any joy from his work, even "though a nation paid it homage" (381). Putting on "a courtly bearing," he hides from the world "his bitter struggles and his loneliness" (387). The "key to his work"—that "almost everything conspicuously great is great in despite" (384)—is also the key to his attenuated self. Aschenbach is the "poet-spokesman of all those who labour at the edge of exhaustion," those "who are already worn out but still hold themselves upright," those "with stunted growth and scanty resources, who yet contrive by skilful husbanding and prodigious spasms of will to produce, at least for a while, the effect of greatness." The heroism Aschenbach celebrates in his art—"heroism born of weakness" (385)—is a projection of his own partitioned self, his simultaneous feelings of grandiosity and enervation.

That archaic fears and needs are subjacent to Aschenbach's desire for artistic mastery and public adulation becomes apparent in his confrontation with the strangers. As narcissistic anxieties spill over into Aschenbach's consciousness and he slips into the uncanny world of the strangers, he experiences a "dreamlike distortion of perspective" (390). Critics have long observed that the reader is invited by clues in the text to interpret these recurring figures as harbingers of evil and death and as psychological manifestations. Read through a self-psychological lens, they represent aspects of Aschenbach's archaic self.

The appearances of the strangers are repetitive and accretive, each stranger repeating and adding to the emerging revelation of Aschenbach's unacknowledged, dark interior. Ironically, the narrator describes how Aschenbach is "brought back to reality" by the sight of the first stranger, a foreign traveler who has a "not quite usual" appearance. Mysteriously and suddenly appearing and then disappearing, the traveler intrudes on Aschenbach's consciousness like a troubling image from a half-forgotten dream. While the traveler is thin and beardless, he also has "a bold and domineering, even a ruthless, air" about him, and his hostile gaze and bared teeth, which give him a predatory look, add to this impression (379). Similarly, the "despotic" and lawless gondolier, though "undersized," has a "gruff, overbearing manner" (394, 393) and he, too, bares his teeth. And the street singer, despite his "slight build" and "thin, undernourished face," has an "impudent, swaggering posture": "half bully, half comedian," he is a "brutal, blustering" figure (424). Meager and undernourished yet brutal and overbearing, the strangers are embodiments of Aschenbach's depleted grandiose self. In the grotesque young-old man, Aschenbach confronts yet another avatar of the self. The young-old man—with his rouged cheeks, his wig, his shrunken neck and false teeth—shamelessly and clamorously demands the attention of those around him just as Aschenbach commands the adulation of his reading public. Similarly, the strolling musician's fawning behavior toward his audience provides a dark and parodic reflection of Aschenbach's urgent need for his public's approval. Existing in the specular world of narcissistic phenomena, Aschenbach encounters in others his own cast-off self-reflections.

At the center of Aschenbach's—and the reader's—gaze is the overdetermined figure of Tadzio. Defensively intellectualizing his narcissistic preoccupation with the boy, Aschenbach marvels at Tadzio's perfection of form and studies the boy until he knows "every line and pose" and "every loveliness" (411). In Tadzio, the aging artist sees the "mirror and image," the "very essence" of beauty: "form as divine thought, the single and pure perfection which resides in the mind, of which an image and likeness, rare and holy, was here raised up for adoration" (412).

"[V]irginally pure and austere" and "beautiful as a tender young god," Tadzio conjures up mythologies in Aschenbach's imagination. The sight of the boy "emerging from the depths of sea and sky" is "like a primeval legend, handed down from the beginning of time, of the birth of form, of the origin of the gods" (403), and Aschenbach associates the boy with a series of mythic figures—Narcissus, Hyacinthus, Hermes. While these comparisons, as André von Gronicka comments, can "in every instance be explained on solidly rational grounds as a figment of Aschenbach's overwrought imagination," the "evocation of the mythical figures and their identification with Tadzio" is so vivid that "we experience their fusion as palpably real and must exert a conscious effort to disengage in our imagination the 'real' boy from the mythical overlay of the divine figures" (55). This interplay between immersion and detachment is central to the reader's transactions with the character and text. Maneuvered to occupy positions both inside and outside the artist's subjectivity, the reader becomes engrossed in the pulse and flow of Aschenbach's mythic and philosophic fantasies and, at the same time, retains an awareness of their defensive function and literary artifice.

In his initial encounters with Tadzio, Aschenbach protectively translates his feelings into thought and literary speech. But he also increasingly reads himself into the boy as he projects onto Tadzio his hidden wishes and fears. An embodiment of human beauty and perfection, Tadzio is also sickly and fragile, and his imperfect teeth, which the text draws our attention to, suggest hidden decay. Tadzio is not unlike those heroes Aschenbach depicts in his art, heroes whose "aristocratic self-command" hides their "biologic decline from the eyes of the world" (385). Pampered and favored by his mother and "sought after, wooed, admired" (402) by his fellow playmates, Tadzio is the center of confirming attention. A child-god, he is superior, proud, imperious. During a moment of "angry disgust," he exhibits the stranger's look of rage: "His brow darkened, his lips curled, one corner of the mouth was drawn down in a harsh line that marred the curve of the cheek, his frown was so heavy that the eyes seemed to sink in as they uttered beneath the black and vicious language of hate" (401). In the psychic notation of the text, Tadzio, in his various guises, comes to represent the artist's perfect/defective self, the idealized selfobject, and the angry, grandiose self.

The allusive and indirect narrative revelation of Aschenbach's obsession with the fetishistic figure of Tadzio reflects the aging artist's lifelong avoidance of his feelings. At one point Aschenbach even flees from Venice only to return, this narrative detour mirroring his delay in confronting his feelings. Solitary and friendless, Aschenbach has lived for years solely in the absent gaze of his public. The actual gaze of Tadzio becomes a fatal lure to the aging artist as he and the boy communicate "only with their eyes" (416) and Aschenbach comes to realize, "not without horror, that he could not exist were the lad to pass from his sight" (420). That Aschenbach's intellectual passion will regress into a desire for sexual merger and possession is suggested in the description of how he, moved by the sight of the boy, writes a "page and a half of choicest prose." Through his writing, he attempts to verbally grasp Tadzio's godlike beauty and perfection. His writing is described as an act of seizure and possession: he wants to "snatch up" Tadzio's beauty "into the realms of the mind." After he completes his work, he feels "exhausted" and "broken" and his conscience reproaches him as if "after a debauch" (413–14). Scott Consigny has noted that in this scene writing is described not as an "act of love" but rather as "an act of lust, a non-reciprocal isolating act whose only satisfaction can be the 'adulation of the masses.' " Writing, then, does not rescue Aschenbach from his "deepening isolation" and "it promises only to bring further empty adulation from the masses to whom it is scattered" ("Aschenbach's 'Page and a Half' " 367). In this work in which the artist never carries on a meaningful conversation with anyone but engages in rich interior monologues and in which the artist's thoughts and perceptions are presented indirectly, filtered through the narrating consciousness, all is interiorized. The lavish, hymnic prose, intertextual borrowings, and self-conscious literary artifice of *Death in Venice* work to mask the mute, menacing horror at the heart of the narrative. One of the narrator's functions is to partially counteract this horror through his frequent addresses to the narratee in which he describes Aschenbach as "our traveller" (390, 398), "our solitary" (413, 422), "our adventurer" (421), and "our solitary watcher" (425). This form of address is designed to momentarily create the illusion of a reading community to which the narrator and the reader belong and which exists outside the isolated, solipsistic world of the artist.

"Who shall unriddle the puzzle of the artist nature? Who understands that mingling of discipline and licence in which it stands so deeply rooted?" asks the narrator (414). Writing himself into the text, the narrator represents himself as the "shrewd critic" (384) whose analysis of the type of hero created by Aschenbach reveals his superior insight into the artist's character. The narrator acts out this role as he invades Aschenbach's subjectivity and explains his defensive behavior. At one point, for example, Aschenbach attempts to approach Tadzio with a friendly word and thus put their relationship on a normal footing. But when he loses his self-command just as he is about to overtake the boy, the narrator, at first voicing Aschenbach's defensive denial, speculates that the artist's breathlessness and pounding heart stem "perhaps from the swift pace of his last few steps." "Too late! Too late!" Aschenbach thinks to himself. "But was it too late?" the narrator asks, suggesting that perhaps the artist "did not want to be cured." Aschenbach, the narrator explains, "was no longer disposed to self-analysis. He had no taste for it; his self-esteem, the attitude of mind proper to his years, his maturity and single-mindedness, disinclined him to look within himself and decide whether it was constraint or puerile sensuality that had prevented him from carrying out his project" (414–15). Describing Aschenbach as "too arrogant to admit fear of an emotion" (415), the narrator condemns him for his lack of self-awareness.

Thus while many of the descriptions of Aschenbach's inner life are so vividly rendered that we momentarily become immersed in his subjectivity, we also are prompted to detach ourselves and view him from the narrator's ironic and increasingly moralistic perspective. Both sympathetic and judgmental, the narrator faithfully renders the artist's experience of a world "transmuted and gilded with mythical significance" (416), but he also persistently criticizes and passes moral judgment on Aschenbach. As we are repeatedly drawn into the seductive world of mythic illusion and then pulled back so that we view that world from an ironic perspective, we become aware of the narrator's fundamental ambivalence toward art. Positioning us as voyeurs, inducing in us his own horrified fascination with "the perverse, the illicit, [and] the absurd" (395), Mann's narrator exposes his own deep attraction to the forbidden and lawless. Consciously, the narrator adheres to the principle of "*Durchhalten*": he holds fast (383). Unconsciously, he is attracted to the dangerous state of mind that "welcomes every blow dealt to the bourgeois structure, every weakening of the social fabric" (419). "[A]ll the seductive arguments" of the novel, as T. E. Apter observes, "are on the side of decadence and extravagance" (*Thomas Mann* 52). At once inscribing and denying his own subversive impulses, the narrator repeats Aschenbach's self-deceptive behavior. Assuming the dual roles of absorbed reader and detached interpreter, critic/readers, while subjecting the text to their critical gaze, also become implicated in its tainted world and entangled in its web of denials.

Because in Aschenbach desire can project itself "visually"

(380), the "language of pictures" (412) provides significant clues to the aging artist's self-drama. As the narrative unfolds, we witness a series of haunting pictures which reverberate in the imagination and which we are induced to decode. What they reveal is the angry negativity—the buried feelings of rage and devouring neediness—that marks Aschenbach's passion. The "eyes of a crouching tiger" gleaming out of a primeval landscape (380)—the first picture that flashes onto the screen of Aschenbach's troubled imagination—prefigure the hypercathexis of the visual mode which surfaces later in Aschenbach's dangerous and predatory preoccupation with Tadzio's gaze. When, in the final scene of the novel, Jaschiu attacks and almost seems to smother Tadzio, he enacts Aschenbach's unacknowledged narcissistic rage against the unavailable love object. In another fantasy, Tadzio is Hyacinthus. "[D]oomed to die because two gods were rivals for his love," Hyacinthus is killed by a blow to the head; subsequently, a beautiful flower springs up in the bloodstained grass, "watered" by the blood of his "broken body" (416). Cast in the role of Hyacinthus, Tadzio embodies not only the unavailable love object that Aschenbach desires to possess and angrily destroy but also the injured, broken self. Intrapsychically, the broken body and beautiful flower are equivalent to the "emaciated, blackened corpses" (428) of the cholera victims, the beauty of myth obscuring the grotesque nature of the broken, deformed self.

What lies behind the beauty of myth is figured in Aschenbach's "fearful" dream where he confronts his primitive underself and consequently finds his European soul—a defensive self-construct—"trampled on, ravaged, and destroyed" (430). Aschenbach's dream is the ur-myth, the myth behind the myths he has consciously indulged in. Here is figured the "stranger god," the godlike, angry, and possessive primal self. In this dream, Aschenbach's fear of his devouring needs, reflected earlier in two images—the crouching tiger and the bared teeth of the strangers—finds open expression. He fantasies himself first seized by a "blind rage" and "whirling lust," then merging with the crowd of bacchic revelers, and, like them, swallowing "smoking gobbets of flesh" and indulging in an "orgy of promiscuous embraces" (431). Aschenbach's thwarted desire to embrace Tadzio ineluctably leads to this cannibalistic, sexualized merger fantasy.

It also leads to something even more dreadful: the void within. When Tadzio smiles, Aschenbach imagines him as Narcissus "bent over the mirroring pool" and gazing at his own lingering smile, his arms outreached as if in an attempt to embrace the shadow of his own reflected beauty (418). Aschenbach's fervent desire to embrace Tadzio—a forbidden wish the narrative allusively and redundantly circles around—ultimately leads to the artist's discovery of his own inner emptiness. As Aschenbach dies, Tadzio, the "pale and lovely Summoner" (437), seems to beckon him into the vast "nothingness" of the sea (401), the amorphous void of the dissolving self. Behind Aschenbach's literary speech, Socratic musings, and lush visual fantasies lie the nonrepresentable nether depths of the broken, vacant self.

While Tadzio stands at the center of Aschenbach's and the reader's awareness, the female is pushed to the periphery: this in an attempt to neutralize her potentially disruptive presence. Tadzio's mother, for example, despite her "cool and measured" manner, has something "faintly fabulous" in her appearance (397) and Aschenbach inherits from his mother's family the "ardent, obscure impulse" (382) that ultimately destroys him. The dark side of the female is figured in Aschenbach's frightening dream-vision of the dancing, shrieking maenads who, their waists surrounded by coiling snakes, suggestively hold their breasts in both hands as if proffering them to the dreamer-artist (430). The appearance of phallic woman—the unreadable composite male/female imago—marks the return of the repressed. While the female is silent and backgrounded, her destabilizing, menacing presence acts as a subversive force in the artist's imagination. To "hold fast" is to eschew the feminine imagination which the text associates with the exotic, the licentious, and the irrational.

To "hold fast" is also to stave off awareness of the ultimate horror of the defective self—the self as distorted and grotesque—which finds expression in the image of the corpses of the cholera victims. Perhaps reflecting an unconscious need to rescue the fragmenting self of his artist-protagonist, Mann does not depict Aschenbach as succumbing to the "most malignant form of the contagion," the " 'dry' type" which causes a ghastly death (428). But the awful image of the shriveled, convulsed bodies of such victims lingers in the reader's imagination as a horrifying possibility. We find further evidence of the author's desire to save his protagonist—or perhaps to evade full awareness of the depths of Aschenbach's self-demise—in the description of the death scene, which prompts the reader to focus on the literary, allusive aspects of the text. André von Gronicka points out that for the "informed reader" Aschenbach's "psychophysical disintegration" is invested with "the dignity and the beauty of apotheosis by being linked with the 'mythic pattern,' the 'mythic return' of a demigod's entrance into the bliss of Elysium" (60–61). The account of the artist's death, observes T. J. Reed, is also based on "Plato's image for the realms into which the spiritual initiate progresses" (161). Apotheosizing Aschenbach's death, Mann transforms the terrifying experience of self-dissolution into grandiose myth and artistic perfection.

This literary translation of Aschenbach's demise stands in direct opposition to the reader's evolving uneasiness in witnessing Aschenbach's loss of self-control and his metamorphosis into the young-old man. "[P]assion paralyses good taste," the narrator observes of Aschenbach, "and makes its victim accept with rapture what a man in his senses would either laugh at or turn from with disgust" (423). Aschenbach's reaction to the young-old man replicates the reader's reaction to Aschenbach when he transforms himself into the young-old man: both are repulsive, grotesque figures provoking feelings of disgust and pity. Also a stand-in for Aschenbach, the street singer, who fawns and cringes before his audience, is similarly an object of shame and scorn, and his "rowdy" song, with its "laughing-refrain" (426), mocks Aschenbach's controlled, hymnic speech. "There he sat, the master . . . ," says the narrator as he condemns the dying Aschenbach and points him out to the reader, almost as a warning. "This was he who had put knowledge underfoot to climb so high . . . whose renown had been officially recognized and his name ennobled . . ." (434).

The final sentence of the novel—which tells how "a shocked and respectful world" receives news of the artist's death (437)—points to the hollowness of the public man who is worshipped by the masses. "The reader," writes Allan McIntyre, "knows the truth, not only about Aschenbach, but about reality, and the illusions of 'the world.' The world does not, indeed cannot, and perhaps should not know these things; it remains permanently deceived, in the dark" (232). This final, ironic observation also returns the reader to the world of the observing ego, the world of social commentary. Though Aschenbach's self collapses, his created public image, a fictional construct, survives in the eyes of his reading audience. The final sentence of the novel, while openly ironic, is also an unacknowledged gesture of denial, a defensive undoing, the narrator's—and Mann's—final attempt to retreat from the disquieting anxieties and fears engendered by Aschenbach's demise.

"[H]e who is beside himself," says the narrator of Aschenbach, "revolts at the idea of self-possession" (429). While Aschenbach ultimately succumbs to his passion, yielding to the amorphous emptiness at the center of his being, the narrator assumes Aschenbach's characteristic pose—that of holding fast. Aschenbach's defensive aestheticism is repeated by the reader who, in decoding the puzzles of the text, feels the same sense of mastery Aschenbach once enjoyed as he created his art. In this text, the mythic and literary act as a barrier, a way of partially blocking the reader's emotional responses to the artist's demise. Through the "rising structural line" of myth, it is argued, Mann successfully counteracts the "falling line" of Aschenbach's progressive decline (Lehnert 116; cited by Bance 149). Graham Good comments that Mann "as a whole, makes good Aschenbach's failure in his triumphant description of it . . ." (52). In Mann's work-notes for the novel, we find this entry: "Dignity is rescued only by death . . ." (cited by T. J. Reed 168). While Mann retreats from his character in the closure by having the narrator pass moral judgment on him, he also, as we have observed, rescues Aschenbach's dignity through his elevated description of his death.

Similarly, many critics have replicated the author's rescue mission. One critic writes that Aschenbach's "death and the weeks preceding it do not detract or destroy anything from the excellence of his works, which are the truly great Aschenbach and which will long survive the Aschenbach in the flesh" (Feuerlicht 125). Another critic writes that despite Aschenbach's final degradation "there remains an aura of nobility" about him (Bance 158). Aschenbach, writes another, "dies a finer, though a less reputable, man than he lived" (Dyson 14). Aschenbach has been lauded as an "exceptional" man because he penetrates "to a place where not the shred of a saving illusion is left" (McIntyre 228), as an artist whose "overly zealous devotion to beauty" causes his "misfortune" (W. Stewart 54), and as a "creative man who follows the danger-beset path . . . which leads by the senses toward the goal of ultimate cognition and beauty" (von Gronicka 59). One commentator's description of the "established critical interpretation" of *Death in Venice* as forming a "unified, coherent whole" (McIntyre 218) provides further evidence of both the need and the ability of critics to shield themselves, through the act of interpretation, from the narcissistic anxieties dramatized in this work. In so doing, critics reenact the text's stratagems: its evasion of its disturbing content and its artistic rescue of Aschenbach's disintegrating self.

"That Aschenbach's sufferings turn to beauty in the telling is . . . a triumph of form," comments A. E. Dyson (14). Mann, according to Walter Stewart, "has perfectly integrated every element of his work into a totality" (50). *Death in Venice*, which moves from an unacknowledged expression of rage to a reactive need for reparation, prompts readers to resist awareness of the ultimate horrors of Aschenbach's plight and to reconstitute the artist's broken self through the process of constructing an interpretation and thus making literary sense of his demise. While *Death in Venice* elaborates on narcissistic fears—in particular disintegration anxiety—it also affords informed readers narcissistic gratification by encouraging them to extract and impose meaning, to decode, to exercise intellectual mastery. Repeating Aschenbach's obsessive search to learn about Venice's "disreputable secret" (422), readers desire to make the text yield its secrets; repeating the artist's defensive denials of his feelings, readers deflect their attention away from the text's emotional and threatening content and onto its literary scaffolding. While Aschenbach loses self-control, readers are empowered as they unlock the novel's mythic code and thus achieve mastery over the literary details of the text. The description of Aschenbach's attempt to grasp, through writing, Tadzio's essence is analogous to the attempt of readers to possess, through the act of interpretation, a perfect understanding, a total reading, of the text. The need to ward off what is threatening and the acts of intellectual mastery and possession—these lie at the center of the novel and at the center of readers' interactions with it.

Taking us into the domain of the isolated, solipsistic self, *Death in Venice* makes us acutely aware of what J. Paul Hunter describes as the inherent loneliness of the reading experience. Describing the act of reading as "an investment in solitude," he points out that "[n]ovels edge into our solitary consciousnesses, not our social ones; we meet their worlds from the perspective of our own certified aloneness . . ." (456). Persistently describing Aschenbach as "our solitary" and "our traveller," Mann's narrator, even as he suggests the existence of a community of readers, also reminds us of our own essential isolation and its lurking dangers. The solitary individual who is "unused to speaking of what he sees and feels," the narrator tells us, "has mental experiences which are at once more intense and less articulate than those of a gregarious man. . . . Solitude gives birth to the original in us, to beauty unfamiliar and perilous—to poetry. But also, it gives birth to the opposite: to the perverse, the illicit, the absurd." Aschenbach is the kind of solitary artist for whom sights and impressions "sink silently in . . . take on meaning . . . [and] become experience, emotion, adventure" (395). The "assumption that Aschenbach holds," comments Daniel Albright, is that "what happens to him is not fortuitous but part of an ongoing revelation" (228). While the solitary habit of mind that transforms the fragmentary and accidental details of life into aesthetic experience can enrich life, it can also lead to the abyss. And excessive isolation, the text warns, can give rise to a dangerous inwardness. By forcing us to acknowledge the allure of imaginative literature, which can take temporary possession of the reader's private consciousness, *Death in Venice* also urges us to be aware of and to interrogate its own seductive fictionality.

In *Death in Venice* we palpably feel the presence of the author as artificer. Mann's description of the "conscious and deliberate mastery" of Aschenbach's art and its "exaggerated sense of beauty" (386) is self-referential. Feuerlicht writes that Mann's style in *Death in Venice* is "masterly" (125). Albright observes that even the descriptions of Venice and of cholera "form an anthem to disease, in the highest style" (234). Involving us in a voyeuristic drama, inducing in us a fascination with the illicit and perverse, Mann implicates us in Aschenbach's solitary world. But he also partially shields us from the narcissistic abyss that exists behind the beauty of words by drawing our attention to the text's mythic and stylistic features. Expressing narcissistic anxieties and converting them into art, Mann, in *Death in Venice*, both exposes us to and defends us against the lurking fears and fantasies of the broken artist.

❋ ❋ ❋ ❋

Part III
Tragic Woman

❋ ❋ ❋ ❋

❀ ❀ ❀ ❀

Seven
The Evasion of Narcissistic Anxieties in Lessing's *Summer Before the Dark*

❀ ❀ ❀ ❀

Doris Lessing's *Summer Before the Dark*, the novel we will now turn to as we begin our analysis of Tragic Woman, brings into strategic focus many of the phenomena we have uncovered thus far in our encounters with the narcissistic character: the need for self-confirming attention and rescue; experiences of narcissistic vulnerability, injury, and rage; and the defensive evasion of narcissistic anxieties and needs. A text that both dramatizes and engenders a rescue fantasy, *The Summer Before the Dark* centers around the plight of Kate Brown, a stylish, suburban housewife who, at forty-five, faces a long-delayed self-crisis. As Kate Brown confronts her female anxieties and anger about being exploited, she discovers that her identity is confined and defined by a patriarchal society which requires of the female selfless duties to others and a smiling acceptance of the equivocations of family life and marriage. A mother, Lessing's protagonist confronts her own essential motherlessness; an attractive woman, she discovers her inner deformity; socially adaptive and successful, she experiences feelings of rage and vulnerability so intense that they take her to the edge of madness. Despite her belief in her self-honesty, Kate has spent her life deferring awareness of her deep-rooted narcissistic anxieties, needs, and hurts. Through her obsessive search for a self-regarding gaze and her acting out of her regressive rage and selfobject needs, she discovers the "monster" which entraps her, the monster of her own self. Encouraged to endorse Kate's struggles against patriarchy, readers of *The Summer Before the Dark* are also prompted to look beyond the novel's political discourse and acknowledge the sealed-off world of Kate's subjectivity and empathically confirm her troubled self. By insistently privileging the inset dream narrative, which contains a completed rescue fantasy, Lessing imposes a happy ending onto Kate's self-crisis. But as we shall see, the critical controversy surrounding the closure provides suggestive evidence of Lessing's own persisting uncertainties about the ultimate fate of her character.

In their response to *The Summer Before the Dark*, critics have revealed themselves to be deeply concerned about Kate's plight.[1] But while Lessing involves her readers in Kate's self-drama, she also erects defenses against the potentially destabilizing experiences that she describes. From the outset and throughout the novel we are made aware of Kate's defensive splitting of herself into observing and experiencing parts. Despite her relentless self-scrutiny and self-analysis, she is, as the novel opens, "uncomfortably conscious" of the discrepancy between her thoughts and feelings (2), between the conventional attitudes toward personal experiences she has consciously adopted—"*Marriage is a compromise. . . . I wouldn't like to be a child again! . . . Love is a woman's whole existence. . .*" (1)—and her subversive feelings. She is aware, the narrator explains, that "a good many of the things she thought, had been taken down off a rack and put on, but that what she really felt was something else again" (2). "I'm telling myself the most dreadful lies!" she thinks to herself. "Why do I do it? There's something here that I simply will not let myself look at. . . . *Now*, look at it all, try and get hold of it, don't go on making up all these attitudes, these stories—stop taking down the same old dresses off the rack . . ." (12). At times, Kate steps back and observes herself from a distance: she watches and notes her own behavior "from behind" her "warm brown eyes" (46). When she scrutinizes herself in the mirror, her glance— described as an "eye-to-eye woman-to-woman collusion" (34)—has this detached quality. Similarly, the narrator both enters Kate's consciousness as she lets "her life—or the words that represented her thoughts about her life—flow through her mind" (27) and periodically stands back and observes her. These at-times-abrupt shifts in angle of vision convey to us Kate's feeling of disconnection. This feeling is evoked in descriptions such as these: "A woman in a white dress, white shoes, a pink scarf on her neck, standing on grass" (7); "A woman stood in front of large mirrors in many shops, looking with a cool, not entirely friendly curiosity at a woman in her early forties..." (34); "She was category Redhead. She had dead-white skin" (72). Because we are readers engrossed in a fictional text, we are inclined to mimic Kate's "passivity, adaptability to others" (18) and thus identify with her and become involved in her self-drama. But we are also persistently positioned at a psychic remove from Lessing's character and thus invited to disengage ourselves and participate in Kate's—and the text's—defensive blocking of unwanted affect. It is symbolically appropriate that Kate, who has "lived among words, and people bred to use and be used by words" (244), is a translator. Behind conventional expressions, she recovers her unarticulated feelings, which are overtly expressed in her serial seal dream and covertly in her unconscious mirror encounters with Jeffrey Merton, Mary Finchley, and Maureen, who represent unacknowledged aspects of Kate's self.

The very first sentence of the novel—"A woman stood on her back step, arms folded, waiting" (1)—reveals to us Kate's characteristic mode of evasion and deferral, her refusal to confront her submerged feelings and anxieties, her passive waiting for things to happen to her. This self-evasive behavior is acted out in her Global Food job and in her repetitive, multiple journeys which are full of postponements, detours, and restless, pointless wanderings. Nothing moves, everything delays and dawdles (32), for instance, when there is difficulty in selecting a site for the Global Food conference. At her temporary job, she compulsively keeps herself occupied with "minor and unimportant obsessions" (29), and she buys herself new dresses and rearranges herself by having her hair done—all in an attempt to stave off her growing awareness of the "violent and uncontrollable swings in her emotions" about her husband and children (33), emotions that emerge when she is cut away from the secure moorings of her London home. Finding her seesaw of emotions "contradictory enough for a madwoman," she begins to wonder if she had always been like this and "was only just beginning to see it" (37). The more aware she becomes of her split-off anger—the "seethe of impatience" behind her "slow sweet smile" (39)—the more she defends herself by keeping busy. In her repetitive, grinding journeys, first to the conference in Turkey and later with her young lover, Jeffrey Merton, in Spain, she acts out her lifelong defensive maneuver, her evasion of her narcissistic neediness and rage. Similarly, the narrative repetitions and detours suggest an authorial desire to defend against the narcissistic wants and fears dramatized in the text.

Kate's narcissistic neediness is initially expressed in her fear of the "cold wind" blowing "straight towards her, from the future" (17). Her anxieties about the cold wind of a loveless old age are associated with the negative feelings which slowly have been surfacing in the past three years, that she is "not wanted" by her family, that she is "unnecessary" (19). Under the pressure of this awareness, she reflects on her life, sifting through and examining the various female roles she has assumed. Recalling her youth, she remembers her grandfather's patriarchal attitudes and how, in his house, she was both "precious and despised" (13). She recalls her admiration for her faultless grandmother, and how, as a young woman, she self-consciously and theatrically enacted the role of the admired, seductive, but unapproachable female. At Global Food, she becomes aware that she is acting out the well-rehearsed roles of "nurse," "nanny," and "tribal mother" (29, 44): she is a "provider of invisible manna, consolations, warmth, 'sympathy'" (46). But she also admits that her image of herself as a "kingpin" (19), as the "warm centre of the family," is "out of date" by some two or three years, as is her "carefully tended" image (52) of her marriage. She has hidden behind her "official memories" (90) in a desperate attempt to ward off self-threatening feelings. As a wife and mother, she has been "at everybody's beck and call, always available, always criticised, always . . . bled to feed these—monsters" (89). She admits that her son Tim's angry accusation that she is suffocating him has injured her and her husband's numerous affairs have diminished her, making her feel "as if a wound had been opened in her from which substance and strength drained from her" (64). Concealed behind her customary, adaptable self are alien feelings of ire and injury. "[S]he had sat often alone in her room, raging under a knowledge of intolerable unfairness. Injustice, the pain of it, had been waiting for her all these last years. But she had *not* allowed herself to feel it, or not for long" (52).

In a narrative which stages a woman's discovery that she feels narcissistically impoverished, starved for affection and attention, the Global Food setting is filled with significance. An organization claiming to be dedicated to solving the hunger problems of the world, Global

Food is, in reality, *"a great con trick . . . a mechanism to earn a few hundred men and women incredible sums of money"* (38). When Kate performs her role as tribal mother at Global Food, her depleted self is, for a while, fed. She basks in the reflected glow of the confirming looks and smiles of others. She feels she is "blooming, expanding, enlarging" because she is "wanted, needed" (51). She is the "ever-available, ever-good-natured, popular Kate Brown" (53). At times her observing self notes the "slow rise of her euphoria" and watches it "drily enough" (51). But she also begins to fear that she is losing control. While "smiling, smiling, in the beam of other people's appreciation" (55), she recognizes that her fear of returning alone to London makes her reactions exaggerated and that her smiling face masks her growing hysteria. She sees herself "as an efficient, high-powered, smiling woman, but spinning around and around on herself like a machine that someone should have switched off" (56). Her condition mirrors that of the airline stewardesses whose "business is to be admired," to be "on show, the focus of hundreds of pairs of eyes, all day" (54) and who, consequently, become "inflated" and "intoxicated" (53). The image of the inflating, expanding self, used throughout the novel, signals the activation of archaic grandiosity. When the airline stewardess gets married and thus, metaphorically, walks offstage, she is deprived of the narcissistic applause that has supported her stunted self and thus she becomes irritable and restless. "She is like a child the grownups have been admiring but now they have got bored with her, they have turned away and started talking and forgotten her, and no matter how she dances, and smiles and poses and shouts, Look at me! Look at me! they seem not to hear" (55). At one and the same time, Kate is the tribal mother and the cast-aside child who desperately craves the attention of others. Though ignored by her family, Kate is the focal point of the reader's empathic interest.

When Kate begins to peel away her smiling mask and delve beneath her "official" memories, she is forced to recognize the tyrannies and trivialities of her customary life. Made privy to Kate's self-discoveries, the reader is also made aware, as Betsy Draine observes, of the narrator's polemical and didactic social message (122–24). When Kate reviews her acquisition of the "hard-to-come-by virtues, self-disciplines" required of the wife and mother, she sees it all as a "gigantic con trick, the most monstrous cynicism" and herself as a "fatted white goose" (91). Her virtues—"Patience. Self-discipline. Self-control. Self-abnegation. Chastity. Adaptability to others—this above all"—she perceives as a "form of dementia" (92). "[O]bsessed, from morning till night, about management, about organisation, about seeing how things ought to go, about the results of not acting like this or of acting like that," she, like other women, has had a "long education in just one thing, fussing" (93). "[T]hrough the long, grinding process of always, always being at other people's beck and call, always having to give out attention to detail, miniscule wants, demands, needs, events, crises," she has been transformed into "an obsessed maniac," someone obsessed with what is "totally unimportant" (94). She feels caught in a sinister pattern, narcissistically injured, invalidated. She is "like a wounded bird, being pecked to death by the healthy birds" (98). "I'm like a cripple or an invalid after years of being your servant, your doormat," she wants but cannot say to her family. "Now help me. I need your help" (95). Kate's mute cry for help is designed to elicit a sympathetic response from the reader. Because she is so much the victim, we want to see her rescued.

In demand at Global Food, Kate temporarily procures the narcissistic sustenance she requires to maintain her impoverished self. But at Global Food she also makes a discovery that will later take her to the brink of self-breakage. For the first time she recognizes that "behind a different facade"—when she lets her body sag and her face droop—she is invisible. To be invisible is to feel "dislocated," as if something has "slipped out of alignment" (43). When others do not mirror her, she feels a slippage of self, this experience an intimation of her later descent into the disconnected world of madness. Narcissistically incomplete, she needs to have her self confirmed by others to feel valid and real.

When Kate goes off with Jeffrey Merton, a younger man who transfers onto her his need for an empathic mother figure, she attempts to run away from her emerging narcissistic anxieties. She has what she calls one of life's "sweet-sour mirror encounters" (103) when she sees an older man and a younger woman and compares their situation with hers. Ultimately, her love affair with Jeffrey proves to be an unacknowledged mirror encounter. Jeffrey's illness, his fever, his restless irritation, his desire for and aversion to food—all are symptomatic, Kate recognizes, of his crisis of identity. He does what she, too, has done. He uses "evasion" as a defense: he retreats inwards, "far away, behind surfaces of flesh, hair, eyes that do not seem to have much to do with one . . ." (112–13). Jeffrey's self-crisis manifests itself physically. He seems to collapse "inwardly"; "corpse-like," he looks "as if the bones in his flesh had collapsed, or had shrunk" (118). In Jeffrey, who alternates between a kind of madness and smiling, courteous behavior, Kate confronts, but does not consciously recognize, a sick version of her own smiling self. Similarly, his restless need "to move, to be going somewhere, to be travelling" (110) dramatizes her own restless and evasive behavior— her compulsive fussing. A key metaphor in Jeffrey's illness is food. Jeffrey is ravenously hungry, for his collapsed self craves narcissistic sustenance, but he also finds food "disgusting or dangerous" (109). Jeffrey's anorexia prefigures Kate's self-starvation. With Jeffrey, Kate unknowingly rehearses her own impending self-collapse.

When Kate suddenly and unaccountably becomes sick, she returns alone to a London hotel to weather her illness. There she pays for nurturing attention "of the very highest quality" (137). In her sickness, the inner feelings she has been avoiding manifest themselves physically. When Kate looks in the mirror, we see her through her own detached perspective. This softens the jolt we get when we witness Kate's appalling transformation: "She stood in front of a glass. . . . She saw a woman all bones and big elbows, with large knees above lanky calves; she had small dark anxious eyes in a white sagging face around which was a rough mat of brassy hair" (141). Kate's stylish public facade is a confection that belies the reality of her attenuated self. The "cold wind" of a loveless, nonempathic future manifests itself as a symptom in her illness. She feels "as if inside her she was cold, very chilled, despite her burning surfaces" (138). Nauseated, unable to eat, "the flesh . . . melting off her" (145), she becomes the image of the deprived, starving child she has harboured within herself all these years.

Kate Brown is a woman who has felt herself onstage all her life, and who has, despite her frequent self-studies, defensively denied her narcissistic wants and fears. Given this, we are not surprised at her choice of setting for publicly acting out her madness—a theater full of people "dressed up in personalities not their own" (152). Momentarily stepping back, the narrator scrutinizes Kate as if she were someone totally unknown to us: "A woman sat prominently in the front row of the stalls, a woman whom other people were observing" (153). This detached perspective, which mimics Kate's self-observing stance, also acts as a shield, partially protecting us against the shame and horror of Kate's bizarre, public behavior. Out of place, Kate openly looks at the people in the audience with "a cocky aggressive sideways cast of her eye" (156), and she mutters at the characters on the stage. An "eccentric to the point of fantasy," she wears a "sacklike" dress, her hair is "multi-hued," and her "gaunt face" is "yellow, and all bones and burning angry eyes" (153). In a self-referential observation, Kate regards the female character in the play as the mirror image of "every woman in the audience who has been the centre of attention and now sees her power slip away from her." The character, she thinks, is "[M]ad. Nuts. Loony. Allowed to be. More, encouraged to be. She should be locked up" (155). Looking at the room full of people through her distorted perception, Kate sees not human beings but "animals covered with cloth and bits of fur, ornamented with stones, their faces and claws painted with colour" (156). When she examines her own face in the mirror, she sees that she, too, is an animal—a sick monkey. Her self is no longer buoyed up by the confirming looks of others. Lost in a nonempathic milieu, she has slipped into a grotesque nonhuman world of meaningless animal behavior and ritual.

As the real world becomes an increasingly hostile and unfamiliar place, Kate begins to live more and more in her dream world, the "country behind the daylit one" (128). Her dream-in-process, she believes, is "as much her business for this time in her life . . . as wrestling with her emotional self, which seemed like a traitor who had come to life inside her. What she was engaged in was the dream, which worked itself out in her" (128–29). Subject to much critical attention, the inset dream text openly provokes the reader to interpret and to locate the correlations between Kate's serial dream and her waking life. We are told that Kate has "always been on good terms with her dreams" and has "always been alert to learn from them" (128). Because the text, in telling us this, indicates "the purpose of the dream within the context of the novel," as Ralph Berets states, "the result should be that Kate and the reader learn something from Kate's persistent dream experiences with the seal" (125). Despite the fact that Kate is an individual who engages in continuous self-analysis, she does not interpret her dream. This task is left to the reader.

The dream is presented as direct, unmediated experience, as a metaphor, a visualization of Kate's wants and anxieties. Her sense of exposure, vulnerability, injury, helplessness, and deformity is conveyed in her dream. A "story" or "journey," "an epic, simple and direct" (29), the seal dream centers around a rescue fantasy, Kate's desire to rescue the seal dramatizing her own need for self-rescue. Like Kate's external journey, her dream journey is full of repetitive delays, false starts, and detours. "How could she be sure of going in the right direction?" (47) she asks during an early dream. "[W]here was the seal? Was it lying abandoned among dry rocks waiting for her, looking for her with its dark eyes?" (68). When Kate looks into its eyes, which are like her own, she encounters her secreted self. Though she momentarily evades her responsibility when she makes "perfect" love to her idealized lover (101)—her husband? Jeffrey Merton?—she soon continues her unremitting, redundant journey in a darkening landscape, a "permanent chilly twilight," a "dark northern country" (119, 123). The "cold wind" Kate has felt blowing from the future becomes figured in her dream. Again and again, she has the nagging feeling that her "inner tutor" wants her "to understand something" which she is "too obtuse" (119) to comprehend. When she, in a condensed dream image, envisions that she and the seal are being attacked by wild animals, she expresses her own violent impulses and her feelings of narcissistic vulnerability and injury. Another dream dramatizes her need to be special, to be singled out, and her concomitant fear of abandonment. In the public gaze, she dances with the king, an older version of her perfect lover, only to be discarded by him, just as her husband repeatedly has discarded her to pursue his numerous sexual liaisons. Again she rescues the abandoned seal and continues her journey "north, always north, away from the sun" (146). Mutilated, alienated, homeless, the seal is an embodiment of Kate's threatened self.

The subterranean, chilly domain of Maureen's basement flat is the final setting of Kate's self-drama and it is here that she finishes her dream. While the text draws attention to Kate's dream-in-process, there is something equally dreamlike in her interactions with the willful, childlike Maureen, and Maureen's rapid shifts in mood and costumes—which range from nursery rhyme and doll-like to Victorian and sexually seductive outfits—add to the surreal quality of this encounter. The narcissistic nature of this relationship is suggested in the first meeting of the two women when Kate, looking at her emaciated body in a mirror, sees the self-absorbed, self-assured Maureen "reflected in the same glass." Maureen's welcoming gesture—the "energetic hopping springing sort of dance" (168) which she performs as she watches herself in the mirror—dramatizes her assertive and exhibitionistic grandiosity. Earlier, before her illness, Kate had recognized that "the future would continue from where she had left off as a child" (125). In her mirror encounter with Maureen, Kate comes face to face with her own child-self. Despite the various locations in the novel— Kate's home, the small hotel rooms she inhabits, Maureen's basement dwelling, the dream terrain of the seal—the true locus of the novel is Kate's subjectivity. The external settings correlate to various aspects of Kate's self-experience. Her London home reflects her adaptive, conventional identity and the small, boxlike rooms she inhabits, which are sparely furnished (but each has a mirror), her introspective and at times claustrophobic self-awareness. The "cave" of Maureen's flat (234) is where Kate finally keeps her long-postponed appointment with her buried self. Here she becomes aware of the "monster inside which she was trapped, a monstrous baby, who had to be soothed and smiled at and given attention on demand" (175). While we may be embarrassed as we witness Kate's subsequent behavior, Lessing assuages our anxiety about being in proximity to her character by positioning us as privileged observers of Kate's turbulent emotions and childish, angry displays.

From the beginning of her psychojourney Kate has been aware of her gnawing hunger, her feeling, which has persisted during the past three years, that she has been "starved" (52) for her family's attention. Kate's anorexia and her resultant weight loss are signifiers of her inner feelings of narcissistic deprivation and rage. What she has never revealed to her family, she openly expresses during her stay with Maureen. Realizing that she should eat, Kate goes to a restaurant and when the waitress ignores her—as her family has done—she nearly succumbs to a childish "tantrum." She wants to shout out, "Look, I'm here, can't you see me?" Angry, unable to eat, she feels "like a small child who has been told to sit in a corner to eat its food because it has been naughty, and then is forgotten" (170). When she subsequently goes shopping for food, she gets so upset because she is buying second-rate goods—"bad dead food" (173)—that she feels like raging and screaming. "She was insane, there was no doubt of it—so spoke her intelligence, while her emotions were those of a small child" (174). Feeling an urgent need to eat so she can "build up energy in order to defeat the monster which had swallowed her whole" (176), she finally consumes the food that Maureen offers her—baby food. She symbolically mothers herself as she attempts to soothe the angry, monstrous child within her. Later when Kate is taken to observe a political demonstration dramatizing the plight of the hungry in London, we hear, in the angry words of a demonstrator, a coded articulation of Kate's plight: "[W]e shall starve publicly, not out of sight. . . . We shall starve ourselves to death where you can see us doing it"; "it's better to . . . starve here in the open, instead of like animals behind shut doors. . . ." (215, 217).

"Why don't you look at me?" (180), Kate wants to cry out when she is totally ignored by men as she walks down the street. Similarly, no one takes "any notice of her" when she enters a cafe. "She knew now, she had to know at last, that all her life she had been held upright by an invisible fluid, the notice of other people. But the fluid had been drained away." She recognizes now that her smile, the "emphatic smile" of Mrs. Michael Brown, is her way of attracting attention by sending out the signal, "I am accustomed to being noticed" (180). Kate becomes conscious of her divided self when she, on the mend, alternately dresses as the stylish and sexually attractive Mrs. Brown and as an invisible, sagging, old woman. "[T]he mask, the charade, the fitting of herself to the template" of Mrs. Michael Brown revives the "old manner, the loving lovely Mrs. Kate Brown" (186–87). Her other identity, her invisible self, is angry, forlorn, vulnerable. She realizes that "[h]er whole surface . . . had been set to receive notice. . . ." When she assumes her invisible identity, she feels dislocated: she is "floating, without ballast," her head is "chaotic, her feelings numbed with confusion" (179). Aware of her split self, Kate, in a conscious mirror encounter, scrutinizes her counterpart, a "lonely woman, her eyes forced full of vivacity, her voice urged full of charm." Following the woman, Kate "was following herself . . . watching how she looked long into every approaching face, male or female, to see how she was being noticed" (187). When Kate acts out her "invisible," unattractive role, she simultaneously watches her other smiling, attractive self being "acknowledged and recognised" and thus basking and growing "subtly fat and happy because of all the note being taken of her" (200). To be looked at and mirrored by others—especially men—is to be fed. This psychic equation between self-regarding eye glances and narcissistic sustenance is symbolized in one of Maureen's more outrageous costumes, the one in which her breasts show behind beige lace revealing nipples that are "painted like eyes" (190). While Kate craves the admiring gaze of men, she also comes to recognize that her customary self conforms, twitches "like a puppet to those strings" of what stimulates men's eyes (186), and thus she consciously determines to free herself from the inauthentic world of female role-playing.

At the outset of her summer experiences, Kate recognizes that only with her friend Mary Finchley does she sometimes "get near" the truth which she has been avoiding by telling herself "dreadful lies" (12). Mary is the only woman Kate knows who refuses to play what Kate comes to see as the con game of female play-acting. Recurrently, Kate's thoughts turn to Mary Finchley and at one point she confesses her need to "understand what Mary meant to her, what she was standing for" (94). When Kate, in response to Maureen's wish to be told a "story" (223), reconstructs the "story" of her life, she begins with pleasant memories of her children and marriage but then subverts this "happy story" by recounting the unsavory exploits of Mary Finchley (225–29). In describing Mary Finchley, Kate inadvertently depicts a split-off part of herself. While Kate thinks that she should understand what Mary represents in her life, she, despite her obsessive self-analysis, never totally solves this riddle. To do so would be too painful.

Mary, as Kate analyzes her friend, gives her another way of looking at things. Love and duty, should and should not—such things, seen through Mary's "perspective," are a "disease" (228–29). In her slide into madness, Kate has shared this perspective. Assertive, invulnerable, and totally lacking the ability to feel guilt or remorse, Mary is a "savage woman" (225), who thoughtlessly, unempathically injures others—most particularly her husband who must accommodate himself to her frequent infidelities just as Kate must overlook her husband's frequent affairs. In Mary, Kate finds an expression of her own never fully acknowledged wish for power and revenge. Kate's passivity and female masochism mask the savagery of her archaic fury. Psychoanalyst Joan Lang's description of female self-development sheds further light on the riddle of what Mary Finchley represents in Kate's psychic life. The "good" female self sanctioned and mirrored by the selfobject milieu, Lang explains, is nonaggressive; female assertiveness, in contrast, is equated with the "bad self." Women are culturally conditioned by their selfobject environment to see their innate aggression as ego-alien, as "not me" (61–63). This is true of Kate whose split-off badness is projected onto others: the childishly aggressive Maureen and the dangerously savage Mary Finchley. What can happen to healthy self-assertiveness when it is not empathically mirrored is also dramatized in the text: it can turn savage and disintegrate into rage.

When she begins to recover her psychic equilibrium, Kate thinks that perhaps her negative feelings of the last few months were nothing more than an expression of her need for attention and appreciation. "She had not been loved enough, noticed enough, licked and stroked enough? Was that all it was?" (231). "[A]ssessing, balancing, weighing" what one thinks and feels—"it's all nonsense" (232), she decides as she recuperates from her "sag into sickness" (201). Her "mood" when she returns home will be "irrelevant," she concludes when she begins to experience a "reversal" of her "black" and "ugly" feelings (231–32). It is at this point that Kate completes her dream and rescues the seal.

"What would be the point of a dream that had to end in me and the seal dying," Kate queries, "just dying, after all that effort?" (210). While Kate's seal dreams have been read as "mechanical and redundant" (Cederstrom 140), many critics, following the text's explicit directives, consider them a fundamental interpretive key to Kate's self-drama. "The culminating dream," states Betsy Draine, "clearly instructs us that Kate was wrong in her assumption that this was her summer before the dark . . ." (129). "The warmth and light at the end of the dream," writes Barbara Waxman, "suggest that this is a moment of triumph as well as of hope for Kate after her struggle in the dark during the summer . . ." (329). Ralph Berets describes the common critical claim that Lessing's novel is unresolved and offers "no alternative to the life of frustration and despair that Kate Brown had experienced earlier before her departure from home" as "suspect because it does not take into account the positive progression of the dream imagery and the growth and development of the seal" (119). For some critics the final dream, in which Kate discovers that the sun—a "brilliant, buoyant, tumultuous sun"—is "in front of her, not behind" (241), points to an underlying religious or spiritual theme. Grace Ann Hovet and Barbara

Lounsberry assert that those who probe "deeply into the mythological and folkloric resonances of Kate's dream images will come to see Kate's seal dream as a sign of her rebirth, and concomitantly of the liberation of spiritual elements within her which can be recombined into new cosmic patterns" (44). Mary Ann Singleton writes that Kate's dreams give her a glimpse of "something within herself that is eternal" (162–63). Often such critics seem intent on rescuing Kate from those readers who find themselves disappointed with her decision to return home.

But given the feminist discourse found in this text and its open criticism of the impositions of marriage and family life, we can see that such disappointment grows out of reader expectations kindled by the text. Often, as Betsy Draine observes, the narrator delivers assertive and didactic commentary about Kate's situation. And in the essaylike discussion of the smiling airline stewardesses "the narrator suggests that the lesson applies generally to women who have accepted the nurturing role": such women are "exhorted to take up Kate's quest—to forego pleasing others" in favor of "learning what will please" themselves (124). Given the polemical tone of such passages, we can understand why a number of critics see Kate's return home as tantamount to her relapse into female passivity and her resumption of the constricting, self-limiting life she has led for years as Mrs. Michael Brown (see, e.g., Lefcowitz 118–19). Or they interpret the return as a sign of her "acceptance of the limits of freedom" (Rubenstein 217). That this text has the power to provoke in readers Kate's assertive anger against patriarchy is suggested by Hovet and Lounsberry in their analysis of why some readers are disappointed with the closure. "Such readers," they write, "would have Kate return from her odyssey, avenge herself on Michael's suitors, indeed on faithless Michael himself, reorder her household and then the world" (48).

Kate's "statement" of defiance, her "widening grey band" of hair (244), is also the subject of much debate. It has been contrastingly described as "trivial" (Cederstrom 145) and as a sign of Kate's "transcending psychic consciousness," the band which "'bisects' her head from mid-scalp to forehead" being interpreted as "an image suggestive of a shattered consciousness moulded and manifesting itself anew" (Hovet and Lounsberry 50). Kate's "statement"—her bisected head—can also be read as an emblem of the persisting split in her self: her external compliance and internal defiance. Although a conscious mission of this text is to illustrate Lessing's belief that madness can be curative and although Kate clearly has gained much in self-awareness by temporarily allowing herself to *feel* her pent up anger and sense of deprivation, there is something unconvincing about her dismissal of her deep-seated need for mirroring attention and her belief that her "mood" when she returns home will be irrelevant. Isn't Kate, in her characteristic way, simply retreating from her "black" and "ugly" feelings? Isn't she submerging the monster of her deeply anchored selfobject needs and anger?

In the final scene, Maureen acts out Kate's persisting narcissistic anxieties. In an unconscious identification with Kate, Maureen cuts off her hair and shapes a harvest doll out of it. With her shorn hair, she looks like a prisoner. Protectively and defiantly, she exhibits her hair puppet to the guests at her party: " 'It's my hair. Can't you see? It's my baby.' Maureen began dancing in front of them, not looking at them at all, but holding up the doll that dangled from her wrist: a bright fragile puppet" (246). In the novel's psychic scheme, the hair doll signifies the inauthentic self—the female self controlled by social stereotypes—and the defiant, inner child-self. When Maureen's lover, William, talks to her about marriage, she suggestively spins the doll "around and around." "Give me that thing, I don't like it," says William. "You aren't supposed to like it," retorts Maureen, guarding the doll. "One could easily imagine them together," we are told, "in their large house . . . deep in plentiful horses, children, and dogs, everything according to the pattern . . ." (247). This final vignette, which we are invited to decode, sends out negative signals. At the outset, Kate felt like a "long-term prisoner" (15) and a puppet; at the end, the childlike Maureen, while openly defiant, seems about to assume these female roles and to repeat the same sinister "pattern" Kate has followed. In effect, the text displaces Kate's female anxieties and anger onto a substitute figure: Maureen.

In a few short months, Kate has visibly grown older, the "light that is the desire to please" having been extinguished. "Her face had aged," Kate thinks to herself. "*They* [her family] could hardly fail to notice it. . . . Her hair—well, no one could overlook that!" (243). Despite her conscious denials, Kate is still bent on gaining the attention of her family. "No one" notices when Kate leaves Maureen's flat to find her way home (247). At once, the narrator implies that Kate no longer needs the self-bolstering regard of others while urging the reader to notice, admire, and endorse Kate. The closure, which is toneless and affectless, also leaves us feeling abruptly disconnected, shut out. The text induces in us Kate's feeling-state as she, distancing herself from her emotions, returns home. "It doesn't matter a damn what you do," Maureen tells Kate. "That is the whole point of everything. It's what no one can face up to" (242). What would be the point, Kate asks herself, of enduring the painful struggle of rescuing the seal only to fail. Implicit in Kate's dream text is the impulse to seek asylum from narcissistic wants and fears by telling a story and thus imposing narrative form onto amorphous anxieties. When Kate spends days telling Maureen the story of her life and then undercuts its hopeful quality by describing Mary Finchley, Maureen, we are told, never again asks to be told a story (229). Maureen's attitude typifies that of many readers who want a happy ending and the working through and resolution of conflict. But Kate's reconstructed story of her life remains incomplete; only in her seal dream does she reach narrative completion and thus achieve the sense of wholeness which she and the reader seek. At the beginning of her summer, Kate is aware that she has little to look forward to but a "dwindling away from full household activity into getting old." What happens to Kate during her fateful summer before the dark, the narrator tells us, is that she experiences, in a "shortened, heightened, concentrated time," the process of growing old (5). When Kate returns home, not as the attractive, young-looking woman she was when she left but as a visibly old woman, she consciously expresses her desire to free herself from female social stereotypes. But she unconsciously signals, through her new appearance, her dependency on selfobject others and her awareness of the dwindling, not the strengthening, of her self.

"Madness and mysticism," observes Jeffrey Berman, "are almost identical phenomena in Lessing's world" (*The Talking Cure* 181). Giving privileged status to the inset dream text, Lessing insistently mythologizes Kate's narcissistic terrors and thus partially shields us from them. In having Kate save the seal, Lessing expresses her own romantic hopes for the rescue of her character. The spiritual solution to Kate's troubled selfhood, implied in the final seal dream, also suggests an authorial desire to resolve Kate's problems by projecting her beyond them. But in counterpoint, we hear the despairing voice of the Maureen-in-Kate saying that all is pointless. The irresolution of the closure suggests Lessing's own lack of certainty about her character's fate as it underscores the central uncertainties of the text. Critics, in their disagreement about the novel's closure, mirror its conscious optimism and unconscious pessimism. While Kate's conscious hopes are shared by readers, her persisting fears, which are acted out by Maureen in the novel's final scene, are also communicated. The receptive reader feels uneasy about the gaps and reticences of this text. "What will happen to Kate and all the women like her?" asks Barbara Lefcowitz. Will she go permanently mad or find " 'the courage to be as a self' "? "Such an outcome," writes Lefcowitz, "is, one suspects, as much up to the others who must meet her part way as it is to Kate herself" (119). Such an outcome also depends on the selfobject support and self-approving regard Kate receives from her family and others.

In *The Summer Before the Dark*, Lessing creates a richly overlaid text as she explores the shuttered world of the narcissistic character. Prompting readers to share Kate's characteristic observing stance, duplicating in us her anger against patriarchy and making us desire her rescue, Lessing invites us to become participant/observers of Kate's ongoing self-drama. Unlike Kate's family, we come to acknowledge and endorse that "thing" Kate has "offered," that "something precious" which those around her have never recognized (126): her needy and fragile self.

✿ ✿ ✿ ✿

Eight

Self-Dispersal and Self-Assemblage:
The Artistic Reconstitution of the Broken
Self in Woolf's *Mrs. Dalloway*

✿ ✿ ✿ ✿

In *Mrs. Dalloway*, Virginia Woolf again and again immerses us in the world we observe from a safe psychic remove in Lessing's novel—the alien world of the disconnected self. But Woolf also uses her art to gain mastery over and partially disguise the narcissistic terrors she fictionalizes. Both in Woolf's comments about *Mrs. Dalloway* and in the critical responses to it, we find suggestive evidence of the narcissistic script it at once enacts and defends against.

"I adumbrate here," Woolf commented in a diary description of *Mrs. Dalloway*, "a study of insanity & suicide: the world seen by the sane & the insane side by side . . ." (*Diary* 2: 207). Because her fictional world is elaborately designed and is populated by unrelated characters who share thoughts and perceptions, the question of authorial presence has recurred like a haunting subtext in critical discussions of the novel as commentators have attempted to account for its strange doubling and blurring of characters and the way the narrating consciousness "hovers . . . between the minds of the characters" or alternately immerses itself into or withdraws from them (Harper 117, 119–20). In the words of Michael Rosenthal, *Mrs. Dalloway* is a novel "steeped in connections and interconnections"; a highly designed work, it depicts the disconnected world of human isolation (88, 90). James Naremore, who observes that "there is no clear boundary between Virginia

Woolf's characters or between the author and her materials" (103), states that the reader of *Mrs. Dalloway* "is never invited to leave the presence of the author, who . . . speaks virtually throughout the novel in a single voice" (91). Woolf, herself, realized this. "Have I the power of conveying the true reality?" she asked herself during the creation of the novel. "Or do I write essays about myself?" (*Diary* 2: 248). The strange alternation between immersion and withdrawal, connection and disconnection experienced by critic/readers is rooted in the narcissistic preoccupations underlying the work: merger needs and apprehensions and disintegration fears. Woolf, as she writes an essay about herself, casts her reader in the roles of the absorbed listener, who becomes immersed in the text's fictional world, and the appreciative critic, who is impressed with the text's intricate design. Behind the magic of *Mrs. Dalloway* with its strange metaphoric pulse, its curious doubling and redoubling of characters, and its romanticizing of madness and suicide lies the agonizing fear that one communicates over an abyss, that words fill in the interstices within the empty, fissuring self.

Placed at the center of our attention, Clarissa Dalloway is a study in contrasts. Alternately situated at several removes from Clarissa and immersed within her subjectivity, we are made aware of the rupture between her public and private selves. In many of the descriptions of Clarissa's public self, some of which verge on satire (see Lee's discussion of this, 103–06), Woolf openly expresses her confessed dislike for the rehearsed public personality of her character. The perfect hostess, "mistress of silver, of linen, of china" (56), Clarissa Dalloway is sentimental about the Crown and tolerant, even admiring, of the Hugh Whitbreads of her world. She is "frivolous" and "empty-minded" (65) and cares "too much for rank and society and getting on in the world" (115). "The doubtful point is I think the character of Mrs Dalloway," Woolf wrote in her diary. "It may be too stiff, too glittering & tinsely—" (*Diary* 2: 272). "I think some distaste for her persisted," Woolf wrote after the book had been published (*Diary* 3: 32). There is something distasteful about Clarissa's coldness and lack of social conscience. "Hunted out of existence, maimed, frozen, the victims of cruelty and injustice . . . no, she could feel nothing for the Albanians, or was it the Armenians? but she loved her roses . . ." (182). While we are made aware of Clarissa's hardness and worldliness, these aspects of her personality are given marginal status. One of Woolf's primary goals is to convey and poetize Clarissa's complicated subjectivity—her fluctuating perceptions and alternating feeling-states.

From the external view, Clarissa Dalloway is unyielding, aloof. But as we learn, her rigid personality structure is a self-construct created to defend against underlying narcissistic anxieties and needs. What readers of *Mrs. Dalloway* are made privy to, observes self psychologist Ernest Wolf, is "the experience of a fragile self as it endures the struggle to preserve its cohesion against the disintegrating stimuli of living through an ordinary day . . ." ("Disconnected Self" 112). Clarissa's impersonation of "the perfect hostess" (9–10, 93) and her "coldness," "woodenness," and "impenetrability" (91) mask her poor self image. She is "hard on people" like the Ellie Hendersons of her world (291) and hates "frumps, fogies, [and] failures" (115) because she herself feels, in some central way, inadequate. She is self-conscious about her "narrow pea-stick figure" and "ridiculous little face, beaked like a bird's" (14) and next to someone like Hugh Whitbread she feels "skimpy" (8). Seeking the self-confirming regard of others, she wants people to "look pleased" when she comes into their presence (13), she desires Peter Walsh's "good opinion" (53), she needs to be liked (185). Just how easily her self-cohesion is threatened is disclosed in her response to rejection. To be rejected, no matter how trivial the cause, is to be plunged to the depths. When Lady Bruton does not invite her to lunch, Clarissa's infirm self shivers, rocks—she suddenly feels "shrivelled, aged, breastless." Her nunlike withdrawal and her perception of the "emptiness about the heart of life" (45) reveal just how deficient her narcissistic reserves are. To be rejected is to feel alone, abandoned. "He has left me; I am alone forever . . . ," Clarissa thinks because Richard is lunching with Lady Bruton and she has been excluded. Isolated, "alone" in her "tower," she is profoundly needy: "Richard, Richard! she cried, as a sleeper in the night starts and stretches a hand in the dark for help" (70). Always she is aware of Peter Walsh in the corner of her mind reproaching her. When Peter, after a long absence, visits her on the morning of her party, she must summon her "self" to "beat off the enemy" of his censure (66). Feeling that she has been criticized unfairly about her parties, she becomes depressed (182–83). While we are apprised of Clarissa's "faults, jealousies, vanities, suspicions" (55) and her concealed anger, what is placed in the forefront of our attention are her elusive and fluid perceptions of self. This foregrounding of the poetic and backgrounding of the negative aspects of Clarissa's personality and their displacement onto others, as we shall see, signals one of the primary defensive strategies of the text.

In the depiction of Clarissa's interiority, the poetic rapture and fluidity of the prose work to partially camouflage the narcissistic anxieties subtending her self-experience. Like Lessing's Kate Brown, Clarissa is split into experiencing and observing selves: she slices "like a knife through everything" and remains "outside, looking on." In Bond Street she becomes absorbed in the vital and crowded ebb and flow of city life, and feels, simultaneously, "far out to sea and alone." It is "very, very dangerous," she senses, "to live even one day" (11). The need to feel connected to others underlies her merger fantasy, her belief that she is part of the life around her and "of people she had never met" (12). Her lack of a stable, cohesive self is underscored when she, looking at her face in a mirror, symbolically attempts to frame and collect "the whole of her at one point" (54). Pursing her lips to give her face "point," she thinks that is "her self—pointed; dartlike; definite." Through force of will, she attempts to assemble the fragmenting parts of her self. She alone is aware of "how different, how incompatible" the shards of her broken self are as she composes herself into "one centre, one diamond, one woman" (55). Her persisting feelings that she is "invisible; unseen; unknown" (14) reveal her sense of disconnection while her fantasy that she is "laid out like a mist between the people she knew best" (12) exposes her need for selfobject support to sustain her fading, dissolving self.

At the psychocenter of the novel and providing hermeneutic clues to the mystery of the empty, dispersed self is an inset, condensed text: Peter Walsh's phantasmagoric dream-vision. "Nothing exists outside us except a state of mind . . . a desire for solace, for relief, for something outside these miserable pigmies, these feeble, these ugly, these craven men and women" (85). With these words the narrating consciousness transcribes the inception of Peter's dream-fantasy in which he takes on the identity of the solitary traveler. The desire for escape from narcissistic distortion and debilitation—from the feeble, the ugly, the craven—gives rise to a vision of the primal mother, described variously as the "giant figure at the end of the ride" and as a figure "made of sky and branches" (85, 86). The solitary traveler feels "a general peace, as if . . . all this fever of living were simplicity itself; and myriads of things merged in one thing" (86). But the wish to fuse with the maternal environment—to "mount" on her streamers and "blow to nothingness"—engenders the associated fear of "annihilation" and the ominous vision of the "figure of the mother whose sons have been killed in the battles of the world." Merger as blissful harmony and as self-dispersal and annihilation—these primitive fears and fantasies are linked to one final signifier in this associative chain: that of the thwarted embrace, the mother figure that the "recollection of cold human contacts forbids us to embrace" (87). Connection and disconnection; absorption and withdrawal—the primary rhythms of the novel find their source in these archaic fantasies of the maternal imago.

In the opening passage in the novel describing Clarissa in Bond Street, we find another coded depiction of the primal imago and also an occulted reference to the authorial presence—the connecting imagination—behind the text. The unknown person in the motor car, a mysterious face fleetingly glimpsed against dove-gray upholstery, is a potent presence, an idealized figure of power and grandeur. For a moment the disconnected lives of Londoners are connected in the awareness that "greatness" is "passing." Inscrutable, unknowable, the face in the motor car will still be known in some remote future when "all those hurrying along the pavement this Wednesday morning are but bones with a few wedding rings mixed up in their dust and the gold stoppings of innumerable decayed teeth" (23). The Mrs. Dalloway in Bond Street description, which was the original germ of the novel, has been lauded for its depiction of the social world of London in the early 1920s. But as in other parts of the novel, the social discourse of this passage is palimpsestic. Insistently, it points to another more primitive and only partially revealed psychonarrative embedded in this layered text.

Similarly, the subtext of Clarissa's interactions with others inscribes a largely concealed self-drama. While Clarissa wants to feel connected with others, she lacks "something central which permeated; something warm which broke up surfaces and rippled the cold contact of man and woman, or of women together" (46). Her special attraction to women is rooted in her unresolved need for her dead, lost mother. This need, as Elizabeth Abel shows, haunts the text by its absence for there are only two passing references to Clarissa's mother in the novel. In Clarissa's emotionally blocked life, one incident, which occurred some thirty years before, stands out as a framed moment of intense emotion. When Sally Seaton kissed her, Clarissa remembers feeling that she had been given a precious gift, a diamond. The orgasmic description of Clarissa's response to women suggests a sense of merger, ecstatic expansion, and self-repair: she momentarily experiences "some pressure of rapture, which split its thin skin and gushed and poured with an extraordinary alleviation over the cracks and sores!" (47). But while Clarissa craves closeness with others, she can express her merger needs only in the safe confines of memory and fantasy. In her social interactions with others she remains aloof. In her marriage she takes comfort in the "gulf" that separates husband and wife (181). And yet despite the fact that Clarissa's husband, Richard, is relegated to the background of her consciousness, she nevertheless perceives him as the "foundation" of her life (43). For he provides needed selfobject support without encroaching on Clarissa who fears closeness as much as she desires it. To safeguard her uncertain self, she has chosen her ever-narrowing virgin's bed, her distant tower where she exists in self-imposed exile. In the old lady opposite, she finds a mirror reflection of her own anchoritic selfhood. As we observe Clarissa observing the old woman, Woolf positions us in such a way that we share Clarissa's experience of disconnection and psychic remove.

To "know her," Clarissa reflects, "one must seek out the people who completed" her (231). Peter Walsh, often described as the middle point on the continuum linking Septimus Smith and Clarissa, is one of the characters who completes her. Preoccupied with Clarissa, Peter feels that she has "influenced him more than any person he had ever known" (232–33), that she is empathically attuned to him, that she understands him, feels with him (68). While Peter is Clarissa's chief critic, he also is the one character who apprehends her "woman's gift"—her ability to make "a world of her own wherever she happened to be" (114). It is Peter's primary role to draw the reader's attention to Clarissa, to single her out, to describe her hidden powers. "She came into a room; she stood, as he had often seen her, in a doorway with lots of people round her. But it was Clarissa one remembered. . . . [T]here she was . . . there she was" (114–15). Existing less as a separate identity than as an extension of Clarissa, Peter, in effect, completes Clarissa by functioning textually as a kind of need-satisfying selfobject. He is also a mirror-reflection. While Peter's narcissistic anxieties are not as intense as Clarissa's, they are similar. Subject to low self-esteem, he perceives himself to be a middle-aged and mediocre failure. "[F]eeling hollowed out, utterly empty within," he thinks "Clarissa refused me" (74). Standing "alone, alive, unknown" in London, he experiences a momentary sense of dislocation. "What is it? Where am I?" he asks (78). Like Clarissa, he senses that "one makes up the better part of life," that one makes up "oneself" (81); when he tells Clarissa about his life in India, he is aware of the "assembly of powers" (66) within him. In his dream-fantasy of the solitary traveler, he shares Clarissa's merger fantasy as he imagines "myriads of things merged in one thing" (86). And Peter also "completes" Clarissa by embodying disowned aspects of her personality. For just as he attempts to impose himself on Clarissa and injures her with his incisive, unempathic remarks, so she imposes herself on others (183) and cuts people up and sticks them together again (157).

While Clarissa aspires to be a "gentle, generous-hearted" woman (58), she is aware of her negative impulses. Acting out of necessity, she attempts to censor or intellectualize away these feelings. Often this leads to split perceptions of others. While one part of her admires Hugh Whitbread, another part of her belittles him for his "perfectly upholstered body" and his "little job at Court" (7). While Clarissa desires to please Evelyn Whitbread, she also perceives the ailing woman as "indescribably dried-up" (13). Determined not to categorize people like Peter Walsh—"she would not say of Peter, she would not say of herself, I am this, I am that"—she nevertheless thinks of him as a failure (11). When Peter tells her he is in love with a woman, Clarissa feels alternately enraged and accepting. "She flattered him; she fooled him, thought Clarissa; shaping the woman . . . with three strokes of a knife" (68). "[T]here's no flesh on his neck; his hands are red . . . her eye flashed back to her; but in her heart she felt, all the same, he is in love" (67). And while Clarissa's hatred for Doris Kilman makes her feel "scraped, hurt in her spine" (17), she shields herself by thinking that it is not Doris Kilman that she hates but "the idea of her, which undoubtedly had gathered in to itself a great deal that was not Miss Kilman" (16). Clarissa perceives her hatred for Doris Kilman as an alien presence, a "monster grubbing at the roots." "It rasped her . . . to have stirring about in her this brutal monster! to hear twigs cracking and feel hooves planted down in the depths of that leaf-encumbered forest, the soul; never to be content quite, or quite secure, for at any moment the brute would be stirring. . . ." Clarissa protects herself from her anger through denial. "Nonsense," she says to her perception that the "whole panoply of content" is "nothing but self love! this hatred!" (17).

One of the destroyer figures inhabiting Clarissa's world, Doris Kilman is a woman who attempts to convert others to her way of thinking. She is a person, Clarissa feels, who would destroy "the privacy of the soul" (192). While Clarissa's aversion to Kilman derives, in part, from her detestation of soul-violators and from her anxiety about being intruded upon, it also has deeper, less obvious, roots. For in Doris Kilman, Clarissa unknowingly confronts hated aspects of her own sequestered self.

A character who "completes" Clarissa, Doris Kilman is physically unattractive. "Heavy, ugly, commonplace" (190), Kilman is inflicted with an "unlovable body which people could not bear to see" (195). She, like Clarissa, suffers from feelings of personal inadequacy and is essentially isolated from others. In her intense desire to possess Clarissa's daughter, Elizabeth—to "make her hers absolutely and forever and then die" (200)—Kilman acts out the concealed dramas of Clarissa's early and remembered relationship with Sally Seaton (see Moon 279–81; also Abel 183). In Kilman's violent response to Elizabeth's desertion—Miss Kilman is "stricken once, twice, thrice by shocks of suffering" (201)—we find a replication of Clarissa's primitive fear of abandonment. In Kilman's desire to dominate and assimilate others to her viewpoint, we find an exaggeration of Clarissa's desire to impose herself on others. Impressing Clarissa with her "largeness, robustness, and power" (203), Kilman is an avatar of the archaic, grandiose self. Her greedy eating, which we are meant to find disgusting and which one critic describes as "utterly and surrealistically repellent" (Rose 149), is a signifier of her devouring neediness. "Ah, how she hated her—hot, hypocritical, corrupt; with all that power . . . ," Clarissa thinks, finding something "satisfying" and "real" in her hatred of Kilman (265).

Following the text's promptings, critics, similarly, have denounced Doris Kilman. She has been found "repulsive" (Rose 147), has been condemned for her "monstrous egotism" (Transue 104), and typecast as a "spiritual vampire" (Fleishman 82). Observing that the "violence" of Clarissa's reaction to Kilman is "endorsed" by Woolf, T. E. Apter comments that "the presentation of Miss Kilman contains an anger which seems to enclose the character, so that one never gets beyond the spectre she represents" (66). Because Kilman "has the hatefulness of a 'loser,'" writes Apter, Woolf has "an unfair advantage in presenting her faults" (67). Doris Kilman's "overmastering desire to overcome" Clarissa, "to unmask her" (189), is acted out by Woolf who, in probing Kilman's consciousness, in splitting her off and rendering her harmless in the narrative, unmasks and masters her.

Similarly, Sir William Bradshaw, who forces the souls of his victims, is unmasked, his soul forced by the author. While advocating "proportion," Bradshaw, we are told, secretly worships conversion, the goddess who "feasts on the wills of the weakly, loving to impress, to impose, adoring her own features stamped on the face of the populace" (150–51). "Naked, defenceless, the exhausted, the friendless received the impress of Sir William's will. He swooped; he devoured. He shut people up" (154). Bradshaw, like Kilman, is "one of those spectres" Clarissa "battles in the night," a spectre that sucks up half her "life-blood" (16–17). And he, like Kilman, is a character who "completes" Clarissa, representing split-off aspects of Clarissa's personality in his desire "to impress, to impose."

The invective behind the verbal portrait of Bradshaw has not escaped critical attention. Indeed it has often been remarked that the extended essay on Conversion and Proportion is "an unusual passage, so conspicuous for its savage indignation that it disrupts the texture of the novel" (Rose 134–35). And yet most critics have failed to recognize the obvious: that, as Beverly Schlack aptly observes, Woolf commits "the same soul-murder on Bradshaw that she charges he committed on Septimus" (55). In the view of Jane Novak this "satiric tirade" serves to relieve "the *reader's own indignation* against the insensitive treatment of Septimus Smith" (125, emphasis added). Echoing Woolf's anger, critics have characterized Bradshaw as a "death-dealing patriarchal man" (Transue 96) and an "arch bully" (Rosenthal 95) and have accused him of "spiritual cannibalism" (Kelley 91). Woolf has inspired reader after reader to feel her rage against what she perceived as coercive social forces and to ignore the fact that she, in her angry attack, repeats what she condemns. An unacknowledged project of this text is to divest the "dominators and tyrants" (17) of their authority and to reallocate that authority in the text's authorial presence.

Enticed to respond favorably to the author's diatribe against

Sir William Bradshaw, reader after reader likewise has been coaxed to foreground the poetic raptures of Septimus Smith's mad ravings and to submerge awareness of his angry depths. In the view of Michael Rosenthal, Septimus Smith, despite his "aberrant" behavior, "retains a kind of inner purity which makes society and its official guardians of mental and moral stability, like Holmes and Bradshaw, seem far more deranged than he" (91). For Avrom Fleishman, Septimus "represents a potential force for revitalization" (90). Suzette Henke sees him as a "visionary madman" with a "messianic mission" (140). For Alice Kelley, he stands for "total vision." Septimus's fantasies, in her view, "carry with them the meaning of vision" which Woolf wishes to present in her novels, a "vision that reveals the unity of man and world" (98–99). Madness, in Barbara Rigney's Laingian rendering of the text, "becomes a kind of refuge for the self rather than its loss" (52), for madness is conceived as "essentially creative rather than destructive" (56). In the novel, Rigney claims, "the psychotic personality is apotheosized" (62). Romanticizing and idealizing Septimus's madness, critics like Alice Kelley focus solely on Septimus's "revelations of universal love and unity" (107) and ignore his manifest loathing for physical life and the disintegrating depths of his anger. Such critical misappraisals and omissions, as we shall see, mirror the author's defensive evasiveness.

In Septimus Smith, the character Virginia Woolf publicly identified as Clarissa's double, the narcissistic anxieties underscoring the novel are given vivid fictional immediacy. Like Clarissa, Septimus suffers from a poor self-image but in him the experience of low self-esteem assumes paranoid, delusional proportions. He feels that others look at him, point at him (21), that he is "a piece of bone" (23), that is he "pocked and marked with vice" (137), and he hallucinates faces "laughing at him, calling him horrible disgusting names" (100). Like Clarissa, Septimus feels detached from others, but while Clarissa can be cold and hard, Septimus suffers from the terrifying perception that he cannot feel at all. In an attempt to stave off feelings of self-unreality and impending fragmentation, he marries Lucrezia, finding her empathic responsiveness a temporary refuge against his radical isolation from other people. Like Clarissa, Septimus fears being abandoned. When Lucrezia initially does not understand his aversion to Dr. Holmes, he feels "alone, condemned, deserted": an "outcast . . . who lay, like a drowned sailor, on the shore of the world" (140). Like Clarissa, Septimus is afraid of having his fragile self encroached upon, this fear expressed in his extreme reaction to Holmes and Bradshaw. Clarissa's transient experiences of merger, self-dispersal, and disintegration anxiety are Septimus's permanent, psychotic nightmare. In a fantasy that captures the global fusion of primal narcissism, he imagines that he is merged with the landscape: "leaves were alive; trees were alive. And the leaves being connected by millions of fibres with his own body, there on the seat, fanned it up and down; when the branch stretched he, too, made that statement" (32). His experience of self-dispersal is agonizingly intense. "His body was macerated until only the nerve fibres were left. It was spread like a veil upon a rock" (102–03). Recurrently, Septimus has the frightening sensation that he is falling—he fantasies himself falling into flames and into the sea—this falling sensation giving experiential immediacy to his fearful experience of self-dissolution. While we sometimes are positioned outside Septimus's experience—for example, we view him through the eyes of his wife and his doctors—we also share his perceptions. Repeatedly immersed in Septimus's subjectivity, we become palpably aware of his narcissistic terrors. Despite the fact that Woolf defensively poetizes Septimus's madness, we come to recognize, as one critic observes, that "[t]o remain immersed in such a consciousness is . . . to drown" (Harper 127).

In his madness, Septimus perceives himself as omnipotent and omniscient: he is the "lord of men" (101) who knows "everything," the "meaning of the world" (100). Behind the beauty of the world, he perceives something frightening and repulsive. "How Shakespeare loathed humanity—the putting on of clothes, the getting of children, the sordidity of the mouth and the belly! This was now revealed to Septimus; the message hidden in the beauty of words. The secret signal which one generation passes, under disguise, to the next is loathing, hatred, despair" (133–34). Plunging into a totally alien, nonhuman world, Septimus envisions a dog turning into a man (102) and men as beasts, as "lustful animals, who have no lasting emotions, but only whims and vanities. . . . They hunt in packs. Their packs scour the desert and vanish screaming into the wilderness" (135). The "repulsive brute, with the blood-red nostrils" (139) which Septimus fears above all else is a compressed image of unempathic others—Holmes and Bradshaw—and of his own archaic wrath. Septimus's mad visions are marked with rage.

A god, a victim, a fugitive, a criminal, Septimus exists in a world of "eternal suffering . . . eternal loneliness" (37). He is "alone forever" and "exposed" (220). When he flings himself "vigorously, violently" onto the area railings (226) and is impaled like a martyr, his self is broken beyond repair. Insistently refusing to acknowledge the full horror of Septimus's plight, the author, instead, heroizes his death and maneuvers the reader, like Lucrezia, to see and understand (226–27). What Lucrezia understands and what we, the readers, are urged to understand, is amplified in Clarissa's reaction to Septimus's suicide. We are prompted to interpret Septimus's suicide as an act of defiance and thwarted heroism. Like Clarissa, we are urged to become connected to Septimus through this, his act of total rupture, his ultimate expression of his total disconnection. Septimus's suicide is transformed into a gesture of self-preservation and self-rescue.

"Why seek pinnacles and stand drenched in fire?" Clarissa asks herself at the outset of her party. "Might it consume her anyhow! Burn her to cinders!" (255). Though surrounded by people, though riding the wave of her social success, Clarissa feels unreal, empty, that "these semblances, these triumphs" are somehow hollow (265). "She had schemed; she had pilfered. She was never wholly admirable. She had wanted success" (282), Clarissa admits to herself after hearing of Septimus's suicide. "A thing there was that mattered; a thing, wreathed about with chatter, defaced, obscured in her own life, let drop every day in corruption, lies, chatter. This he had preserved" (280). Confronting her narcissistic anxieties, Clarissa recognizes her own "terror," her sense of "overwhelming incapacity" in the face of life, her sense of "awful fear" (281). In her empathic response to Septimus Smith's suicide Clarissa experiences, by proxy, her own self-dissolution. "Always her body went through it first . . . her dress flamed, her body burnt. He had thrown himself from a window. Up had flashed the ground; through him, blundering, bruising, went the rusty spikes" (280). "Death," Clarissa feels, is "defiance," an "attempt to communicate," to reach the elusive centre. "[R]apture faded, one was alone. There was an embrace in death" (280–81).

In Clarissa's and the narrator's consciousness, Septimus's agonizing narcissistic terror, despair, and self-lacerating rage are warded off. "She felt glad that he had done it; thrown it away. . . . He made her feel the beauty; made her feel the fun. But she must go back. She must assemble" (283–84). Similarly, many readers, guided by the text, read Septimus's death positively: as a "desperate act of affirmation" (Shields 85), as a way of preserving "his autonomy, his idealism, and his spiritual freedom" (Henke 143), as a "restorative act" (Fleishman 93), and as "the ultimate union" (Naremore 107). In Woolf's original conception of the novel, Clarissa was to have died at the end. Septimus dies in her place. The "message" Septimus finds "hidden in the beauty of words" is "loathing, hatred, despair" (134). Clarissa's misrecognition of his message—his death makes her feel the beauty and fun of life—mirrors the text's evasion of its own subversive negativity. Septimus's broken self is apotheosized, his apprehension of the sordidity of life avoided in the final summation of his act—that he died to preserve the "treasure" of the inviolate self (281). At one and the same time, Septimus's menacing, destabilizing presence is purged from the text and his broken self is symbolically repaired, reassembled by the connecting powers of the narrating consciousness, the interpreting, artistic imagination.

The novel's closing scene, as it denies the dreadful reality of the threatened, isolated self, also acts out Woolf's intention to "bring . . . other characters" to Clarissa's "support" (*Diary* 2: 272). Woolf also brings her readers to Clarissa's support. Perceiving Clarissa through Peter Walsh's consciousness, we are directed to admire her, to recognize her potent magic, her hidden grandiosity:

> What is this terror? what is this ecstasy? he thought to himself.
> What is it that fills me with extraordinary excitement?
> It is Clarissa, he said.
> For there she was. (296)

As the final words in the novel and the author's final interpretive act, these words are compelling, celebratory. But given the pulsating rhythms of the novel, with its movement from self-cohesion to self-dispersal, from ecstasy to blank horror, this final moment of rapture signifies not a permanent reconstitution and affirmation of the self but a fleeting moment of being. For what subtends this framed and staged moment are the narcissistic anxieties so poignantly dramatized in the text. Behind Clarissa's potent presence lies an inner void, the "emptiness about the heart of life" which she perceives at the center of her self-experience. The closure is imposed. It does not resolve the incipient sense of threat to Clarissa's self conveyed in the novel's multiple forewarnings of her death. Instead it displaces and acts out that threat on a substitute figure, Septimus Smith, the author's fictional projection and scapegoat.[1]

Creating characters who share thoughts and fantasies, the narrating-artist dissolves clear-cut boundaries between them. "Nothing exists outside us except a state of mind . . . ," says the narrating consciousness at the outset of Peter Walsh's vision of the solitary traveler (85). This is more than metaphysical speculation. It also points to the solipsistic nature of this text in which the characters exist solely in the hall-of-mirrors world of the artist's subjectivity. The narcissistic anxieties concerning self-fragmenting merger, isolation, and rage that permeate the novel find their most intense expression in the character of Septimus Smith, the madman who interprets "with effort, with agony, to mankind" (103) on his scraps of paper and who stands as the unacknowledged double of the artist. Septimus's disconnected messages are an inversion of the artist's self-conscious, carefully wrought art of interconnection. His apotheosis in death and his containment in art enact the central psychological impulse behind the novel: the artistic repair of the broken self. But for Woolf, artistic construction, though potent, does not have any real sense of permanency. The broken self of the artist, symbolically reassembled in the work of art, constantly exists under threat of self-dispersal.

Through her prose style and narrative voice, Woolf verbally transmits her search for connection and wholeness. One critic writes that in the description of Clarissa Dalloway on Bond Street, the "liquidity and flow" of Woolf's prose, as "image melts into image, combining, not separating," suggest "union and fusion" (Gillen 485–86). Another critic writes that the "watery world, where identity is muted and the self seems to blend with the outside . . . this world *is* Virginia Woolf's style" (Naremore 111). Yet another comments that "the narrative voice is an expansive voice, a voice which dominates the novel and avoids the limitations of the individual characters at the same time that it incorporates those characters into its design" (Frye 44). But whereas Woolf's text is highly designed, the reader experiences its fictional world as unfixed, unstable, finding in it "not stable meaning but meaningful and coherent instability . . ." (Frye 55–56). To become absorbed in the text's strange fluctuation of moods and perceptions is to temporarily experience the instability of the narcissistically threatened self. Suicide, madness, isolation, and a radical sense of disconnection—Woolf at once makes these the subject of her novel as she verbally enacts an urgent need for interconnection and cohesion. The rich prose poetry of this text serves both to re-create the central merger fantasy it inscribes and to efface the terror and rage at its core by blunting and muting the dreadful "message" concealed in the "beauty of words."

In the skywriting episode that begins the novel, we find a covert staging of the writing and reading processes. Like a grandiose, omnipotent writer, the airplane inscribes its message across the sky, compelling the attention of the onlookers. As the letters blur and fade, another word—perhaps the same, indecipherable word—expands across the sky. The overlaid words are evanescent, their meaning forever effaced as the letters fade and dissolve. Breathtaking but forever on the verge of dispersal, the writer's message stands as a metaphor for the empty, dissolving self.

J. Hillis Miller writes that although the characters are unaware of the novel's "narrating presence, they are at every moment possessed and known, in a sense violated, by an invisible mind, a mind more powerful than their own" (178). While aware of the novel's narrating presence, most critic/readers have not recognized the extent to which Woolf attempts to assimilate her reading audience to her point of view, urging reader after reader to deemphasize the novel's manifest negativity and poetize its embedded themes: disintegration anxiety, madness, and suicide. Communicating her vision, Woolf entices her reader to affirm her central character, Clarissa Dalloway, and also to respond sympathetically to Septimus, whose madness is modeled after Woolf's own mental breakdowns. In apotheosizing and imaginatively killing off her mad fictional projection, Woolf acts out her defensive need to shield herself from the fearful spectres of madness, rage, and suicide. Writing an essay about herself in *Mrs. Dalloway*, Woolf solicits her reader's approval as she publicly exposes her deepest anxieties about her own unstable self. Warding off Septimus's negativity, she symbolically rehabilitates her self in the potent, magical figure of Clarissa, who becomes the ultimate focus of the reader's empathic attention.

In *Mrs. Dalloway* Woolf creates a complicated, layered text as she thrusts us into the solipsistic world of the narcissistic character.

Conveying to us Clarissa's sense that it is "very, very dangerous to live even one day" and her tragic perception of the "emptiness about the heart of life," Woolf coaxes us to come to the aid of her character. As we, through our critical art, attempt to compose Clarissa into "one woman," we fill the void that exists at the center of her self. Critic-rescuers, we enact a negotiated role as we "complete" Clarissa, acknowledge her hidden grandiosity, and empathically confirm her troubled self.

✤ ✤ ✤ ✤

Nine

Comic Storytelling as Escape and Narcissistic Self-Expression in Atwood's *Lady Oracle*

✤ ✤ ✤ ✤

A novel that provides a fitting conclusion to our study of the narcissistic character, Margaret Atwood's *Lady Oracle* has tantalized, amused, and baffled critics who are fascinated with its duplicitous, protean narrator-heroine. "The task of fitting the pieces of the puzzle together, the puzzle of Joan Foster," writes one critic, "is left to the reader" (MacLean 187). As Joan narrates the story of her life and exposes her narcissistic anxieties, hurts, and rage, she is undeniably funny. But even while we laugh at her comic descriptions of her mother-dominated childhood, her childhood obesity, her recurring fat lady fantasies, and her troubled relationships with men, we are aware that her comedic voice "covers a prolonged scream of pain" (Smith 144). Like the opera singer, Joan wants to "stand up there in front of everyone and shriek as loud" as possible "about hatred and love and rage and despair," to "scream at the top" of her lungs "and have it come out music" (83). The kind of storyteller we've encountered before, Joan wants to seduce her listeners, compel their attention. Creating a character who amuses and disarms, keeping reader attention riveted on Joan, Atwood enjoins us to become accomplices, an appreciative audience for Joan's secret but nevertheless exhibitionistic exploits. Urging us into a pact with her storyteller-heroine, Atwood takes us into a comic version of a world we've come to know well in the course of this study: the solipsistic, hall-of-mirrors world of the narcissistic character.

A text replete with messages and clues for the psychoanalytic inquirer, *Lady Oracle* focuses attention on a troubled mother-daughter relationship. The preestablished plot Joan acts out finds its source in her mother-controlled and tormented childhood, a world in which the "huge but ill-defined figure" of her mother blocks "the foreground" (134) while her father is essentially an "absence" (73). An autobiographer, Joan tells the story of her childhood in an attempt to understand and thus master her memories of the corrosive emotional hurts of her past and also to verbally retaliate against her mother. Cast in the role of sympathetic listener, the reader is encouraged to take Joan's side in the mother-daughter conflict. Part of the text's agenda is to use comic accusation to expose and undercut the lethal powers of the unempathic, and hence dangerous, mother figure.

Her mother is "the manager, the creator, the agent," and she "the product," says Joan as she reconstructs her childhood relationship with her mother (70). Motherly "concern" in Joan's childhood is equated with "pain" (121), her mother's anger barely camouflaged by her public pose as the concerned mother. "On her hands, in her hair," these are the metaphors Joan's mother uses to describe her, even though she "seldom" touches her (95). Unconsciously, her mother conspires to deny Joan's healthy childhood assertiveness and curtail her development of feelings of self-worth and authenticity. She wants Joan to "change into someone else" (56), continually berates and finds fault with her, and always tries to teach her "some lesson or other" (85). When Joan becomes an overweight child, she becomes a "reproach" to her mother, the "embodiment" of her mother's "failure and depression, a huge edgeless cloud of inchoate matter which refused to be shaped into anything" for which her mother "could get a prize" (71). Joan's dreams depict her childhood anxieties about her self-absorbed, nonresponsive, and angry mother. In one dream, she envisions herself struggling on a collapsing bridge; as she falls into a ravine, her nearby mother remains oblivious of the fact that "anything unusual" is happening (68). In another dream, Joan's memory of her mother putting on make-up in front of her three-sided mirror surfaces as a nightmare in which her mother metamorphoses into a three-headed monster and only Joan is aware of her "secret" monstrousness (70). And in her most terrifying dream, Joan, overhearing voices talking about her and realizing that "something very bad" is about to happen, feels utterly "helpless" (239). The persecutory fears that Joan fictionalizes in her Gothic novels and that plague her as an adult in her dreams and real life—like her Gothic heroines, she feels vulnerable, exposed, haunted and hunted down by malevolent, spectral pursuers—find their source in her crippling childhood encounters with her mother. With her childhood contemporaries, her companion Brownies who take special delight in persecuting her since she makes such a good victim and cries so readily, she repeats her troubled relationship with her mother. Later, when she meets Marlene, one of her childhood tormentors, these painful memories erupt. "Like a virus meeting an exhausted throat, my dormant past burst into rank life. . . . I was trapped again in the nightmare of my childhood, where I ran eternally after the others, the oblivious or scornful ones, hands outstretched, begging for a word of praise" (255). What Joan attempts to elicit from others is the confirming attention she never received in childhood. Like Atwood, who plays the "good mother" to Joan by making her the focal point of attention, the reader is encouraged to enact the "good mother" role by becoming an appreciative audience for Joan's comic misadventures. Divulging to us her character's needs and hurts, positioning us as confidants, Atwood invites our active listening and empathic interest.

Joan's early pursuit of audience recognition is dramatized in her childhood experiences as an overweight, would-be ballet dancer. Exposing herself to control her fear of exposure, laughing at herself to disarm those who would laugh at her, Joan describes her childhood fascination with ballet dancers. "I idealized ballet dancers . . . ," she recalls, "and I used to press my short piggy nose up against jewelry store windows and goggle at the china music-box figurines of shiny ladies in brittle pink skirts, with roses on their hard ceramic heads, and imagine myself leaping through the air . . . my hair full of rhinestones and glittering like hope" (44). Enrolled in Miss Flegg's dancing school, Joan eagerly awaits the recital performance of the "Butterfly Frolic," which is her "favorite" dance and which features her favorite costume: a short pink skirt, a headpiece with insect antennae, and a pair of cellophane wings. In her outfit, as she later reconstructs this incident, she looks "grotesque": "with my jiggly thighs and the bulges of fat where breasts would later be and my plump upper arms and floppy waist, I must have looked obscene, senile almost, indecent . . ." (47). Provoked to laugh as Joan makes wisecrack after wisecrack about her weight, Atwood forces us to confront, even as we laugh at Joan's jokes about her obesity, our own—and the text's—latent cruelty.

After her embarrassed mother betrays her to Miss Flegg, Joan is given a new role in the dance: that of a mothball. Joan's "humiliation [is] disguised as a privilege" (51), for Miss Flegg tells her it is a special part that she has been selected to dance. "There were no steps to my dance, as I hadn't been taught any, so I made it up as I went along. . . . I threw myself into the part, it was a dance of rage and destruction, tears rolled down my cheeks behind the fur, the butterflies would die. . . . 'This isn't me,' I kept saying to myself, 'they're making me do it'; yet even though I was concealed in the teddy-bear suit . . . I felt naked and exposed, as if this ridiculous dance was the truth about me and everyone could see it" (51–52). Though thwarted in her desire to have wings, she does provoke both laughter and vigorous applause. Left alone, center stage, she is a special person, a grotesque clown.

At the time, she is filled with "rage, helplessness and [a] sense of betrayal," but she gradually comes to view this episode as "preposterous," most particularly when she thinks about telling others about it. "Instead of denouncing my mother's injustice, they would probably laugh at me. It's hard to feel undiluted sympathy for an overweight seven-year-old stuffed into a mothball suit and forced to dance; the image is simply too ludicrous" (53). While we are invited to laugh at this episode, we also are meant to feel sorry for Joan and disapprove of her mother's unempathic behavior. As one critic observes, "Joan swings back and forth between self-pity and self-mockery. She thinks of herself as a victim and the 'pity the unwanted child' tone is very strong, but she also sees and shows herself to be ridiculous as well as pathetic" (Thomas 165). Despite Joan's comic dismissal, this incident causes a deep narcissistic wound. It later resurfaces in her recurring fat lady fantasy and gives birth to her identity as the escape artist who fears exposure and thus compulsively assumes a series of identities, each identity becoming a new trap. And here we find the precursor of the writer who achieves narcissistic revenge via her art and the comedian who later learns how to disarmingly throw the cloak of humor over her rage to win the approval of others. This also points to one of the defensive strategies of the narrative: the use of humor to partially contain and diffuse the explosive anger that threatens to erupt from just beneath the surface of the text. "All that screaming with your mouth closed," Joan says, her depiction of an Italian fotoromanzo an apt depiction of her own inner life (206).

As Joan battles her hostile and intrusive mother during adolescence, she transforms herself into a grotesque monster. Insistently, the text draws attention to Joan's defective body. A physical statement, Joan's obesity is a visible signifier of her thwarted and angry grandiosity, her inner defectiveness and hollowness,[1] and her introjection of her mother's monstrousness. "Eat, eat, that's all you ever do," Joan recalls her mother saying. "You're disgusting, you really are, if I were you I'd be ashamed to show my face outside the house" (136). Using eating as a weapon, Joan eats "steadily, doggedly, stubbornly." "The war between myself and my mother was on in earnest; the disputed territory was my body," as she later analyzes it. "I swelled visibly, relentlessly, before her very eyes, I rose like dough, my body advanced inch by inch towards her across the dining-room table, in this at least I was undefeated" (73). Determined not to be "diminished, neutralized" by the nondescript clothes her mother wants her to wear, she chooses outfits of "a peculiar and offensive hideousness, violently colored, horizontally striped" (94). Her confidence undercut when she recognizes that others view her obesity as an "unfortunate handicap," she comes to derive a "morose pleasure" from her weight "only in relation" to her mother. In particular, she enjoys her ability to clutter up her mother's "gracious-hostess act" (78). Putting on her fashion shows "in reverse," she calls attention to herself by "clomping silently but very visibly" through the rooms where her mother sits. "[I]t was a display, I wanted her to see and recognize what little effect her nagging and pleas were having" (75). Eating to "defy" her mother, Joan also eats from "panic": "Sometimes I was afraid I wasn't really there, I was an accident; I'd heard her call me an accident. Did I want to become solid, solid as a stone so she wouldn't be able to get rid of me?" (82–83). Conflating her memory of herself as a fat ballerina and her fantasy of the fat lady in the freak show, she envisions herself as a fat lady in a pink ballerina costume walking the high wire, proceeding inch by inch across Canada, the initial jeers of the audience transforming into the roar of applause when she triumphantly completes her death-defying feat. Dramatizing Joan's need to exhibit her grandiose self and gain self-confirming attention, this fantasy also depicts her anxieties about her fragile self-stability, which is expressed as the fear of falling.

When Joan, left two thousand dollars by her Aunt Lou on condition that she lose one hundred pounds, goes on a diet, the mother-daughter battle enters a new phase. "Well, it's about time, but it's probably too late," her mother says at first. But when Joan begins to successfully shed her fat, her mother becomes progressively "distraught and uncertain," for as Joan grows thinner and thinner her mother loses control over her (135). "About the only explanation I could think of for this behavior of hers was that making me thin was her last available project. She'd finished all the houses, there was nothing left for her to do, and she had counted on me to last her forever" (136). After Joan has stripped away most of her protective covering of fat, her mother's "cutting remarks" (73) are finally literalized: she attacks Joan with a knife, this actual infliction of a narcissistic wound concretizing the verbal wounds Joan has suffered for years. Consequently, Joan leaves home, determined to sever her connection with her mother and to discard her past with all its "acute concealed misery" (103).

Discovering that she is the "right shape" but has "the wrong past," she determines "to get rid of it entirely" and create "a different" and "more agreeable one" for herself (157). Thus she begins her life-long habit of compulsive lying and storytelling, as she invents, first for her lover Paul and later for Arthur and her adoring public, a "more agreeable" personal history. Consciously, she attempts to divest herself of her past. But she remains haunted by it, and she constantly fears exposure. No matter what she achieves, she feels that she is an impostor, a fraud, and that others will uncover her persisting defectiveness. She is also unable to escape her mother's malevolent presence and her own buried rage. When Joan receives a telegram announcing her mother's death, she thinks it might be a trap, her mother's attempt to bring her "back within striking distance" (195). Subsequently, she imagines that she somehow has killed her mother for unconsciously she perceives her angry thoughts as lethal. Strategically "killed off" and banished from the text, the mother figure resurfaces in a potentially more dangerous form. Twice after her mother's death Joan hallucinates what she thinks is her mother's astral body. Married to Arthur, she remains a partial prisoner of her noxious past. "All this time," she recalls, "I carried my mother around my neck like a rotting albatross. I dreamed about her often, my three-headed mother, menacing and cold" (238). When she looks at herself in the mirror, she does not see what others see. Instead, she imagines the "outline" of her "former body" still surrounding her "like a mist, like a phantom moon, like the image of Dumbo the Flying Elephant superimposed on my own. I wanted to forget the past, but it refused to forget me; it waited for sleep, then cornered me" (239). That the narrative seemingly delivers Joan from her mother's noxious presence and from her own grotesque shape only to sabotage the rescue points to a drama which recurs in the text: the thwarted rescue.

In Joan's relationships with men, we find a repetition of this narrative pattern of thwarted rescues. Desiring magic transformations, wishing to escape from her past, Joan imagines that the men in her life are like the romantic figures populating her Gothic novels. When she meets Paul, the Polish count, and listens to his story, she thinks she has met "a liar as compulsive and romantic" as herself (165). Arthur, at first, seems a "melancholy fighter for almost-lost causes, idealistic and doomed, sort of like Lord Byron" (184). Similarly, the Royal Porcupine has "something Byronic about him" (283). But when the romance wears off and these men become "gray and multidimensional and complicated like everyone else" (300), the inevitable happens: Joan relives her past in her relationships with men.

Her husband, Arthur, for example, is an amalgam of her father's aloofness and her mother's disapproving behavior. Arthur faults Joan for being obtuse and disorganized, is in the habit of giving expositions on her failures, and, like her mother, is "full of plans" for her (235). Fearing that Arthur will find her unworthy, she protects her fragile self-esteem by keeping secret her childhood obesity and her identity as Louisa K. Delacourt, the writer of costume Gothics. Both Arthur and Paul, her first lover, seem bent on changing her, transforming her into their own likenesses. While Arthur enjoys her defeats in the kitchen—"[m]y failure was a performance and Arthur was the audience. His applause kept me going" (235)—she also comes to feel that no matter what she does Arthur is "bound to despise" her and that she can never be what he wants (275).

What Joan seeks from the men in her life is the mirroring attention she never got from her mother. "I'd polished them with my love," as she puts it, "and expected them to shine, brightly enough to return my own reflection, enhanced and sparkling" (315). But the men she loves are also objects of fear. She realizes that all the men she has been involved with have had "two selves" (325): her father, a doctor-savior and wartime killer; the man in the tweed coat, her childhood rescuer but also possibly the daffodil man, a pervert; Paul, an author of innocuous nurse novels and a man she suspects of having a secret sinister life; the Royal Porcupine, her fantasy lover and feared "homicidal maniac" (303); and Arthur, her loving husband and suspected madman, possibly the unknown tormentor sending her death threats. She splits men into dual identities: the apparently good man is a lurking menace, a hidden pervert, a secret killer. In the text's code, men are an embodiment of Joan's split good/bad mother and her own hidden energies and killing rage. What Arthur doesn't know about her, she tells us, is that behind her "compassionate smile" is "a set of tightly clenched teeth, and behind that a legion of voices, crying, *What about me? What about my own pain? When is it my turn?* But I'd learned to stifle these voices, to be calm and receptive" (100).

Perpetually trapped, Joan perpetually attempts to escape as she assumes a series of identities and becomes a writer of Gothic novels. "Escape literature," Paul tells Joan, "should be an escape for the writer as well as the reader" (173). While Joan uses her writing to escape her daily life, she also persistently dramatizes in her work her amorphous anxieties, her conflicted selfhood, and her need for self-rescue. For while her heroine is perpetually "in peril" and "on the run" (146), she is also, of course, always rescued. In her work-in-progress, *Stalked By Love*, Joan fictionalizes her contrasting selves. Charlotte represents her socially compliant, conventional female self, the role that she assumes with Paul and Arthur, while the possessive, angry, powerful Felicia embodies her camouflaged grandiosity. Publicly, Joan plays the role of Arthur's self-effacing, inept, always-apologizing wife; in secret, she becomes Louisa Delacourt, writer of Gothic novels. As time passes, Joan's desire for public acknowledgment grows. But she also fears that if she brings the two parts of her life together there will be "an explosion" (242). And in a sense there is.

In an episode designed to compel reader attention and provoke the critic's speculative gaze, Atwood describes Joan's discovery of her own "lethal energies" (242) when she experiments with automatic writing. Sitting in the dark in front of her triple mirror and staring at a candle, Joan, in a symbolic act of narcissistic introversion, imagines herself journeying into the world of the mirror. "There was the sense of going along a narrow passage that led downward," she recalls, "the certainty that if I could only turn the next corner or the next—for these journeys became longer—I would find the thing, the truth or word or person that was mine, that was waiting for me" (247). On the trail of an elusive stranger, she discovers, in the subterranean world of the unconscious, a woman unlike anybody she's "ever imagined," a woman who, she feels, has "nothing to do" with her. "[S]he lived under the earth somewhere, or inside something, a cave or a huge building. . . . She was enormously powerful, almost like a goddess, but it was an unhappy power" (248):

> She sits on the iron throne
> She is one and three
> The dark lady   the redgold lady
> the blank lady   oracle
> of blood, she who must be
> obeyed   forever.   (252)

Figured as the mother-goddess Demeter, Lady Oracle—who is potent and blank—is a composite of the internalized mother and Joan's grandiose, empty self. It is the Lady Oracle in Joan that compels her to endlessly construct herself, to create a series of fictional lives for herself, each new creation ultimately becoming a new trap, a new replication of her past. "There was always," she remarks, "that shadowy twin, thin when I was fat, fat when I was thin, myself in silvery negative, with dark teeth and shining white pupils glowing in the black sunlight of that other world" (274).

When Joan publishes her Lady Oracle poems and consequently becomes a cult figure, she achieves the recognition she has always craved. But this only serves to deepen the cracks in her fractured self. Again the narrative pattern of the thwarted rescue is repeated. Joan's celebrity self, which takes on a deadly energy of its own, seems alien.[2] "[I]t was as if someone with my name were out there in the real world, impersonating me . . . doing things for which I had to take the consequences: my dark twin, my fun-house-mirror reflection. She was taller than I was, more beautiful, more threatening. She wanted to kill me and take my place . . ." (279). At long last Joan acts out her archaic grandiosity only to feel unreal, that she is "hollow, a hoax, a delusion"

(280). In a new variation on her recurrent fat lady fantasy, she expresses her growing recognition of her subjective emptiness. Fantasying the fat lady floating up like a helium balloon, she realizes that the fat lady, despite her large size, is "very light" for she is "hollow." "*Why am I doing this? . . . Who's doing this to me?*" Joan asks herself (305). Unable to "turn off" her "out-of-control fantasies," she is forced to "watch them through to the end" (280). Although we find Joan's apparent lack of control unsettling, we also sense that as a storyteller she is perpetually playing up to her audience, embroidering her preposterous fantasies. "As the teller of a humorous tale," writes Sybil Vincent, "Joan gains a sense of power. She deliberately manipulates her audience and experiences a sense of control lacking in her actual life" (154–55). Situated as appreciative listeners and suspicious critics, we sense that one of the text's errands is to rivet reader attention on Joan and thus, as it were, to gratify her grandiose-exhibitionistic needs.

When all the convoluted plots of Joan's life converge—her current lover, the Royal Porcupine, wants her to marry him; Paul, her former lover, traces her and wants her back; a blackmailer hounds her; she imagines that Arthur is the persecutor sending her death threats— she determines to escape her life which has become "a snarl, a rat's nest of dangling threads and loose ends" (326). Accordingly, she fakes her death by drowning and lives, incognito she thinks, in Italy. In a symbolic gesture, she buries her clothes, attempting to shed her past identity. But what she can never escape is her inner sense of defectiveness. In one of her more lurid fantasies, she imagines her buried clothes growing a body, which shapes itself into "a creature composed of all the flesh that used to be mine and which must have gone somewhere." Transforming into a featureless monstrous form, it engulfs her. "It was the Fat Lady. She rose into the air and descended on me. . . . For a moment she hovered around me like ectoplasm, like a gelatin shell, my ghost, my angel; then she settled and I was absorbed into her. Within my former body, I gasped for air. Disguised, concealed. . . . Obliterated" (353). When Joan suspects that Mr. Vitroni may be in league with her secret pursuers, she fantasies herself spending the rest of her life "in a cage, as a fat whore, a captive Earth Mother for whom somebody else collected the admission tickets" (362). As her narcissistic anxieties become more and more ungovernable, not only do her Gothic fantasies intrude into her real life, her real life invades her art: Felicia metamorphoses into the bloated, drowned fat lady and is rejected by her husband, Redmond-Arthur.

As the narrative progresses and Atwood carries us deeper and deeper into Joan's fun-house, hall-of-mirrors world, a kind of infinite regression occurs as fantasy and reality coalesce and we gradually come to the realization that Joan's descriptions of others—those in her life and her art—are autorepresentational. Joan's final and terrifying dream encounter with the "dark vacuum" of her mother forces her to recognize that her mother is her own reflection. "She'd never really let go of me because I had never let her go. It had been she standing behind me in the mirror, she was the one who was waiting around each turn, her voice whispered the words. . . . [S]he had been my reflection too long" (363). In her Gothic novel, *Stalked by Love*, Joan's stand-in, Felicia, is compulsively drawn into the labyrinth's "central plot" (375). At the psychocenter of the novel, the "central plot" of the maze depicted in the inset Gothic text provides interpretive clues to the narrative plot of the text we are reading. For at the maze's center, Joan-Felicia encounters her mirror selves. There she finds the ubiquitous fat lady, her defective self; there she also finds an embodiment of her identity as Louisa Delacourt, the middle-aged writer of Gothic novels and her dual red-haired, green-eyed self: Joan, the self-effacing wife and Joan the powerful poet cult figure. And there behind a closed door which she imagines is her pathway to freedom, her escape from the trap of self-entanglement, she discovers yet another alter-ego, fictional self, Redmond, who transforms sequentially into the men in her life—her father, Paul, the Royal Porcupine, Arthur—and then into a death's skull. In the specular world of the maze, Joan encounters, recursively, images of self. As Redmond reaches out to grab her, she experiences, once again, the smothering, self-fragmenting dominance of her childhood mother who unconsciously sought to obliterate Joan's fledgling self.[3] Twice before—first during her Lady Oracle experiments with automatic writing and then in a terrifying nightmare in which she seemed about to be sucked into the "vortex" of her mother (363)—Joan approached this world of suffocating darkness, the self-annihilating world of the engulfing, destructive mother. Joan's faked drowning, in effect, is stage managed by her dead but potent mother, who remains a menacing presence in Joan's psyche. But Joan's faked death *is* faked. She is the escape artist who uses deception to appease her lethal, interiorized mother-self. Her faked suicide is a signifier of her desire to live, to rescue and repair her self.

To the Italian village women, the resurrected Joan becomes an object of fear. Joan imagines that they see her as a kind of science fiction creature, "[a] female monster, larger than life . . . striding down the hill, her hair standing on end with electrical force, volts of malevolent energy shooting from her fingers . . ." (370). The monster of her own narcissistic ire possesses her like an alien presence. In her anger, she resembles her mother. No wonder she is bent on escape, on comic diffusion of her deadly rage. In a comic denouement, Joan, fearing that her murderous pursuer is at the door, exposes her wrath when she attacks a reporter who has come to interview her. "I've begun to feel," she comments, "he's the only person who knows anything about me. Maybe because I've never hit anyone else with a bottle, so they never got to see that part of me" (379–80). As the novel ends, Joan determines to stop writing Gothic novels and to turn, instead, to science fiction, a process she has already begun in her comic, self-parodic depiction of herself as a science fiction monster.

The victim of repeated maternal denials of her self, Joan, as she repeatedly fabricates her life, constructs a series of fictional identities which she disposes of at will. Through this symbolic act of self-creation and self-annihilation, she replicates and replaces her mother and becomes the guarantor of her own identity. The victim of maternal betrayal and control, Joan becomes a dissembler who secretly betrays and controls others. When Joan describes herself as "essentially devious, with a patina of honesty" (328), readers may suspect that they, too, despite their privileged perspective, are being deceived. Again and again, critics have remarked on this. One critic comments that Joan's "absolute honesty in confessing her lies, tricks, and deceptions becomes, in itself, a confidence game which lulls the reader into a misguided trust in Joan's ability to interpret her experiences" (Freibert 25); another insists that readers "have more reason to suspect Joan than to believe her" (Grace 124); and yet another says that Atwood's novel leaves readers with "the vague suspicion" that they have been "duped" (MacLean 179). In their uneasy feeling that they are being gulled and manipulated, critic/readers repeat Joan's childhood and persisting experiences of being deceived and controlled by others, by her mother and the men in her life. Depicted as a confessed liar, Joan escapes reader control and stubbornly resists being made into a stable, literary property.

"Most said soonest mended" (133)—this garbled rendering of one of her Aunt Lou's trite sayings provides a central clue to the impulse behind Joan's autobiographical writing. Admitting, at one point, that she could never say the word "fat" aloud (230), Joan describes, in a vivid, comic-angry way, her childhood obesity and her persisting fat lady fantasies. Her self-exposure and self-condemnation repeat her mother's cutting remarks and also act as a form of verbal exorcism. Verbally striking back at the mother who verbally abused her as a child, Joan, as a wielder of words, fictively mothers and then obliterates the mother who attempted to annihilate her. In a similar vein, readers of *Lady Oracle* are urged to collude in the narrational plot to fictively "kill off" Joan's mother, who is represented in the text, in the words of one critic, "not as a woman, but as a fetish or witch-doll" (Thomas 166). Achieving verbal mastery over the men in her life who attempted to master her, Joan secretly attacks her perceived attackers and becomes a hidden menace to those who menace her. She acts this out in the novel's final scene when she assaults the reporter. When she consequently gives a bunch of wilted flowers to the hospitalized reporter as she plays nurse to him, she unconsciously signals her identification not only with the Mavis Quilp nurse heroines, but also with the daffodil man, an exhibitionist. Her artistry springs, in part, from her covert exhibitionism and rage, both expressed in her genesis as an artist—her mothball dance—and in her Lady Oracle manifestation.

In *Lady Oracle* autobiographical creation allows Joan to assert her grandiosity, vent her anger, and express her autonomy. Situated as a witness of Joan's conspiracy against others, the reader revels in her disguises and concocted plots and laughs at her descriptions of political activism, spiritualism, the publishing establishment, artistic creation, and faddish artists. Again and again Joan confesses her inability to control her overactive imagination, describing how her fantasies must play themselves out to their appointed ends. Indeed there are undertones of hysteria in her Gothic imaginings—her fears about being pursued in Italy—and in her fat lady fantasies, which progressively grow more and more ludicrous and elaborate. But just as Joan, as a Gothic storyteller, adroitly manipulates her audience, so she, as a comic character, compels our attention. At the outset of the novel, Joan, newly arrived in Italy, imagines all the people she has left behind. She envisions them grouped on the seashore talking to each other and ignoring her. But one thing the reader cannot do is ignore Joan. Atwood prompts us to give Joan the smiling attention that her mother never gave to her and that Arthur, who is subject to periodic depression—he gives off a "gray aura . . . like a halo in reverse," as she puts it (286)— gives her less and less frequently.

"I longed for happy endings," Joan remarks, "I needed the feeling of release when everything turned out right and I could scatter joy like rice all over my characters and dismiss them into bliss" (352). While some readers of *Lady Oracle* might share Joan's longing and wish to see a conclusive ending to her story and a final rescue, Atwood frustrates such a desire. "[T]here is no way for the reader to be certain that anything has changed by the end of Joan's narration," observes one critic (Grace 127). At the end "the reader suspects that there are more Joans to come," writes another (MacLean 195); the reader watches "in helpless recognition," writes yet another, as Joan assumes a new role at the novel's end (Rosowski 97). Thwarting our desire for happy endings, for artistic coherence, for neat foreclosures, for final rescues, Atwood creates a plot like her character: one that is entangled and full of loose ends.

Installed as appreciative listeners, collaborators, and accomplices, we revel in Joan's zany exploits, her proliferating mirror encounters and angry-comic rhetoric. Joan's confessions are designed to entertain us, to win our smiling approbation of her thwarted grandiosity. But we are also implicitly led to reflect on our own need to escape through and live vicariously in art and to ask ourselves whether we, like Joan the compulsive creator of plots, are compulsive readers of plots. We are also led to ask ourselves to what extent we read ourselves into a fictional text just as Joan writes herself into her art. Coaxed throughout the novel to see the parallels between Joan's fictional and real worlds, we are also urged to consider to what extent we blur fact and fantasy as we construct the plots and texts of our own lives.

"I might as well face it," Joan admits in the novel's conclusion, "I was an artist, an escape artist. . . . [T]he real romance of my life was that between Houdini and his ropes and locked trunk; entering the embrace of bondage, slithering out again" (367). So, too, she escapes our grasp as she multiplies before our eyes. As the realistic surface of her autobiographical account dissolves into a richly complex and redundant subjective fantasy, we gain momentary access to the shapeshifting world of the narcissist. Swerving out of our grasp, Joan lures us into a strange world in and beyond the looking glass: the multiple, mirrored, decertainized world of the narcissistic character.

❉ ❉ ❉ ❉

In Conclusion
Empathic Reading and the Critic/Reader

❉ ❉ ❉ ❉

Describing her difficulty in making sense of the discourse of her patient, Mrs. G., psychoanalyst Evelyne Schwaber comments: "It spoke to the feeling I had that I so often seemed to lose her, to how I had to grope and struggle to find my place in *her* experiential world, while yet trying to maintain my own self-reflective vigil . . ." ("Empathy" 164). In quoting from Schwaber's account of her analytic exchange with Mrs. G., I invoke here, as I did at the beginning of this study, the real world of the consulting room. What is central to the empathic mode of listening, as Schwaber indicates, is the analyst's ability both to step inside the patient's subjective world and to reflect on what he or she has heard and experienced. In a parallel sense, the critic/reader must both enter into and reflect on the experiential world proffered by the text.

To negotiate with a fictional work as a critic/reader is to assume different relations to the text and to occupy shifting positions. Again and again critics have characterized reading as a process of absorption and dispossession. "To some extent, we fuse with the literary work. In absorbing it, we become absorbed" (Holland, *Dynamics* 80). The text is described as an "enrapturing aesthetic object" (Krieger 17) and reading as an "aroused merging" (Hartman 50), as an experience of "fusion-illusion" in which the "reader's consciousness is completely filled by the work" being read (Bernheimer 10),[1] and as an act in which the reader's subjectivity is "on loan to another" who "thinks, feels, suffers, and acts within" the reader (Poulet 45). If to read is to feel temporarily merged with and carried away by a text, to criticize is to be "back in one's own mind," to act "upon the work rather than being acted upon" (Slatoff 377). Unlike the reader who "attempts to negate the space between the text and himself" and "strives for fusion with the text via internalization," the critic, distances, reifies, and appropriates (George Steiner 443).

"To be immersed," "to be distanced"—these descriptions of the reading and critical processes bear crucial similarities to accounts of the empathic event in psychoanalytic discourse. In the burgeoning literature on empathy, the empathic event is characterized variously: as temporary oneness followed by separateness, as thinking both with and about the patient, as the dynamic interaction between merging and separating pressures, as emotional contagion plus understanding (Jaffe 229–32; see also Lichtenberg, *Empathy*). What is common to such descriptions is the notion that empathy involves a transient or trial merger experience, a temporary relinquishing of the self/nonself boundary. In psychoanalytic discourse, the word "empathy," as Gail Reed observes, is used to suggest both a passive and an active process. The passive is associated with "resonating, sudden illumination, losing the self" and the active with "grasping meaning, understanding, and interpreting." The passive mode of empathy Reed tentatively represents "by the mythological figure of the perfectly attuned, resonating, responsive mother" and the active "by the mythological figure of the dispassionate, rational scientist of 'calibrated' ego." In clinical practice, according to Reed, "some combination of these modes is a necessary part of each analyst's work character" ("Antithetical Meaning" 16, 20). Similarly, the critic/reader uses a combination of these modes, becoming the temporarily immersed, passive reader but also the detached, active interpreter. "Although the critic is first a reader, absorbed in some way with a text, experiencing it unreflectively," as Murray Schwartz observes, "he is also (and may even simultaneously be) transforming that experience in the service of conscious interpretation. . . . [C]riticism is something *done* with reading, a mixture of reconstructive and constructive activity" ("Literary Use of Transference" 40–41).

Our situation as critic/readers, which resembles in significant ways that of psychoanalysts, is vastly complex. Like analysts in the analytic transaction (see Wolf, "Transferences and Countertransference" 585–87), we, in entering the world of the text, may undergo some controlled regression, a situation in which the self becomes more vulnerable and residual narcissistic needs can be activated. Like analysts who may transiently experience their patients as selfobjects, we may experience characters and texts as selfobjects, as self-extensions or props that allow us to fulfill our selfobject needs. We may, for example, temporarily bolster the self by identifying with idealized characters or we may find ourselves sustained by establishing twinship relationships with characters who seem like the self or with grandiose characters who seem to reflect back the desired greatness of the self. While Tragic Man and Woman generally frustrate such needs, they do involve us in a complicated transaction. Like analysts who, in placing themselves in their patients' intrapsychic reality, are "used and responded to as part of the context of that reality" (Schwaber, "Narcissism" 125), we are cast in a recipient/coparticipant role when we enter the sequestered space of the text. We are encouraged to become implicated in the self-dramas staged in texts and to respond to the characters' needs for confirmation, wholeness, and rescue. In an essential way, the meaning of a literary work, as we have observed in the course of this study, grows out of the empathic event that occurs between the critic/reader and the text. At once affective and cognitive, the empathic event involves a dynamic interplay between objective and subjective, conscious and unconscious, the verbalizable and the unverbalizable. One of the goals of empathic reading is to make us aware of the narcissistic dramas encoded in texts. Empathic reading also makes us aware of our affective and collusive involvements with literature, of the various negotiated roles we are invited to play as we respond to fictional characters, and of the ways in which we may act out our own self-dramas when we interpret literary works.

Optimally, critical interpretation is an empathic art and the space occupied by criticism is that which Murray Schwartz, borrowing a concept from D. W. Winnicott, calls the "potential space" of literature. This is "the area between objectivity and subjectivity . . . in which we are free to engage in active interplay between ourselves and the external world of persons and objects" ("Where Is Literature?" 763). In the "potential space" of literature and literary criticism we discover both the other and mirror reflections of our selves. As literary critics we are engaged in the same project Kohut conducted: the search for the self and for the nuclear essence of humanness. As empathic critic/readers we become absorbed and we observe, we become engrossed and we seek to understand the characters we meet in literary texts. And as empathic critic/readers we seek to inhabit and illuminate the world that both gives us pleasure and can make us anxious: the vast and inward "potential space" of the literary text, a strange, shapeshifting, and at times threatening hall-of-mirrors world inhabited by authors, characters, readers, and critics.

Literature, observes self psychologist Ernest Wolf, is a "created" selfobject whose "selfobject function can be universally shared and with which . . . humanly alive empathic resonances can be established" ("Concluding Statement" 504). In our transactions with literature, we experience that empathic "resonance of essential human alikeness," the "accepting, confirming, and understanding human echo evoked by the self" ("The Psychoanalyst" 713, 705) which Kohut considers so essential to our humanity. Indeed, what ultimately draws us to the fictional world of the text and underlies our relationship to the characters we encounter there is empathy, the resonant human echo to a shared experience.

✤ ✤ ✤ ✤

Notes

✤ ✤ ✤ ✤

1 / Kohut's Psychology of the Self, Empathy, and the Reading Process

1 There is an on-going discussion among analysts as to whether self psychology complements, encompasses, or supersedes Freudian drive theory. While Kohut described his theory as "complementary" to classical theory, in the view of Stephen Mitchell, Kohut's "principle of complementarity" seemed "less designed to integrate two compatible and mutually enriching perspectives, and more designed to preserve an older framework" that was "conceptually incompatible" with the new self-psychological model (181). Mitchell speculates that Kohut wanted to avoid "too abrupt a de-idealization" of the "original, idealized, but no longer fully adequate conceptual framework" in order to preserve the "cohesion" of the "psychoanalytic 'group self'" (182). According to Michael Basch, Kohut initially "believed he was making only a clinical contribution" to psychoanalysis and "only after years of further clinical work did he come to recognize and finally to accept that his findings necessitated postulation of a single theory of development organized around the maturation of the self that encompassed but transcended Freud's instinct theory" ("Selfobject Theory" 15). Melvin Bornstein observes that self psychology, which "started out to be an addition to existing psychoanalytic theory" and was later seen as offering a "sizable alteration in existing theory" but one to which "a complementary accommodation could be made," ultimately came to be regarded "by some as constituting a new general theory or at least an alternative theory to both ego psychology and object relations theory" (283).

173

And finally, John Gedo describes Kohut's self psychology as "the most powerful dissident movement on the contemporary psychoanalytic scene" (99). For further discussion of these issues see Lichtenberg and Kaplan 283–416 and Gedo 99–131. And for Kohut's conjectures on the narcissistic aspects of Freud's personality see *Restoration* 292–98 and *How?* 54.

2 In "self-state" dreams, "archaic self-states are presented in an undisguised (or only minimally disguised) form." Associations to such dreams "do not lead to unconscious hidden layers of the mind" but "at best" provide the analyst with "further imagery which remains on the same level as the manifest content of the dream." The "act of portraying" narcissistic fears and anxieties in such dreams "constitutes an attempt to deal with the psychological danger by covering frightening nameless processes with namable visual imagery" (*Restoration* 110, 109). Kohut provides some examples of self-state dreams in *Analysis* 4–5, 149. See also Goldberg, *Psychology*.

3 For more detailed discussions and illustrations of this phenomenon see the casebook *The Psychology of the Self*, edited by Goldberg, and Wolf and Wilson's "The 'Monday Crust' in the Disorders of the Self."

4 Kohut theorizes that changes in family patterns—such as the increased number of smaller families and the absence of both parents from the home—have led to a growing number of children whose empathic selfobject environment is far from optimal and thus who are at greater risk for developing the self-disorder (see, e.g., *Restoration* 269–78).

5 "The need for the life-sustaining psychological presence of self-objects, like the need for the life-sustaining physical presence of oxygen and other nutriments," writes Ernest Wolf, "remains throughout life, though the psychological self-objects can gradually be present at greater distances and can, with increasing maturity, be represented by symbols which substitute for the person whose presence was needed originally. For example, self-object constancy is reached when the child's capability for symbolic representation has achieved a point of solidity where the self-object's visual or auditory physical presence is no longer needed to maintain the functional psychologic presence of the self-object. By the time adulthood is attained, the symbolic yet functional presence of self-objects usually has been taken over by a multitude of partial self-objects, such as one's whole family, community, membership in various groups, etc. . . ." ("Transferences and Countertransferences" 584).

6 One of the basic tenets of the classical nineteenth-century science adhered to by Freud, Kohut comments, "was the clear distinction between observer and observed." Freud, in Kohut's words, "took the ultimate step that could still be taken by 'objective' science: he investigated the inner life of man, including—and especially—his own. But—and here lies the crucial issue—he gazed at man's inner life with the objectivity of an external observer, i.e., from

the viewpoint that the scientist of his day had perfected vis-à-vis man's external surroundings, in the biological sciences and, above all, in physics" (*Restoration* 67).

7   For an excellent discussion of and response to the criticisms currently being leveled against the empathic-introspective stance in psychoanalysis see Post and Miller 222–28 and 232–34. For a brief discussion of Freud's view on the analyst's use of empathy as a therapeutic tool see Wolf, "Empathy and Countertransference" 309–11. "A path leads," said Freud, "from identification by way of imitation to empathy, that is, to the comprehension of the mechanism by means of which we are enabled to take up any attitude at all towards another mental life" ("Group Psychology and the Analysis of the Ego" [1921], 110, n. 2; *Standard Edition* 18: 69–143). But while Freud thought empathy to be central to the analytic transaction, he made only passing references to the concept in his writing. Wolf provides some interesting speculations on why this is so.

8   Schwaber gives a number of clinical illustrations of this listening perspective in "Narcissism, Self Psychology" 119–24. For a frank discussion of the strains and difficulties of using empathic-immersion as a therapeutic technique see Post and Miller 233.

9   Ironically, Freud's actual clinical techniques, as has often been observed, would be deemed unorthodox by his disciples. Freud "conducted therapy," Janet Malcolm remarks, "as no classical Freudian analyst would conduct it today—as if it were an ordinary human interaction, in which the analyst could shout at the patient, praise him, argue with him, accept flowers from him on his birthday, lend him money, and even gossip with him about other patients" (37). In contrast, Freud, in his "Recommendations to Physicians Practicing Psycho-analysis" (1912; *Standard Edition* 12: 111–20), likens the psychoanalyst to the surgeon "who puts aside all his feelings, even his human sympathy, and concentrates his mental forces on the single aim of performing the operation as skilfully as possible" (115). The analyst, Freud metaphorically states, "should be opaque to his patients and, like a mirror, should show them nothing but what is shown to him" (118).

10   For some surveys of the literature on countertransference, see Kernberg 49–67, McLaughlin 644–53, and Epstein and Feiner. As Epstein and Feiner point out in their historical survey of countertransference, the "two thematic strands—countertransference as a hindrance, and the doctor's use of his own unconscious to understand the patient" (1)—find their source in Freud's writings. But until the late 1940s and early 1950s the "prevailing classical view" held that countertransference "was simply a hindrance to effective psychoanalytic work" (1). These authors also observe that there has been a reawakening of interest in countertransference "following the period of

dormancy from the 1950s to the 1970s" (17). As analysts have become aware
that their "more intense countertransference reactions are usually generated by
the more severely disturbed type of patient," countertransference has come to
be viewed "as a normal, natural interpersonal event, rather than as an idiosyncratic pathological phenomenon. This has facilitated the shift from viewing
countertransference reactions solely as a hindrance, to viewing them for their
potential value in understanding the patient and the therapeutic relationship . . ." (18–19).

11   "The reader of *The Turn of the Screw*," writes Felman, "can
choose either to *believe* the governess, and thus to behave like Mrs. Grose, or
not to believe the governess, and thus to behave precisely *like the governess*.
Since it is the governess who, within the text, plays the role of the suspicious
reader, occupies the *place* of the interpreter, to *suspect* that place and that
position is, thereby, *to take it*. To demystify the governess is only possible on
one condition: the condition of *repeating* the governess's very gesture" (190).

12   Clarifying what is meant by temporary or trial identification,
Michael Basch points out that the word "identification" is not used in the
"metapsychological sense, i.e., of a transmutation of character so as to become
like the other in some significant respect." Rather, the "identification that takes
place in an empathic encounter is not with the other person *per se*, but with
what he is experiencing. It is a matter of concluding that one's own affective
state duplicates that of the other, the presumed similarity permitting one to
identify one's own affective position as representative of the other's mental
state at a particular moment." In Basch's view, empathy, "the ability to put
oneself in the place of another, represents . . . the final potential transformation
of affective communication." "I would suggest," says Basch, "that our affective
life lends itself to being divided on the basis of progressive development into
states of affect, feeling, emotion, and empathic understanding" ("Empathic
Understanding" 105, 118–19, 116).

13   In Holland's identity-theme theory of reading, each reader as-
similates and enacts the text through his or her own idiosyncratic perceptive,
defensive, and affective modes of organization. The "overarching principle"
involved in reading, according to Holland, "is: identity recreates itself. . . . That
is, all of us, as we read, use the literary work to symbolize and finally to
replicate ourselves" ("Unity" 124; see also 5 *Readers Reading*). For Holland, as
Wendy Deutelbaum accurately observes, "the text is seen either as a receptacle,
a lack, or [as] a mere materiality, with no meaning or unity until the reader's
active subjectivity fills it up . . ." (98).

Describing his own identity theme, Holland comments on how his
"passionate desire to know about the insides of things" is in conflict with "an
equally strong feeling that one is, finally, safer on the outside." "My identity

theme," writes Holland, "[has] to do with preserving a sense of self and securing self-esteem by gaining power over relations between things, in particular, mastering them by knowing or seeing them from outside rather than being actually in the relationships" ("Literary Interpretation" 232–33). For an interesting reaction to Holland's identity theme statement, see Nelson, "Psychology of Criticism" 52–54.

14 David Bleich, describing how he taught his students to record "response statements," comments that "[r]ecording a response requires the relaxation of cultivated analytical habits, especially the habit of automatic objectification of the work of literature. When this is done, we become aware of what we know happens anyway—an affective evaluation that accompanies perception. Normally, the act of objectification inhibits awareness of response in the service of continuing to read" (147). Readers' responses, Bleich also observes, are "negotiable into knowledge": in a "pedagogical community, response statements vary in character according to how each reader considers himself a member of that community" (168).

2 / Narcissistic Vulnerability and Rage

1 It is speculated that *Notes*, which uses insult as a mode, had its origins in Dostoevsky's reaction to what he perceived as an insult. One of the impulses behind the novel may have been Dostoevsky's desire to pay back Nicoli Chernyshevsky—author of *What Is To Be Done?*, the utopian novel *Notes* actively mocks—after Chernyshevsky turned against him (see, e.g., Weisberg 559, n. 22).

2 The psychological critics were among the first to focus particular attention on the Underground Man's character and to recognize the compulsive aspects of his behavior. For Barbara Smalley, the Underground Man acts out, "[t]o a marked degree," the "patterns of a paranoid personality" (390). Michael Sperber, using the theories of Otto Kernberg, labels the anti-hero as a borderline personality. Bernard Paris, in a Horneyan analysis, describes him as a "withdrawn man," a neurotic who protects himself through detachment. And for Richard Weisberg, the Underground Man acts out his deeply rooted sense of *ressentiment*, his sense of unresolved insult. "The '*ressentient*' man," writes Weisberg, "lives through, again and again, the event which has rendered him bitter and revealed his impotence, [and] re-senses and re-intellectualizes it to the point of creating a false ethic from it" (555).

3 / Insect Transformation as a Narcissistic Metaphor

1 For an overview of the critical response to *The Metamorphosis* up to 1972 see Stanley Corngold's critical bibliography—*The Commentators'*

Despair—which includes the work of American, English, Spanish, French, German, and Italian critics.

2 The Samson allusion has been noted, for example, by Norman Holland (148–49) and Jean Jofen (349). In a conversation with Kafka, Gustav Janouch commented that the name Samsa sounded "like a cryptogram for Kafka. Five letters in each word. The S in the word Samsa has the same position as the K in the word Kafka. The A. . . ." To this, Kafka replied: "It is not a cryptogram. Samsa is not merely Kafka, and nothing else" (32).

3 Gregor's hiding under the couch recalls the behavior of one of the infants observed by Margaret Mahler and her collaborators. "[W]hen in distress," writes Mahler, "she would lie flat against the surface of the floor, or on the mattress on the floor, or would squeeze herself into a narrow space; it was as if she wanted to be enclosed (held together) in this way, which would afford her some of the sense of coherence and security that she was missing in the relationship with her mother" (94).

4 Essentially a family story, *The Metamorphosis* reflects, as many critics have noted, aspects of Kafka's life: his submissive relationship to his father, his alienation from his mother, his hidden anger and resentment, his hypochondria, depression, feelings of worthlessness, powerlessness, physical imperfection, loneliness, and isolation. Although most discussions of the biographical elements of *The Metamorphosis* focus on Kafka's relationship to his insensitive, domineering father, which is well documented in Kafka's *Letter to His Father*, Margarete Mitscherlich-Nielsen, in her "Psychoanalytic Notes" on Kafka, offers an interesting speculation on his early relationship with his mother, pointing to a disturbance in the early mother-child relationship. "The early death of his [Kafka's] brothers and his mother's reaction to their loss— probably warding off emotion on the surface but deeply depressed beneath—," she writes, "must have had a profound effect on Kafka . . ." (5). Equally suggestive are recent discussions of Kafka's narcissistic relationships with Milena (see Böhme) and Felice (see Bernheimer 152–61).

Kafka, in the words of biographer Ronald Hayman, used writing to "give him the illusion of inching his way towards his objective of being understood, of bringing the reader to know him as well as he knew himself" (198). In *The Metamorphosis*, Hayman comments, Kafka allegorized "his relationship with the family, building out from his sense of being a disappointment, a burden" (151). That Kafka was thinking of his own family situation when he wrote *The Metamorphosis* is revealed in the few recorded comments he made about the story. After its publication, he remarked to an acquaintance, "What do you have to say about the dreadful things happening in our house?" (Urzidil 18). In a conversation with Gustav Janouch, he described the story as an "indiscretion." "Is it perhaps delicate and discreet," he asked, "to talk about the bugs in one's own family?" When Janouch described the story as "a terrible dream, a terrible conception," Kafka responded, "The dream reveals the reality, which conception lags behind. That is the horror of life—the terror of art" (Janouch 32).

5 / Storytelling as Attempted Self-Rescue

1 For a rare and spirited defense of Archbold see Michael Murphy, " 'The Secret Sharer': Conrad's Turn of the Winch."

2 The story, I suspect, also dramatizes Conrad's deep involvement with his fictional characters. Conrad commented on this in a letter to his publishers: "[S]hould you find Jim unconscionably long," he wrote about *Lord Jim*, "I am ready to shorten (what remains) by excision. I am however in such a state of mind about the story—so inextricably mixed up with it in my daily life—that I feel unequal to doing the cutting myself . . ." (*Letters to William Blackwood* 90). Describing the breakdown Conrad had after finishing *Under Western Eyes*, Jessie Conrad describes how Conrad lived "mixed up in the scenes" and held "converse with the characters" (*Letters to William Blackwood* 192).

Psychobiographer Bernard Meyer, describing the beginning of Conrad's literary career, comments that in "taking up his pen" Conrad sought to "combat his loneliness by creating a world of fiction teeming with people and bursting with action" (92). Writing constituted a "rescue of the self through a creative act which in time to come afforded him the companionship not only of invented characters but of fellow artists and an ever-increasing reading public" (92–93).

3 In "The Secret Sharer" and "Heart of Darkness," we find a re-enactment of what Jeffrey Berman describes as Conrad's "need for writing as rescue" and his systematic killing off of his "fictional projections, especially the ones with whom he most closely identified" ("Writing as Rescue" 68, 74). "[A] novelist," Conrad wrote, "lives in his work" (*A Personal Record* xv). A complex and contradictory personality, Conrad, in his fiction, disclosed much about his own psychology. As psychobiographer Bernard Meyer shows, Conrad was a man who had a deep sense of isolation coupled with an intense yearning for human warmth, who had a "highly unstable and shifting conception" of self and a "hazy sense" of identity (288), who needed to borrow "tokens of individuality and strength" from others to sustain his "sense of identity and manliness," and who was "menaced" with a "sense of inner dissolution" throughout his life (104). While Conrad had a "grandiose ambition to become a savior and a hero of world renown" (96), he was also prone to hypochondriacal complaints, suicidal preoccupations, uncontrollable rage re-

sponses and feelings of utter helplessness. With Ford Madox Ford, he developed an intense twinship relationship, finding in Ford both a "secret sharer" and an empathic companion (see Meyer 133–53, 166–67, et passim).

6 / Defensive Aestheticism and Self-Dissolution

1   In 1948, almost twenty years before he published his first essay on narcissism, Kohut wrote an analysis of *Death in Venice* which was ultimately published in 1957 (see *Search* 1: 107–30). One of Kohut's central focuses in this early classical analysis of the work is on its "father theme." Kohut argues, for example, that the four strangers Aschenbach encounters are embodiments of the "bad, threatening, sexually active father" and that Aschenbach identifies himself with the "good" father who "forgoes threats and punishment and heterosexual love" and "loves only the son." In his love for Tadzio, Aschenbach portrays "what he wished he had received from his father" but his "ambivalence is intensified by the narcissistic, envious recognition that another is getting what he really wished for himself, and hostile, destructive elements enter into his feelings toward Tadzio" (124). The "decisive threat to Aschenbach's defensive system" is caused not "by the traces of envious hostility against Tadzio" or "hatred against the father" but instead "by the breakdown of sublimated homosexual tenderness and the nearly unchecked onrush of unsublimated homosexual desire in the aging writer" (125).

In 1976, in another essay, Kohut made passing reference to *Death in Venice*, reinterpreting it in light of his evolving theory of narcissism (see "Creativeness, Charisma, Group Psychology" 821–22). The focus of this second analysis is on Aschenbach's loss of the ability to provide himself with the "experience of basic self-esteem" (821) through artistic creation. In Tadzio, Kohut finds the "revival of the sexualized precursor of the artistic product: the beautiful boy (though frail and already marked for destruction) who is the symbolic stand-in for the core of the still unaltered childhood self which craves love and admiration" (822).

For several brief discussions of Kohut's 1948 and 1976 analyses of the novel, see Paul Ornstein's "Introduction" to Kohut's *Search for the Self* (10–12) and Ernest Wolf's "Psychoanalytic Psychology of the Self and Literature" (47–48). Both Ornstein and Wolf find foreshadowings of Kohut's later theoretical findings on narcissism in the early essay.

7 / The Evasion of Narcissistic Anxieties

1   The one notable exception to this is Lorelei Cederstrom who reads the novel as an exercise in satire. Kate Brown, in Cederstrom's view, "is a

very frail vessel for a message of importance." Lessing "has chosen a limited woman as her protagonist in order that the reader will not identify with her" (132, 133). In contrast, Betsy Draine, whose response to the novel is typical, states that *The Summer Before the Dark* "*engages* its readers—with the main character, Kate, with the issues she confronts, and with the propositions concerning those issues that the action, dream-allegory, and narrative commentary all conspire to assert" (112).

8 / Self-Dispersal and Self-Assemblage

1   Discussing how Woolf devised a "sacrificial double" to "do the dying" for Clarissa, Mark Spilka observes that Woolf gave Septimus her maiden name, Stephen Smith, at one point in the writing of the novel and then renamed him "with nearly sufficient lettering to match her full present name— Septimus Warren Smith, Virginia Stephen Woolf—and to disperse the name Stephen into a hidden anagram" (52–53).

As critics long have observed, Septimus's experiences are directly related to Woolf's breakdowns of 1904 and 1913–14. "[T]he mad part," she wrote in her diary during the creation of the novel, "tries me so much, makes my mind squint so badly that I can hardly face spending the next weeks at it" (*Diary* 2: 248). It is no wonder that Woolf found these passages difficult. For during her breakdowns, she was paranoiac, anorexic, suicidal, and, at times, violent and psychotic. During the 1904 episode, she, like Septimus Smith, heard the birds singing in Greek and, in a suicide attempt, she, like Septimus, threw herself from a window (Bell 1: 89–90). And during the 1913 episode, she, like Septimus Smith, "became convinced that her body was in some way monstrous, the sordid mouth and sordid belly demanding food. . . . Material things assumed sinister and unpredictable aspects, beastly and terrifying or— sometimes—of fearful beauty" (Bell 2: 15).

9 / Comic Storytelling as Escape and Narcissistic Self-Expression

1   The compulsive overeating that leads to obesity, according to Richard Chessick, often is a narcissistic phenomenon, a reaction to feelings of empty depletion and diffuse rage. It represents a self-soothing effort to protect against the fragmentation of the sense of self. Compulsive overeating "drains off the rage and paranoia (more or less) and focuses the patient's attention away from the empty, depleted self and onto preoccupation with gastrointestinal-tract sensations. In this manner some sort of sense of being alive is maintained" (306). "It is the extremely negative self image and self hatred—or in

Kohut's terms the depleted self with the disintegration product of narcissistic rage—that *precede* the development of obesity ..." (312). Low self-esteem and compensatory grandiose fantasies are also common among those with eating disorders, according to Chessick (313).

2   This description of Joan's potent celebrity self recalls Kohut's description of the "overstimulated self." According to Kohut, in cases in which the responses of the selfobjects focus "prematurely and unrealistically on the fantasied performance or the fantasied products of the self" and fail "to respond appropriately to the exhibitionism of the nascent nuclear self of the child as the initiator of the performance and as the shaper of products, the self will, throughout life, be experienced as separate from its own actions and weak in comparison with them. Such people will tend to shy away from giving themselves over to creative activities because their self is in danger of destruction by being siphoned into its own performance or into the product it is shaping" (Kohut and Wolf 419).

3   Claire Kahane's insight into the psychodynamics of Gothic literature sheds light on Joan's Gothic preoccupations. "What I see repeatedly locked into the forbidden center of the Gothic which draws me inward," writes Kahane, "is the spectral presence of a dead-undead mother, archaic and all-encompassing, a ghost signifying the problematics of femininity which the heroine must confront" (336).

In Conclusion

1   "[O]nly rarely," writes Bernheimer, are we able "to take full advantage of the text's maternal offer. The fusion of self and other in the act of reading is the result of a temporary spell, of an aesthetic moment that may be thought of as recreating the mother's 'holding environment,' that is, her system of care and protection" (10–11). Bernheimer's analysis of the primitive sources of the aesthetic moment is partly derived from that of psychoanalyst Christopher Bollas who holds that the "uncanny fusion" an individual transiently experiences in the aesthetic moment (98) is a memory trace of the "*transformational object*," i.e., "an object that is experientially identified by the infant with the process of the alteration of self experience; an identification that emerges from symbiotic relating, where the first object is . . . known as a recurrent experience of being—a kind of existential, as opposed to representational, knowing" (97).

✻ ✻ ✻ ✻

Works Cited

✻ ✻ ✻ ✻

Abel, Elizabeth. "Narrative Structure(s) and Female Development: The Case of *Mrs. Dalloway*." *The Voyage In: Fictions of Female Development.* Ed. Elizabeth Abel, Marianne Hirsch, and Elizabeth Langland. Hanover: University Press of New England, 1983. 161–85.

Adorno, Theodor. "Notes on Kafka." Trans. Samuel and Shierry Weber. *Prisms.* Cambridge: MIT Press, 1981. 243–71.

Albright, Daniel. *Personality and Impersonality: Lawrence, Woolf, and Mann.* Chicago: University of Chicago Press, 1978.

Alter, Robert. *Motives for Fiction.* Cambridge: Harvard University Press, 1984.

Anders, Günther. *Franz Kafka.* Trans. A. Steer and A. K. Thorlby. London: Bowes and Bowes, 1960.

Angus, Douglas. "Kafka's *Metamorphosis* and 'The Beauty and the Beast' Tale." *Journal of English and Germanic Philology* 53 (1954): 69–71.

Apter, T. E. *Thomas Mann: The Devil's Advocate.* New York: New York University Press, 1979.

——. *Virginia Woolf: A Study of Her Novels.* New York: New York University Press, 1979.

Atwood, Margaret. *Lady Oracle.* New York: Avon, 1976.

Bakhtin, Mikhail. *Problems of Dostoevsky's Poetics.* Trans. R. W. Rotsel. Ann Arbor: Ardis, 1973.

Bance, A. F. "*Der Tod in Venedig* and the Triadic Structure." *Forum for Modern Language Studies* 8 (1972): 148–61.

Basch, Michael Franz. "The Concept of 'Self': An Operational Definition."

Developmental Approaches to the Self. Ed. Benjamin Lee and Gil G. Noam. New York: Plenum, 1983. 7–58.

———. "Empathic Understanding: A Review of the Concept and Some Theoretical Considerations." *Journal of the American Psychoanalytic Association* 31 (1983): 101–26.

———. "Memorial For Heinz Kohut, M.D., October 31, 1981." *The Annual of Psychoanalysis.* New York: International Universities Press, 1985. 12/13: 5–7.

———. "The Selfobject Theory of Motivation and the History of Psychoanalysis." *Kohut's Legacy: Contributions to Self Psychology.* Ed. Paul E. Stepansky and Arnold Goldberg. Hillsdale: Analytic Press, 1984. 3–17.

Bell, Quentin. *Virginia Woolf: A Biography.* 2 vols. New York: Harcourt Brace, 1972.

Bellow, Saul. *Seize the Day.* New York: Penguin Books, 1956.

Beres, David, and Jacob Arlow. "Fantasy and Identification in Empathy." *Psychoanalytic Quarterly* 43 (1974): 26–50.

Berets, Ralph. "A Jungian Interpretation of the Dream Sequence in Doris Lessing's *The Summer Before the Dark.*" *Modern Fiction Studies* 26 (Spring 1980): 117–29.

Berman, Jeffrey. *The Talking Cure: Literary Representations of Psychoanalysis.* New York: New York University Press, 1985.

———. "Writing as Rescue: Conrad's Escape from the Heart of Darkness." *Literature and Psychology* 25 (1975): 65–78.

Bernheimer, Charles. *Flaubert and Kafka: Studies in Psychopoetic Structure.* New Haven: Yale University Press, 1982.

Bidwell, Paul. "Leggatt and the Promised Land: A New Reading of 'The Secret Sharer.'" *Conradiana* 3 (1971–72): 26–34.

Bleich, David. *Subjective Criticism.* Baltimore: Johns Hopkins University Press, 1978.

Böhme, Hartmut. "Mother Milena: On Kafka's Narcissism." Trans. John Winkelman. *The Kafka Debate: New Perspectives for Our Time.* Ed. Angel Flores. New York: Gordian, 1977. 80–99.

Bollas, Christopher. "The Transformational Object." *International Journal of Psycho-Analysis* 60 (1978): 97–107.

Bornstein, Melvin. "Prologue" to "Self Psychology: Implications for Psychoanalytic Theory." Lichtenberg and Kaplan, 283–86.

Brooks, Peter. *Reading for the Plot: Design and Intention in Narrative.* New York: Random House, 1984; Vintage Books edition, 1985.

Cantrell, Carol. "*The Metamorphosis*: Kafka's Study of a Family." *Modern Fiction Studies* 23 (1977–78): 578–86.

184

Cederstrom, Lorelei. "Doris Lessing's Use of Satire in *The Summer Before the Dark*." *Modern Fiction Studies* 26 (Spring 1980): 131–45.

Chessick, Richard D. "Clinical Notes toward the Understanding and Intensive Psychotherapy of Adult Eating Disorders." *The Annual of Psychoanalysis*. New York: International Universities Press, 1985. 12/13: 301–22.

Clayton, John J. "Saul Bellow's *Seize the Day*: A Study in Mid-Life Transition." *Saul Bellow Journal* 5 (Fall/Winter 1986): 34–47.

Cohen, Sarah. *Saul Bellow's Enigmatic Laughter*. Urbana: University of Illinois Press, 1974.

Conrad, Joseph. *Heart of Darkness. Youth and Two Other Stories*. Garden City: Doubleday, Page, 1903. 51–184.

——. *Letters to William Blackwood and David S. Meldrum*. Ed. William Blackburn. Durham: Duke University Press, 1958.

——. *A Personal Record*. New York: Doubleday, Page, 1924.

——. "The Secret Sharer." *'Twixt Land and Sea*. Garden City: Doubleday, Page, 1912. 91–143.

Consigny, Scott. "Aschenbach's 'Page and a Half of Choicest Prose': Mann's Rhetoric of Irony." *Studies in Short Fiction* 14 (1977): 359–67.

——. "The Paradox of Textuality: Writing as Entrapment and Deliverance in *Notes From Underground*. *Canadian-American Slavic Studies* 12 (Fall 1978): 341–52.

Corngold, Stanley. *The Commentators' Despair: The Interpretation of Kafka's Metamorphosis*. Port Washington: Kennikat Press, 1973.

Cox, C. B. *Joseph Conrad: The Modern Imagination*. London: Dent, 1974.

Cronin, Gloria. "The Seduction of Tommy Wilhelm: A Post-Modernist Appraisal of *Seize the Day*." *Saul Bellow Journal* 3 (Fall/Winter 1983): 18–27.

Culler, Jonathan. *On Deconstruction: Theory and Criticism after Structuralism*. Ithaca: Cornell University Press, 1982.

Curley, Daniel. "Legate of the Ideal." *Conrad's Secret Sharer and the Critics*. Ed. Bruce Harkness. Belmont: Wadsworth, 1962. 75–82.

Daleski, H. M. "'The Secret Sharer': Questions of Command." *Critical Quarterly* 17 (1975): 268–79.

Deutelbaum, Wendy. "Two Psychoanalytic Approaches to Reading Literature." *Theories of Reading, Looking, and Listening*. Ed. Harry R. Garvin. Lewisburg: Bucknell University Press, 1981. 89–101.

Dobrinsky, Joseph. "The Two Lives of Joseph Conrad in 'The Secret Sharer.'" *Cahiers Victoriens & Edouardiens* 21 (1985): 33–49.

Doody, Terrence. "The Underground Man's Confession and His Audience." *Rice University Studies* 61 (Winter 1975): 27–38.

Dostoevsky, Fyodor. *Notes From Underground*. Trans. Constance Garnett. *The Short Novels of Dostoevsky*. New York: Dial Press, 1945. 129–222.

Draine, Betsy. *Substance under Pressure: Artistic Coherence and Evolving Form in the Novels of Doris Lessing*. Madison: University of Wisconsin Press, 1983.

Dussinger, Gloria. " 'The Secret Sharer': Conrad's Psychological Study." *Texas Studies in Literature and Language* 10 (Winter 1969): 599–608.

Dyson, A. E. "The Stranger God: 'Death in Venice.' " *Critical Quarterly* 13 (Spring 1971): 5–20.

Edel, Edmund. "Franz Kafka: *Die Verwandlung*, Eine Auslegung." *Wirkendes Wort* 4 (1957–58): 217–26. Trans. and summarized by Corngold, 101–06.

Eggenschwiler, David. "*The Metamorphosis*, Freud, and the Chains of Odysseus." *Modern Language Quarterly* 39 (1978): 363–85. Rpt. in *Modern Critical Views: Franz Kafka*. Ed. Harold Bloom. New York: Chelsea House, 1986. 199–219.

———. "Narcissus in 'The Secret Sharer': A Secondary Point of View." *Conradiana* 11 (1979): 23–40.

Emrich, Wilhelm. *Franz Kafka: A Critical Study of His Writings*. Trans. Sheema Zeben Buehne. New York: Frederick Ungar, 1968.

Epstein, Lawrence, and Arthur H. Feiner. "Introduction." *Countertransference: The Therapist's Contribution to the Therapeutic Situation*. Ed. Lawrence Epstein and Arthur Feiner. New York: Jason Aronson, 1983. 1–23.

Felman, Shoshana. "Turning the Screw of Interpretation." *Literature and Psychoanalysis: The Question of Reading: Otherwise*. Ed. Shoshana Felman. Baltimore: Johns Hopkins University Press, 1982. 94–207.

Feuerlicht, Ignace. *Thomas Mann*. New York: Twayne, 1968.

Fleishman, Avrom. *Virginia Woolf: A Critical Reading*. Baltimore: Johns Hopkins University Press, 1975.

Fortin, Rene. "Responsive Form: Dostoyevsky's *Notes From Underground* and the Confessional Tradition." *Essays in Literature* 7 (Fall 1980): 225–45.

Frank, Joseph. *Dostoevsky: The Stir of Liberation: 1860–1865*. Princeton: Princeton University Press, 1986.

———. "Nihilism and *Notes From Underground*." *Sewanee Review* 69 (1961): 1–33.

Freibert, Lucy. "The Artist as Picaro: The Revelation of Margaret Atwood's 'Lady Oracle.' " *Canadian Literature* 92 (Spring 1982): 23–33.

Freud, Sigmund. *The Standard Edition of the Complete Psychological Works of Sigmund Freud.* Trans. and ed. James Strachey. 24 vols. London: Hogarth Press, 1953–74.

Frye, Joanne S. "*Mrs. Dalloway* as Lyrical Paradox." *Ball State University Forum* 23 (1982): 42–56.

Fuchs, Daniel. *Saul Bellow: Vision and Revision.* Durham: Duke University Press, 1984.

Geary, Edward A. "An Ashy Halo: Woman as Symbol in 'Heart of Darkness.'" *Studies in Short Fiction* 13 (Fall 1976): 499–506.

Gedo, John E. *Conceptual Issues in Psychoanalysis: Essays in History and Method.* Hillsdale: Analytic Press, 1986.

Giannone, Richard. "Saul Bellow's Idea of Self: A Reading of *Seize the Day.*" *Renascence* 27 (Summer 1975): 193–205.

Gillen, Francis. "'I Am This, I Am That': Shifting Distance and Movement in *Mrs. Dalloway.*" *Studies in the Novel* 4 (1972): 484–93.

Girard, René. *Deceit, Desire, and the Novel: Self and Other in Literary Structure.* Trans. Yvonne Freccero. Baltimore: Johns Hopkins University Press, 1965.

Goldberg, Arnold, ed. *Advances in Self Psychology.* New York: International Universities Press, 1980.

———. *The Future of Psychoanalysis: Essays in Honor of Heinz Kohut.* New York: International Universities Press, 1983.

———. *The Psychology of the Self: A Casebook.* New York: International Universities Press, 1978.

Good, Graham. "The Death of Language in *Death in Venice.*" *Mosaic* 5 (Spring 1972): 43–52.

Grace, Sherrill. *Violent Duality: A Study of Margaret Atwood.* Montreal: Véhicule Press, 1980.

Graff, Gerald. *Professing Literature: An Institutional History.* Chicago: University of Chicago Press, 1987.

Graver, Lawrence. *Conrad's Short Fiction.* Berkeley: University of California Press, 1969.

Greenberg, Martin. *The Terror of Art: Kafka and Modern Literature.* New York: Basic Books, 1968.

Greenstein, Susan. "Dear Reader, Dear Friend: Richardson's Readers and the Social Response to Character." *College English* 41 (January 1980): 524–34.

von Gronicka, André. "Myth Plus Psychology: A Stylistic Analysis of *Death in Venice.*" *Thomas Mann: A Collection of Critical Essays.* Ed. Henry Hatfield. Englewood Cliffs: Prentice-Hall, 1964. 46–61.

Guerard, Albert J. *Conrad the Novelist.* Cambridge: Harvard University Press, 1958.

Works Cited

Hall, J. R. "Abstraction in Dostoyevsky's 'Notes From the Underground.'" *Modern Language Review* 76 (1981): 129–37.

Harper, Howard. *Between Language and Silence: The Novels of Virginia Woolf.* Baton Rouge: Louisiana State University Press, 1982.

Hartman, Geoffrey. *Criticism in the Wilderness: The Study of Literature Today.* New Haven: Yale University Press, 1980.

Hassan, Ihab. *Radical Innocence: Studies in the Contemporary American Novel.* Princeton: Princeton University Press, 1961.

Hayman, Ronald. *Kafka: A Biography.* New York: Oxford University Press, 1982.

Heller, Erich. "Autobiography and Literature." Afterword to *Death In Venice by Thomas Mann.* New York: Random House, 1970. 101–27.

Henel, Ingeborg. "Die Deutbarkeit von Kafkas Werken." *Zeitschrift für deutsche Philologie* 86, no. 2, 250–66. Trans. and summarized by Corngold, 134–35.

Henke, Suzette A. "*Mrs. Dalloway*: The Communion of Saints." *New Feminist Essays on Virginia Woolf.* Ed. Jane Marcus. Lincoln: University of Nebraska Press, 1981. 125–47.

Hewitt, Douglas. "Reassessment of 'Heart of Darkness.'" *Conrad's Heart of Darkness and the Critics.* Ed. Bruce Harkness. San Francisco: Wadsworth, 1960. 103–11.

Hochman, Baruch. *Character in Literature.* Ithaca: Cornell University Press, 1985.

Holland, Norman. *The Dynamics of Literary Response.* 1968. New York: Norton, 1975.

———. *5 Readers Reading.* New Haven: Yale University Press, 1975.

———. "Literary Interpretation and Three Phases of Psychoanalysis." *Critical Inquiry* 3 (Winter 1976): 221–33.

———. "Realism and Unrealism: Kafka's 'Metamorphosis.'" *Modern Fiction Studies* 4 (1958): 143–50.

———. "UnityIdentityTextSelf." *PMLA* 90 (1975): 813–22. Rpt. in *Reader-Response Criticism: From Formalism to Post-Structuralism.* Ed. Jane P. Tompkins. Baltimore: Johns Hopkins University Press, 1980. 118–33.

Honig, Edwin. *Dark Conceit: The Making of Allegory.* Evanston: Northwestern University Press, 1959.

Hovet, Grace Ann, and Barbara Lounsberry. "The Affirmation of Signs in Doris Lessing's *The Summer Before the Dark*." *Wascana Review* 16 (Fall 1981): 41–52.

Hunter, J. Paul. "The Loneliness of the Long-Distance Reader." *Genre* 10 (Winter 1977): 455–84.

188

Jackson, Robert Louis. *The Art of Dostoevsky: Deliriums and Nocturnes.* Princeton: Princeton University Press, 1981.

Jaffe, Daniel S. "Empathy, Counteridentification, Countertransference: A Review, with Some Personal Perspectives on the 'Analytic Instrument.'" *Psychoanalytic Quarterly* 55 (1986): 215–43.

Janouch, Gustav. *Conversations with Kafka.* Trans. Goronwy Rees. 2nd ed. New York: New Directions, 1971.

Jean-Aubry, G. *Joseph Conrad: Life and Letters.* 2 vols. Garden City: Doubleday, Page, 1927.

Jofen, Jean. "Metamorphosis." *American Imago* 35 (Winter 1978): 347–56.

Johnson, Bruce. *Conrad's Models of Mind.* Minneapolis: University of Minnesota Press, 1971.

Kafka, Franz. *Letter to His Father.* Trans. Ernst Kaiser and Eithne Wilkins. New York: Schocken, 1966.

———. *The Metamorphosis.* Trans. and ed. Stanley Corngold. New York: Bantam, 1972.

Kahane, Claire. "The Gothic Mirror." *The (M)other Tongue: Essays in Feminist Psychoanalytic Interpretation.* Ed. Shirley Nelson Garner, Claire Kahane, Madelon Sprengnether. Ithaca: Cornell University Press, 1985. 334–51.

Karl, Frederick. *A Reader's Guide to Joseph Conrad.* New York: Noonday, 1960.

Kaufmann, Walter, ed. *Existentialism from Dostoevsky to Sartre.* Cleveland: World, 1956.

Kavanagh, Thomas M. "Dostoyevsky's *Notes From Underground*: The Form of the Fiction." *Texas Studies in Literature and Language* 14 (Fall 1972): 491–507.

Kelley, Alice van Buren. *The Novels of Virginia Woolf: Fact and Vision.* Chicago: University of Chicago Press, 1973.

Kernberg, Otto. *Borderline Conditions and Pathological Narcissism.* New York: Jason Aronson, 1975.

Kirschner, Paul. *Conrad: The Psychologist as Artist.* Edinburgh: Oliver and Boyd, 1968.

Köhler, Lotte. "On Selfobject Countertransference." *The Annual of Psychoanalysis.* New York: International Universities Press, 1985. 12/13: 39–56.

Kohut, Heinz. *The Analysis of the Self.* New York: International Universities Press, Inc., 1971.

———. "Creativeness, Charisma, Group Psychology: Reflections on the Self-analysis of Freud." *Search* 2: 793–843.

———. "*Death in Venice* by Thomas Mann: A Story about the Disintegration of Artistic Sublimation." *Search* 1: 107–30.

———. "Forms and Transformations of Narcissism." *Search* 1: 427–60.

———. "The Future of Psychoanalysis." *Search* 2: 663–84.

———. *How Does Analysis Cure?* Chicago: University of Chicago Press, 1984.

———. "Introspection, Empathy, and the Semicircle of Mental Health." *International Journal of Psycho-analysis* 63 (1982): 395–408. Rpt. in Lichtenberg, *Empathy* 1: 81–100.

———. "Narcissism as a Resistance and as a Driving Force in Psychoanalysis." *Search* 2: 547–61.

———. "The Psychoanalyst in the Community of Scholars." *Search* 2: 685–724.

———. "Reflections on *Advances in Self Psychology.*" Goldberg, *Advances* 473–554.

———. "Remarks about the Formation of the Self." *Search* 2: 737–70.

———. *The Restoration of the Self.* New York: International Universities Press, 1977.

———. *The Search for the Self: Selected Writings of Heinz Kohut 1950–1978.* Ed. Paul H. Ornstein. 2 vols. New York: International Universities Press, 1978. Vols. 3 and 4 are forthcoming.

———. "Selected Problems of Self Psychological Theory." *Reflections on Self Psychology.* Ed. Joseph Lichtenberg and Samuel Kaplan. Hillsdale: Analytic Press, 1983. 387–416.

———. *Self Psychology and the Humanities: Reflections on a New Psychoanalytic Approach.* Ed. Charles B. Strozier. New York: Norton, 1985.

———. "Thoughts on Narcissism and Narcissistic Rage." *Search* 2: 615–58.

Kohut, Heinz, and Ernest S. Wolf. "The Disorders of the Self and Their Treatment: An Outline." *International Journal of Psycho-Analysis* 59 (1978): 413–25.

Krieger, Murray. *Theory of Criticism: A Tradition and Its System.* Baltimore: Johns Hopkins University Press, 1976.

Kuna, Franz. *Franz Kafka: Literature as Corrective Punishment.* Bloomington: Indiana University Press, 1974.

Landsberg, Paul. " 'The Metamorphosis.' " Trans. Caroline Muhlenberg. *The Kafka Problem.* Ed. Angel Flores. New York: Octagon, 1963. 122–33.

Lang, Joan. "Notes toward a Psychology of the Feminine Self." *Kohut's Legacy: Contributions to Self Psychology.* Ed. Paul E. Stepansky and Arnold Goldberg. Hillsdale: Analytic Press, 1984. 51–69.

Layton, Lynne, and Barbara Schapiro, eds. *Narcissism and the Text: Studies in*

Literature and the Psychology of Self. New York: New York University Press, 1986.

Leavis, F. R. *The Great Tradition*. London: Chatto and Windus, 1948.

Lee, Hermione. *The Novels of Virginia Woolf*. New York: Holmes and Meier, 1977.

Lefcowitz, Barbara F. "Dream and Action in Lessing's *The Summer Before the Dark*." *Critique* 17 (1975): 107–20.

Lehnert, Herbert. *Thomas Mann: Fiktion, Mythos, Religion*. Stuttgart: Kohlhammer, 1965.

Lessing, Doris. *The Summer Before the Dark*. New York: Vintage Books, 1973.

Levenson, Michael. "On the Edge of the Heart of Darkness." *Studies in Short Fiction* 23 (Spring 1986): 153–57.

Lichtenberg, Joseph, Melvin Bornstein, and Donald Silver, eds. *Empathy*. 2 vols. Hillsdale: Analytic Press, 1984.

Lichtenberg, Joseph, and Samuel Kaplan, eds. *Reflections on Self Psychology*. Hillsdale: Analytic Press, 1983.

MacLean, Susan. "*Lady Oracle*: The Art of Reality and the Reality of Art." *Journal of Canadian Fiction* 28–29 (1980): 179–97.

Mahler, Margaret, Fred Pine, and Anni Bergman. *The Psychological Birth of the Human Infant: Symbiosis and Individuation*. New York: Basic Books, 1975.

Malcolm, Janet. *Psychoanalysis: The Impossible Profession*. New York: Knopf, 1981.

Mann, Thomas. *Death in Venice*. *Thomas Mann: Stories of Three Decades*. Trans. H. T. Lowe-Porter. New York: Knopf, 1936. 378–437.

McCadden, Joseph F. *The Flight from Women in the Fiction of Saul Bellow*. Washington: University Press of America, 1980.

McIntyre, Allan. "Psychology and Symbol: Correspondences between *Heart of Darkness* and *Death in Venice*." *Hartford Studies in Literature* 7 (1975): 216–35.

McLauchlan, Juliet. "The 'Value' and 'Significance' of *Heart of Darkness*." *Conradiana* 15 (1983): 3–21.

McLaughlin, James. "Transference, Psychic Reality, and Countertransference." *Psychoanalytic Quarterly* 50 (1981): 639–64.

Meckier, Jerome. "The Truth about Marlow." *Studies in Short Fiction* 19 (Fall 1982): 373–79.

Merrill, Reed. "The Mistaken Endeavor: Dostoevsky's *Notes From Underground*." *Modern Fiction Studies* 18 (Winter 1972–73): 505–16.

Meyer, Bernard. *Joseph Conrad: A Psychoanalytic Biography*. Princeton: Princeton University Press, 1967.

Miller, J. Hillis. *Fiction and Repetition: Seven English Novels*. Cambridge: Harvard University Press, 1982.

Mitchell, Stephen A. "Twilight of the Idols: Change and Preservation in the Writings of Heinz Kohut." *Contemporary Psychoanalysis* 15 (1979): 170–89.

Mitscherlich-Nielsen, Margarete. "Psychoanalytic Notes on Franz Kafka." *Psychocultural Review* 3 (1979): 1–23.

Montag, George E. "Marlow Tells the Truth: The Nature of Evil in *Heart of Darkness*." *Conradiana* 3 (1971–72): 93–97.

Moon, Kenneth. "Where Is Clarissa? Doris Kilman and Recoil from the Flesh in Virginia Woolf's *Mrs. Dalloway*." *College Language Association Journal* 23 (1980): 273–86.

Morahg, Gilead. "The Art of Dr. Tamkin: Matter and Manner in *Seize the Day*." *Modern Fiction Studies* 25 (Spring 1979): 103–16.

Murphy, Michael. " 'The Secret Sharer': Conrad's Turn of the Winch." *Conradiana* 18 (1986): 193–200.

Naremore, James. *The World without a Self: Virginia Woolf and the Novel*. New Haven: Yale University Press, 1973.

Nelson, Cary. "The Psychology of Criticism, or What Can Be Said." *Psychoanalysis and the Question of the Text*. Ed. Geoffrey Hartman. Baltimore: Johns Hopkins University Press, 1978. 45–61.

———. "Reading Criticism." *PMLA* 91 (1976): 801–15.

Norman, Liane. "Risk and Redundancy." *PMLA* 90 (1975): 285–91.

Novak, Jane. *The Razor Edge of Balance: A Study of Virginia Woolf*. Coral Gables: University of Miami Press, 1975.

Opdahl, Keith. *The Novels of Saul Bellow: An Introduction*. University Park: Pennsylvania State University Press, 1967.

Ornstein, Paul H. "Introduction: The Evolution of Heinz Kohut's Psychoanalytic Psychology of the Self." Kohut, *Search* 1: 1–106.

Paris, Bernard J. *A Psychological Approach to Fiction: Studies in Thackeray, Stendhal, George Eliot, Dostoevsky, and Conrad*. Bloomington: Indiana University Press, 1974.

Pascal, Roy. *Kafka's Narrators: A Study of His Stories and Sketches*. Cambridge: Cambridge University Press, 1982.

Pecora, Vincent. "*Heart of Darkness* and the Phenomenology of Narrative Voice." *ELH* 52 (Winter 1985): 993–1015.

Porter, M. Gilbert. *Whence the Power? The Artistry and Humanity of Saul Bellow*. Columbia: University of Missouri Press, 1974.

Post, Stephen L., and Jule P. Miller, Jr. "Apprehensions of Empathy." Lichtenberg, *Empathy* 1: 217–35.

Poulet, Georges. "Criticism and the Experience of Interiority." Trans. Catherine and Richard Macksey. *Reader-Response Criticism: From Formalism to Post-Structuralism.* Ed. Jane P. Tompkins. Baltimore: Johns Hopkins University Press, 1980. 41–49.

Raper, J. R. "Running Contrary Ways: Saul Bellow's *Seize the Day.*" *Southern Humanities Review* 10 (Spring 1976): 157–68.

Raval, Suresh. *The Art of Failure: Conrad's Fiction.* Boston: Allen & Unwin, 1986.

Reed, Gail. "The Antithetical Meaning of the Term 'Empathy' in Psychoanalytic Discourse." Lichtenberg, *Empathy* 1: 7–24.

———. "*Candide*: Radical Simplicity and the Impact of Evil." *Literature and Psychoanalysis.* Ed. Edith Kurzweil and William Phillips. New York: Columbia University Press, 1983. 189–200.

———. "Toward a Methodology for Applying Psychoanalysis to Literature." *Psychoanalytic Quarterly* 51 (1982): 19–42.

Reed, T. J. *Thomas Mann: The Uses of Tradition.* Oxford: Clarendon Press, 1974.

Ressler, Steve. "Conrad's 'The Secret Sharer': Affirmation of Action." *Conradiana* 16 (1984): 195–214.

Richmond, Lee. "The Maladroit, the Medico, and the Magician: Saul Bellow's *Seize the Day.*" *Twentieth Century Literature* 19 (1973): 15–26.

Rigney, Barbara Hill. *Madness and Sexual Politics in the Feminist Novel: Studies in Brontë, Woolf, Lessing, and Atwood.* Madison: University of Wisconsin Press, 1978.

Rodrigues, Eusebio. *Quest for the Human: An Exploration of Saul Bellow's Fiction.* Lewisburg: Bucknell University Press, 1981.

Rolleston, James. *Kafka's Narrative Theater.* University Park: Pennsylvania State University Press, 1974.

Rose, Phyllis. *Woman of Letters: A Life of Virginia Woolf.* New York: Oxford University Press, 1978.

Rosenshield, Gary. "The Fate of Dostoevskij's Underground Man: The Case for an Open Ending." *Slavic and East European Journal* 28 (Fall 1984): 324–39.

Rosenthal, Michael. *Virginia Woolf.* New York: Columbia University Press, 1979.

Rosowski, Susan. "Margaret Atwood's *Lady Oracle*: Social Mythology and the Gothic Novel." *Research Studies* 49 (1981): 87–98.

Roudané, Matthew. "An Interview with Saul Bellow." *Contemporary Literature* 25 (Fall 1984): 265–80.

Rubenstein, Roberta. *The Novelistic Vision of Doris Lessing: Breaking the Forms of Consciousness.* Urbana: University of Illinois Press, 1979.

Schlack, Beverly Ann. "A Freudian Look at *Mrs. Dalloway.*" *Literature and Pychology* 23 (1973): 49–58.

Schlesinger, Herbert. "The Process of Empathic Response." Lichtenberg, *Empathy* 2: 187–210.

Schwaber, Evelyne. "Construction, Reconstruction, and the Mode of Clinical Attunement." Goldberg, *Future* 273–91.

———. "Empathy: A Mode of Analytic Listening." *Psychoanalytic Inquiry* 1 (1981): 357–92 . Rpt. in Lichtenberg, *Empathy* 2: 143–72.

———. "Narcissism, Self Psychology, and the Listening Perspective." *The Annual of Psychoanalysis*. New York: International Universities Press, 1981. 9: 115–31.

———. "On the 'Self' Within the Matrix of Analytic Theory—Some Clinical Reflections and Reconsiderations." *International Journal of Psychoanalysis* 60 (1979): 467–79.

———. "Self Psychology and the Concept of Psychopathology: A Case Presentation." Goldberg, *Advances* 215–42.

Schwartz, Murray. "The Literary Use of Transference." *Psychoanalysis and Contemporary Thought* 5 (1982): 35–44.

———. "Where Is Literature?" *College English* 36 (1975): 756–65.

Shields, E. F. "Death and Individual Values in 'Mrs. Dalloway.'" *Queens Quarterly* 80 (Spring 1973): 79–89.

Sicherman, Carol. "Bellow's *Seize the Day*: Reverberations and Hollow Sounds." *Studies in the Twentieth-Century* 15 (Spring 1975): 1–31.

Singleton, Mary Ann. *The City and the Veld: The Fiction of Doris Lessing.* Lewisburg: Bucknell University Press, 1977.

Slatoff, Walter. "Some of My Best Friends Are Interpreters." *New Literary History* 4 (Winter 1973): 375–80.

Smalley, Barbara. "The Compulsive Patterns of Dostoevsky's Underground Man." *Studies in Short Fiction* 10 (Fall 1973): 389–96.

Smith, Rowland. "Margaret Atwood: The Stoic Comedian." *Malahat Review* 41 (1977): 134–44.

Spann, Meno. *Franz Kafka.* Boston: Twayne, 1976.

Sperber, Michael. "Symptoms and Structure of Borderline Personality Organization: Camus' *The Fall* and Dostoevsky's 'Notes From Underground.'" *Literature and Psychology* 23 (1973): 102–13.

Spilka, Mark. *Dickens and Kafka: A Mutual Interpretation.* Bloomington: Indiana University Press, 1963.

———. *Virginia Woolf's Quarrel with Grieving.* Lincoln: University of Nebraska Press, 1980.

Stallman, R. W. "Conrad and 'The Secret Sharer.'" *The Art of Joseph Conrad: A Critical Symposium.* Ed. R. W. Stallman. Encore edition. Athens: Ohio University Press, 1982. 275–95.

Stark, Bruce R. "Kurtz's Intended: The Heart of *Heart of Darkness.*" *Texas Studies in Literature and Language* 16 (Fall 1974): 535–55.

Steiner, George. "Critic"/"Reader." *New Literary History* 10 (Spring 1979): 423–52.

Steiner, Joan. "Conrad's 'The Secret Sharer': Complexities of the Doubling Relationship." *Conradiana* 12 (1980): 173–86.

Stewart, Garrett. "Lying as Dying in *Heart of Darkness.*" *PMLA* 95 (1980): 319–31.

Stewart, Walter K. "*Der Tod in Venedig*: The Path to Insight." *Germanic Review* 53 (1978): 50–55.

Stolorow, Robert D. "Varieties of Selfobject Experience." *Kohut's Legacy: Contributions to Self Psychology.* Ed. Paul E. Stepansky and Arnold Goldberg. Hillsdale: Analytic Press, 1984. 43–50

Strozier, Charles B. "Glimpses of a Life: Heinz Kohut (1913–1981)." *Progress in Self Psychology.* Ed. Arnold Goldberg. New York: Guilford, 1985. 1: 3–12.

Thomas, Clara. "*Lady Oracle*: The Narrative of a Fool-Heroine." *The Art of Margaret Atwood: Essays in Criticism.* Ed. Arnold E. Davidson and Cathy N. Davidson. Toronto: Anansi, 1981. 159–75.

Thorburn, David. *Conrad's Romanticism.* New Haven: Yale University Press, 1974.

Tindall, W. Y. "Apology for Marlow." *Conrad's Heart of Darkness and the Critics.* Ed. Bruce Harkness. San Francisco: Wadsworth, 1960. 123–33.

Tompkins, Jane P. "Criticism and Feeling." *College English* 39 (1977): 169–78.

Transue, Pamela. *Virginia Woolf and the Politics of Style.* Albany: State University of New York Press, 1986.

Trowbridge, Clinton. "Water Imagery in *Seize the Day.*" *Critique* 9 (Spring 1967): 62–73.

Urzidil, Johannes. *There Goes Kafka.* Trans. Harold A. Basilius. Detroit: Wayne State University Press, 1968.

Vietta, Silvio. "Franz Kafka, Expressionism, and Reification." *Passion and Rebellion: The Expressionist Heritage.* Ed. Stephen Eric Bronner and Douglas Kellner. New York: Universe, 1983. 201–16.

Vincent, Sybil Koroff. "The Mirror and the Cameo: Margaret Atwood's Comic/Gothic Novel, *Lady Oracle.*" *The Female Gothic.* Ed. Juliann E. Fleenor. Montréal: Eden, 1983. 153–63.

Wasiolek, Edward. *Dostoevsky: The Major Fiction.* Cambridge: MIT Press, 1964.

Watts, Cedric. *The Deceptive Text: An Introduction to Covert Plots.* Sussex: Harvester; Totowa: Barnes and Noble, 1984.

———. "The Mirror-Tale: An Ethico-Structural Analysis of Conrad's 'The Secret Sharer.'" *Critical Quarterly* 19 (Autumn 1977): 25–37.

Waxman, Barbara Frey. "From *Bildungsroman* to *Reifungsroman*: Aging in Doris Lessing's Fiction." *Soundings* 68 (Fall 1985): 318–34.

Weisberg, Richard. "An Example Not to Follow: *Ressentiment* and the Underground Man." *Modern Fiction Studies* 21 (Winter 1975–76): 553–63.

Weiss, Daniel. "Caliban on Prospero: A Psychoanalytic Study on the Novel *Seize the Day*, by Saul Bellow." *Saul Bellow and the Critics*. Ed. Irving Malin. New York: New York University Press, 1967. 114–41.

Von Wiese, Benno. "Franz Kafka: *Die Verwandlung*." *Die deutsche Novelle von Goethe bis Kafka, II*. Düsseldorf: Bagel, 1962. 319–45. Trans. and summarized by Corngold, 247–54.

Wilson, Jonathan. *On Bellow's Planet: Readings from the Dark Side*. London and Toronto: Associated University Presses, 1985.

Wilson, Samuel. "The Self-Pity Response: A Reconsideration." *Progress in Self Psychology*. Ed. Arnold Goldberg. New York: Guilford, 1985. 1: 178–90.

Winnicott, D. W. *Playing and Reality*. London: Tavistock, 1971.

Wolf, Ernest. "Concluding Statement." Goldberg, *Future* 495–505.

———. "The Disconnected Self." *Psychoanalysis, Creativity, and Literature: A French-American Inquiry*. Ed. Alan Roland. New York: Columbia University Press, 1978. 103–14.

———. "Empathy and Countertransference." Goldberg, *Future* 309–26.

———. "On the Developmental Line of Selfobject Relations." Goldberg, *Advances* 117–30.

———. "Psychoanalytic Psychology of the Self and Literature." *New Literary History* 12 (Autumn 1980): 41–60.

———. "Transferences and Countertransferences in the Analysis of Disorders of the Self." *Contemporary Psychoanalysis* 15 (1979): 577–94.

Wolf, Ernest, and James Wilson. "The 'Monday Crust' in the Disorders of the Self." *The Annual of Psychoanalysis, 1980*. New York: International Universities Press, 1981. 8: 197–213.

Woolf, Virginia. *The Diary of Virginia Woolf*. Ed. Anne Olivier Bell. 5 vols. New York: Harcourt Brace, 1977–84.

———. *Mrs. Dalloway*. New York: Harcourt Brace, 1925.

Wright, Elizabeth. *Psychoanalytic Criticism: Theory in Practice*. London: Methuen, 1984.

Yoder, Albert C. "Oral Artistry in Conrad's 'Heart of Darkness': A Study of Oral Aggression." *Conradiana* 2 (1969–70): 65–78.

Index

❋ ❋ ❋ ❋

Index

Grandiosity, archaic: and narcissistic dis-
order, 16–17, 18, 19; normal develop-
ment of, 14–15
Graver, Lawrence, 82–83, 86, 90, 91
Greenberg, Martin, 54
Greenstein, Susan, 28–29
von Gronicka, André, 108–09, 114, 115
Guerard, Albert, J., 83, 86
Guilty Man. See Kohut

Hall, J. R., 46
Harper, Howard, 138, 148
Hartman, Geoffrey, 169
Hassan, Ihab, 78
Hayman, Ronald, 178
"Heart of Darkness" (Conrad): act of
storytelling in, 5, 93, 98; African landscape in, 94; closure of, 98–100; Conrad on, 100; critical responses to, 92–
93, 95, 98, 100, 101, 103; doubles in,
92–93; female figure in, 93–94, 98–
100; inconclusiveness of, 103; lying in,
99, 100; maternal imago in, 93–94;
reader/text transaction in, 93, 95–96,
98, 100, 101, 102, 103, 104
—Kurtz: archaic grandiosity of, 94, 95,
96, 97, 98, 99; critical split on, 92, 95;
emptiness of, 95, 97; greed of, 95, 97;
as Marlow's double, 92, 95, 96, 100–
102; narcissistic rage of, 96, 97; self-
fragmentation of, 97
—Marlow: African journey of, 94; and
African natives, 94–95; anger of, 100,
101; defenses of, 94, 98, 99, 100, 101,
102, 103; emptiness of, 100, 103; and
Europeans, 95; grandiose desires of,
101, 102; and the Intended, 98–100;
isolation of, 101, 102, 103; and Kurtz,
92, 94, 95–98, 100–102; narrative
postponements of, 94; rescue mission
of, 95, 96, 100; and Russian harlequin,
94, 96; self-disintegration, fear of, 97–
98; as storyteller, 93, 98, 100–103;
and unnamed narrator-listener, 93,
102, 103
Heller, Erich, 105, 106
Henel, Ingeborg, 54
Henke, Suzette, 147, 150
Hewitt, Douglas, 92

Hochman, Baruch, 28
Holland, Norman, 25, 27, 169, 176–77,
178
Honig, Edwin, 61
Hovet, Grace Ann, 133–34
Hunter, J. Paul, 116

Idealization, archaic: and narcissistic dis-
order, 16–17, 18, 19; normal develop-
ment of, 14–15
Idealized parent imago, 14
Idealizing transference, 18, 23
Identification, transient, 22–23, 25, 176
Imago. See Idealized parent imago
Iser, Wolfgang, 27

Jackson, Robert Louis, 48
Jaffe, Daniel, 22, 170
Janouch, Gustav, 178–79
Jean-Aubry, G., 91
Jofen, Jean, 178
Johnson, Bruce, 86

Kafka, Franz. See Metamorphosis, The
Kahane, Claire, 182
Kaplan, Samuel, 174
Karl, Frederick, 91
Kaufmann, Walter, 33–34, 48
Kavanagh, Thomas M., 49
Kelley, Alice van Buren, 146, 147
Kernberg, Otto, 24, 175, 177
Kirschner, Paul, 86, 90
Köhler, Lotte, 24
Kohut, Heinz, 3–4, 6, 11–24, 28, 29, 39,
41, 44, 50, 52, 55, 56, 60–61, 84, 89,
107, 172, 173, 174–75, 180, 182; on
American psychoanalysis, 12; on artis-
tic anticipation of narcissistic disorder,
50; classical psychoanalytic method,
reliance on, 13; development of self
psychology, 11–24; on empathy, 4, 22,
28, 172; on Freudian theory and practice, 11–13, 14, 16, 19–20, 21–22,
174–75; on Guilty Man and Tragic
Man, 4, 12–13; on narcissistic disorder, 16–22; on oedipal phase, 21; on
Oedipus myth, 21–22; on psychoanalytic cure, 19–21; on the self, 13–15;
on self-development, 13–17; on self-

199

138, 139, 142, 149, 151–52; critical responses to, 138–39, 145, 146, 147, 148, 150, 151, 152, 181; defensive strategies of, 138, 139, 141, 146, 147, 148, 149–50, 151, 152; maternal imago depicted in, 141–42; narrating consciousness of, 138, 141, 149, 151, 152; reader/text transaction in, 138–39, 140, 143, 145, 146, 147, 148, 149, 150, 151, 152, 153; romanticizing of madness and suicide in, 139, 147, 148, 149, 150; skywriting episode in, 152; solitary traveler fantasy in, 141–42, 144; style of, 151–52; Woolf's comments on, 138, 139, 150, 181
—Clarissa Dalloway: abandonment, fear of, 140, 145, 147; attraction to women, 142–43, 145; connection, need for, 141, 142, 143; disconnection, sense of, 141, 143; and Doris Kilman, 144, 145; emptiness, sense of, 149, 150–51; experiencing and observing selves of, 141; merger needs and fears of, 141, 143, 144, 148; narcissistic vulnerabilities of, 140–41, 143–44, 145, 147–48, 149, 150–51; negativity of, 140–41, 144–45, 146; and Peter Walsh, 140, 143–44, 150; public and private selves of, 139–41; rejection, sensitivity to, 140; and Richard Dalloway, 140, 143; self-cohesion, fragility of, 140, 141, 148, 149; and Septimus Smith, 143, 147–50, 151; and Sir William Bradshaw, 146
Murphy, Michael, 179

Narcissism: development of, 14–15; healthy, 14–15; parent-child relationship and, 14–16; pathologic, 16–19
Narcissistic disorder: development of, 16–17; disintegration anxiety, 4, 17; empathic milieu, need for, 4, 16, 18, 20; fragmentation of the self, 17, 18; grandiosity, archaic, 16–17, 18, 19; idealization, archaic, 16–17, 18; parenting and, 16, 174; patient discourse, 3–4, 18–19; personality types, 19; predominance of, 19
—symptomatology: attention, need for,

4, 16, 17, 18, 19; dominance, desire to exercise, 16, 18, 19; emptiness, feelings of, 16, 17; eye glance, desire for, 55; loneliness, 4; megalomaniac fantasies of, 4, 18; merger apprehensions of, 17, 19; merger with idealized figure, desire for, 16, 17, 18; overburdenness, 17; overstimulation, 17, 18; powerlessness, feelings of, 16, 19; rage reaction, 17, 18, 20, 21, 41; rejection, hypersensitivity to, 17, 18, 19, 20; self-esteem, shakiness of, 4, 17, 18, 19; shameproneness, 17, 41; understimulation, 17; worthlessness, sense of, 19
Narcissistic injury, 18, 20, 21. *See also* Narcissistic rage
Narcissistic rage, 17, 18, 20, 21
Naremore, James, 138–39, 150, 151
Nelson, Cary, 26, 177
Norman, Liane, 33, 34, 49
Notes From Underground (Dostoevsky): closure of, 49; critical responses to, 33–34, 35, 39, 47–49; rage in, 33, 35, 36, 42, 46–47; reader/text transaction in, 33, 34, 35, 36, 37–38, 39, 40–41, 42, 46–50; storytelling in, 36, 39, 42–43, 46–47
—The Underground Man: attention, need for, 33, 35, 37, 38, 39, 40, 41–42, 43, 44, 45–46, 50; compulsive behavior of, 34–35, 36, 39, 40, 43–44, 45, 46, 48; depletion, sense of, 38, 42, 43; eye contact, desire for, 37, 41–42; free-will rhetoric of, 34–35, 43–44; and the gentlemen narratees, 34, 35, 36, 37–38, 39, 40, 43, 44–47; grandiose fantasies of, 35, 37–38, 40, 46; grandiosity of, 35, 36, 37, 38, 40, 41, 42, 43, 44, 45, 46; narcissistic injuries of, 36, 39, 41, 43, 44; narcissistic rage of, 5, 33, 35, 38, 39, 40, 41, 42, 43, 44, 46–47; rejection, sensitivity to, 33, 36, 37, 38, 40–41, 42, 43; relationship with Liza, 35, 41–43, 46–47; relationship with the officer, 35, 39–40; relationship with Zverkov, 35, 40–41; self-esteem, vacillations of, 33, 36, 37; shame, sense of, 36, 39–40, 41, 43; as

Index

DATE DUE

FEB 4 '92			

DEMCO 38-297